Andri Gerber, Ulrich Götz (eds.)
Architectonics of Game Spaces

Andri Gerber (PhD), born in 1974, is Professor for the History of Urban Design at the ZHAW in Winterthur. He is an expert of metaphors in the context of architecture and urban design. His research interests turn around the concept of space, from a phenomenological, a political and more recently from a cognitive perspective.

Ulrich Götz, born in 1971, is Professor at the ZHdK Zurich University of the Arts, heading the ZHdK Subject Area in Game Design. Trained as an architect, he discusses comparable strategies of spatial design in architecture and game spaces. He has built up extensive experience in research and development of serious and applied games. His university teaching focuses on the analysis and design of game mechanics, game concepts, motivation design, and spatial design in virtual environments.

ANDRI GERBER, ULRICH GÖTZ (EDS.)

Architectonics of Game Spaces

The Spatial Logic of the Virtual and Its Meaning for the Real

[transcript]

Bibliographic information published by the Deutsche Nationalbibliothek
The Deutsche Nationalbibliothek lists this publication in the Deutsche Nationalbibliografie; detailed bibliographic data are available in the Internet at http://dnb.d-nb.de

Cover concept: Kordula Röckenhaus, Bielefeld
Cover illustration: Max Moswitzer
Proofread by Lindsay Blair Howe

Print-ISBN 978-3-8376-4802-7
PDF-ISBN 978-3-8394-4802-1
https://doi.org/10.14361/9783839448021

Contents

Introduction

Andri Gerber and Ulrich Götz

> "The decisive question of how a free human be-
> ing—the homo ludens—will live his or her life can-
> not be adequately answered until an idea
> about the artificial world is formulated—the
> world that these humans will build when they are
> not required to work."
> Constant, 1964[1]

INTRODUCTION LEVEL ONE: PRESS ARCHITECTURE TO START

Let us begin with something that might sound far-fetched: the children's book *King Nutcracker and Poor Reinhold*, by Heinrich Hoffmann.[2] In this story, a poor, sick boy is visited by an angel on Christmas Eve. The angel leads the boy away from his home, into a room with a small box full of wooden building blocks. Reinhold takes the blocks out of the box; after stacking them with the church in the center of his city, the blocks began to grow until they surrounded him—toy buildings that became "real." In this fantastic city, Reinhold encounters a series of strange and unusual inhabitants, including a king who introduces the boy to his subjects.

Later, the angel takes Reinhold back and announces that "the game is over." Upon returning home, he falls asleep—and when he wakes up next

---

1 | Constant Nieuwenhuys, New-Babylon: imaginäre Stadtlandschaften (Krefeld: Scherpe, 1964).

2 | Heinrich Hoffmann, *König Nussknacker und der arme Reinhold* (Frankfurt am Main: Literarische Anstalt Rütten & Löning, 1851). Hoffmann was psychiatrist and children's author, and the creator of the famous character of Struwwelpeter.

morning, he discovers a wonderful Christmas tree, alongside the toys he had played with the night before.

Play opens the door to fantasy and illusion. The etymology of "illusion" originates from the Latin *in-ludere*, referring to "play". Games demand illusion: we either play with the image of a game in our minds—like the German expression *Gedankenspiel*—or by literally jumping *into* the game. While at first, the Heinrich Hoffmann example may seem off-topic, it illustrates the agenda of this book: It reminds us that play, in fact, has a long history, and by playing, we are transported into the world of games. This world is always related to our everyday reality—and yet it is of another dimension, in which a different set of rules, perhaps better or fewer ones, take control.

Fig. 1: Hoffmann, Heinrich, König Nussknacker und der arme Reinhold, 1851

Architecture defines spaces, which unfold before us and envelop us. Architecture is a complex discipline, yet also one of the most "solid" disciplines ever, as its results manifest themselves in bricks and mortar. At the same time, architecture has always been plagued by contradictions and crises—the resulting instability of it all is a wonderful paradox indeed. Because of this fundamental condition, architecture has always been open to external discourses, embracing new directions and definitions in search of its own nature—as it has never been able to answer this central question on its own. Since architecture primarily expresses itself in the form of spatial structures, it has always had to share concepts of "space" with related interpretations from other disciplines, and in a complex entanglement with society. From movies to literature, philosophy, technology, sciences, politics, the military, economics, even music—all have made seminal contributions to the evolution of architecture and its discourses, often shifting the focus from purely architectural questions to hybrid applications.

Yet some of these interdisciplinary shifts may have served as more of an escapist movement than an actual attempt to translate the findings back into architectural designs. In contrast, other strategies tend to explain architecture *through* architecture, which often results in sterile, self-reflecting monuments—almost like architectural mirrors. These tendencies lead either to a condition of heteronomy that removes architecture from its foundations, or to a state of autonomy, making genuine communication with society equally impossible.[3]

As a consequence, architecture has created various forms of "utopia": playgrounds of both the introverted and extroverted, fantastic possibilities, all of which avoid a true confrontation with reality. By its own nature, architecture has a longstanding tradition of creating virtual spaces, of searching for its own forms of virtuality—particularly within the design process itself. Even though, in many ways, architecture was the precursor of digital metaphors (such as networks, clouds, or flows), its referential qualities remain. Architecture has always had virtual doubles—spatial structures in disguise.

On one hand, these doppelgangers served to blur the concept of architecture itself; on the other, they helped to better understand it. Because of this complex condition, we decided to borrow Immanuel Kants term *architectonics* for this book. Kant presented the phenomenon of an "impossibility of architecture" in his *Critique of Pure Reason* (1781), naming this "architectonics": in order to fulfill all criteria of architecture, it would have to be designed, planned, and built at the same time—which is, of course, impossible. According to Kant, this impossibility of existing while simultaneously being created will never result in *architecture*, but rather, in *ruins* and *failure*. This definition of architectonics therefore refers to

---

3 | Italian architectural historian Manfredo Tafuri named these two poles "labyrinth" and "sphere." Manfredo Tafuri, *Teorie e storia dell'architettura* (Bari: Laterza, 1968).

architecture as a system, which Kant uses to reflect upon philosophy. In this book, we use it to reflect upon architecture in games.

This line of inquiry is urgent, because over the past several decades, yet another counterpart to architecture has emerged, one which constantly comments on the venerable discipline: video games. They have vastly extended the references of spatial design, enriching the discussion with powerful simulations of environments in general, and of architecture in particular. Architecture has always been closely linked to the production of fantastic imagery, transferring traditional forms of virtuality (drawings, books, movies, etc.) into the constructed spaces of reality. The virtual spaces of games have to be designed, constructed, narrated, and filled with action—much in the way that architects attempt to anticipate how its occupants will appropriate architecture. If reality is a construction—and architecture is part of it—then the virtual spaces of games can teach us about architecture, and the role it plays in and for society.

Games reproduce portions of the world and define the framework that governs them. This also includes the rules for the construction and design of such worlds. This book discusses the "architectonics of game spaces," grounded in the understanding of architecture as an unstable discipline, one which cannot be reduced to mere structural design. Architecture transforms into duplicates, enters a game space, and—from this position—reverberates back into architecture.

INTRODUCTION LEVEL TWO: MAIN QUESTS AND SIDE QUESTS

These transitions and processes are not smooth at all. Cross-media artist Aram Bartholl (*1972) exploits the tension of this topic by using elements of video games that originated in "reality" and translating them back into "reality." In his project *DUST* (2011), Bartholl identified level design elements from the user-generated map *Dust* (by David Johnston) of *Counter-Strike* (1999), and planned to build it in reality. The functional design for a game, made out of virtual materials, was to appear in "reality," as a concrete construction!

While working on this book, we identified different ways in which games reflect reality in their designs. Interestingly, similar categories can be detected in the utopian projects of architecture and urban design.

Fig. 2: Aram Bartholl, DUST, 2011

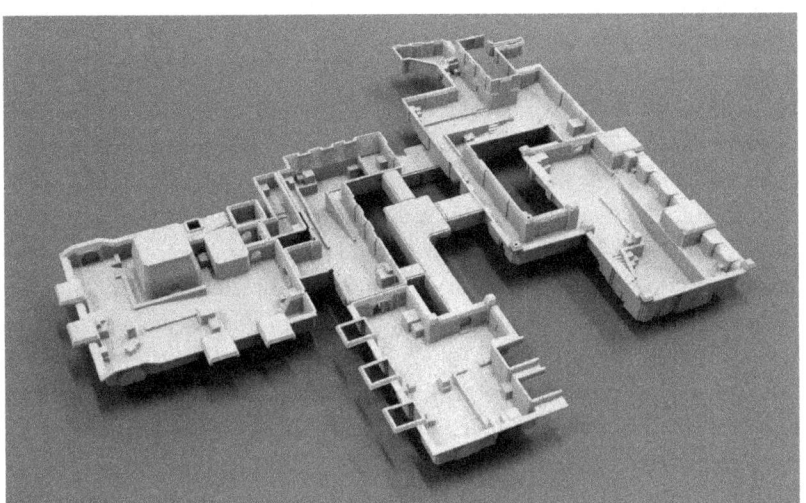

First, there is nostalgia, in which the narratives of games refer to alleged better, or older, worlds. Second, games serve as socio-analytical, critical, or subversive commentary. Of course, in most productions, both of these positions mix and cannot be strictly separated. However, we found that the work of Johan Huizinga (1872-1945) and Roger Caillois (1913-1978), the famous meta-theorists of game and play, could be distinguished from these two positions. Huizinga was a historian, with a background in linguistics. His major work, *Herfsttij der Middeleeuwen* (1919), describes the society of the Middle Ages; in it, he claims that people were closer to "things" and "reality" back then than they are now—for example, in the way children relate to their environment through play.[4] Caillois, on the other hand, was influenced by avant-garde movements such as the Surrealists, for whom artistic practice, play, and games played a pivotal role (e.g. in the *cadavre*

---

4 | "To the world when it was half a thousand years younger, the outlines of all things seemed more clearly marked than to us. The contrast between suffering and joy, between adversity and happiness, appeared more striking. All experience had yet to the minds of men the directness and absoluteness of the pleasure and pain of child-life." Johan Huizinga, *The Waning of the Middle Ages. A Study of the Form of Life, Thought and Art in France and the Netherlands in the XIVth and XVth centuries* (New York: Doubleday Anchor Books, 1954[1919]), p. 9.

exquis game).[5] Callois' approach to play reflects questions of and subversions of reality.

In *Architectonics of Game Spaces*, we want to demonstrate that discussing architecture from the perspective of video games leads to entirely different frameworks than the architectonic references from other disciplines. Much can be learned from the interrelated, yet diverse strategies of designing space for architecture and video games. We postulate that an understanding of design processes in virtual worlds, as well as the act of playing games themselves, could become an important asset for architectural education. Also, designing and experiencing virtual spaces with virtual reality (VR) devices permits an empirical investigation into the perception and impact such designs have on users—the kind of knowledge that could be fed back into architecture. Similar insight can also be gained from applying lessons from architecture and urban design to video games.

The designs of games often refer to designs from the real world. Creating such virtual "doubles" implies a thorough understanding and selection of circumstances, parameters, and rules, derived from the real and implemented in the virtual. Just imagine how the design of in-game fortresses would upset Francesco di Giorgio Martini (1439-1501), a pioneer military architect! (It might be of special interest to gamers that in his *Trattato di architettura civile e militare* (ca. 1478-1481), di Giorgio Martini not only described the construction of a secure stronghold, but also where to place explosives for their most effective destruction.)

On a more serious note, the transposition of buildings or scenery into the virtual, and the consequent distortions required to make them fit their new game purposes, is a highly interesting topic in and of itself. Ubisoft's version of Florence during the Renaissance, recreated for *Assassin's Creed II* (2009), perfectly illustrates typical *Architectonics of Game Spaces*. The virtual replica of the historic city is stunning, while at the same time major differences to the original emerge: the plan of Renaissance Florence was determined by the roman castrum, subsequent urban planning, and, finally, by the collapse of these structures during the Middle Ages. There-

---

5 | A game introduced by the Surrealists, in which a paper is folded many times and each participant adds a written or drawn element without knowing the contributions of the other players. The result is an often hilarious and absurd text or drawing.

fore, today's city map of Florence reveals a vague orthogonal city structure, overwritten by irregularities. However, the map of the video game postulates a spatial logic of its own, since it primarily consists of curved streets, to suit the typical movement of the assassin and enhancing a spatial experience. Even though most Renaissance buildings were low-rise, Assassin's Creed II features many buildings with more than two levels in order to facilitate the main character's climbing actions. In this case, form does follow function—but it is reality adapted to the necessities of the game. María Elisa Navarro, a professor of architectural history and theory who acted as consultant during the development of the game, explains that "each decision to deviate from historical accuracy was always done with some part of the game in mind".[6]

Architecture, urban design, and landscape design have always been closely linked to their economic feasibility—despite all attempts to ignore this evidence. Considering the budgets of many video games, there is hardly any danger of accidentally overlooking the economic aspects of their development, and the impact their financing has on the act of play. While the often simple imperialistic narratives of games focusing on economic game mechanics are evident[7], games can also question and rethink economic, political, or other normative circumstances. The Greek economist Yanis Varoufakis (*1961) was once asked by *Valve Corporation* to analyze economic systems in multiplayer games. In his words, it was "a dream come true for an economist." He said: "It's like being God, who has access to everything and to what every member of the social economy is doing".[8] Current practices in architecture and urban design are being invaded by the belief in algorithms and statistics, by *BIM*—Building Information Modeling—and *Smart Cities*—development models based on data and

---

6 | Maria Elísa Novaro, "What It's Like to Be an Architectural Consultant for Assassin's Creed II," interview by Manuel Saga, translated by Matthew Valata (October 7, 2015), https://www.archdaily.com/774210/maria-elisa-navarro-the-architectural-consultant-for-assassins-creed-ii (accessed July 7, 2019).

7 | See for example: Nick Dyer-Whiteford and Greig de Peuter, *Games of Empire: Global Capitalism and Video Games* (Minneapolis: University of Minnesota Press, 2009).

8 | Peter Suderman, "A Multiplayer Game Environment Is Actually a Dream Come true for an Economist" (June 2014), https://reason.com/archives/2014/05/07/a-multiplayer-game-environment (accessed July 7, 2019).

statistics, which are supposed to allow cities to become more inclusive and sustainable. Such approaches promise all kinds of problem-free spaces, but will eventually lead to cities of boredom. In contrast, playing with data might be a way to escape this bureaucratic, data-fanatic, and perfect future (see the contribution of James Delaney and Luke Pearson in this book)! Architecture and urban design can be so much more than mere functionalist calculations. The goal of architecture and urban design is not to accommodate society, but to express its inherent flaws, tension, and frictions; and to help ease these problems.

Fig. 3: Red Bull Air Drop at the entrance to Zurich University of the Arts, 2018

Games have developed the capacity to express such tensions, and to translate them back into "reality." Players of *Pokémon GO* (2016), a game which enhances public spaces with augmented reality objects, are warned when starting the game: "Do not trespass while playing Pokémon GO." The game's territory suggests a continuous playing ground, as buildings are not represented in a borderless game space. This concept sometimes results in awkward situations, when shops or cafés have positioned themselves in the public spaces, where players summon in "game-arenas". In such cases, virtual objects actually have an impact on the real spaces of cities, revealing the ongoing conflicts between public spaces and spaces of trade and commerce. An even further twist might be represented by the university campus marketing campaign by the Red Bull Company, in which crates of product samples were placed as obstacles in universities' entrances, which they referred to as "Red Bull Air Drops." To most students, the references to multiplayer games like *PlayerUnknown's Battlegrounds* (2017) or *Fortnite* (2017) were evident in the "air drops"—extra resources distributed by parachute. Despite the aforementioned warnings, trespassing does occur—from virtuality to reality, and vice versa.

INTRODUCTION LEVEL THREE: A USER MANUAL

The publication *Space Time Play*[9] provided an extensive selection of articles in 2007 addressing the relationship between architecture and video games, and they remain a valid reference today. Since then, publications on this topic tended to discuss specific details, rather than providing broad-based access to the topic. For this reason, we felt it was necessary to present a wide-ranging selection of interviews and essays anew, delineating the state-of-the-art on the many perspectives and aspects of today's interlinked practices in architecture and video game design.

Architectonics of Game Spaces was written for architects and architectural students interested in video games, and in utilizing them for their own architectural practice. Many authors of this book provide excellent examples of how to take this step. Also, the publication is intended for game designers and game design students who actively explore the design possibilities between real and virtual spaces. The book is divided into two sections: the first part contains interviews, and the second part contains essays. Both tackle the relationship between architecture and games, between "reality" and "fiction," between "actuality" and "virtuality." *Architectonics of Game Spaces* continues the discussion of the conference *The Architectonics of Virtual Spaces*, which was held on June 9, 2018 at the Werner Oechslin Library Foundation in Einsiedeln, Switzerland.

---

9 | Friedrich von Borries, Steffen P. Walz, and Matthias Böttger (eds.), *Space Time Play. Computer Games, Architecture and Urbanism: The Next Level* (Basel/Boston/Berlin: Birkhäuser, 2007).

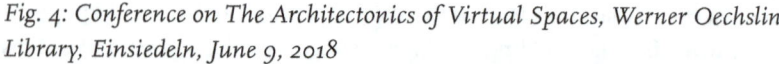

Fig. 4: Conference on The Architectonics of Virtual Spaces, Werner Oechslin Library, Einsiedeln, June 9, 2018

INTERVIEWS

In a series of interviews, experts from different fields provide an overview of the role architecture plays in their practice. Among these interviewees, Paolo Pedercini, Konstantinos Dimopoulos and Francine Rotzetter are experts on gaming. The remaining interviewees are not directly involved in the practice of developing games, but they are interested in questions of virtuality and in contributing new perspectives to game theory.

It may be hard to imagine **Werner Oechslin** gaming away on a PlayStation. As a former professor of the history and theory of architecture, long-time head of the gta institute at the ETH Zurich, and founder of the *Bibliothek Werner Oechslin,* he is one of the few truly universal scholars of our time. Amid the stunning collection of architectural and non-architectural books in his library (a building by Mario Botta, *1943), one might think him far removed from engaging with topics such as game and play. Yet, as his interview reveals, he has great interest in such activities: he understands them as possibilities with which to approach knowledge that is inductive, not deductive. Referring to historical examples, such as *aenigma* and *verisimilia,* and emphasizing the role of fiction and poetry, he argues for a more playful approach to science and culture in general. To his understanding, the main lesson we should learn from games is that playing always implies taking risks; in a society obsessed with security norms, we should learn to take more risks!

Paolo Pedercini distributes the games he designs under the label *Molleindustria*. His productions are great examples of how games can be used to critically assess society, culture, and politics. Pedercini claims that his games are instruments for a critique of power, and that they can help the player become aware of the forces to which he is subjected. Pedercini makes an interesting analogy between the relationship of the human scale in architecture to the time spent in video games. He likes to compare the relation of a gamer and in-game architecture to someone using skateparks or doing parkour. When asked about his architectural references, surprisingly, he does not cite history books, but immersive art installations and the pedagogical (and really funny) *101 Things I Learned In Architecture School* (2007) instead.

Konstantinos Dimopoulos was originally trained as a surveyor, and as an urban and regional planner in geography. But a long time ago, he transposed his knowledge about real cities and landscapes to virtual spaces, not missing "corruption, red tape, and maddening officials" at all. He recently published *The Virtual Cities Atlas*, a collection of virtual cities from games, in which he affords them a quasi-real status. Having worked in the field, he argues for the creation of in-world realism, which—related to J.R.R. Tolkien's (1892-1973) idea of a second reality—should be defined by imagination, character, and believability. Furthermore, he advocates the need to admit history and time a more relevant role in games.

Johannes Binotto is a media and culture theorist, who lives in a spatial multiverse ranging from cinema to architecture. Discussing video games in relation to film, he emphasizes the differences between the media of "film" and "video," and what this distinction means for games. From his perspective, the relationship between architects and media artists or game designers leads to an interesting chiasm: whereas the former envy the possibilities of manipulating reality, the latter envy the "reality" of architecture. Binotto's dream would be a boring game, with only subtle differences to reality, moving the game closer towards film. He would love to play such a game, against its own rules, just exploring its space—yet aware that he probably would be the only one enjoying it.

Silke Steets is not a gamer, but when she played tennis on *wii*, she was surprised about her sore muscles the day after. As a sociologist, she has investigated architectural objects as "social realities." This led her to focus on the spaces of games, their architecture, and their impact on reality (as in sore muscles). Steets describes the relationship of game spaces and architecture in terms of signs and symbols, but also through their spatial experience, which she compares to the layout of the English landscape garden or to skating (like Paolo Pedercini). As a sociologist, she explains how the sphere of everyday life and the sphere of games are always connected, even though this relationship is not always evident.

Philipp Schaerer is a master in manipulating imagery. Having previously worked as an architect to create architectural renderings, he later decided to subvert this kind of production by questioning the means generating these images. While at first sight, the results appear to be conventional architectural images and renderings, really they show to what extent 3D renderings have established a culture of copy-paste. His images are both a strong criticism on the processes of designing architecture in a digital and capitalist era, and they also remind us of the decisive influences of tools in design practice. His approach is strongly oriented towards practice, yet his images emit a seductive aura and open a door to visions of a different kind of architecture. If only Schaerer could someday be involved in the development of a video game...

After studying architecture at the ETH Zurich, **Francine Rotzetter** enrolled in the master's program in game design at the Zurich University of the Arts. Currently, she is working with VR experiences in architectural visualizations. Trained as an architect, she is aware of the specific knowledge necessary for the development of virtual and game spaces: the emotional dimension of space. She admits to having learned a lot about architecture through her work and research on video games, for example, the meticulous consideration of a future user's actions—a practice she found strongly underrepresented in the study of architecture. Her background as an architect and a game designer allows her to obtain deep insight into both disciplines, and also to identify typical mistakes. During her interview, we discussed a proposal to open up the creation of virtual cities to architects and urban planners, unfolding "sandbox" environments to mirror the complexity of reality in virtuality.

François Charbonnet and **Patrick Heiz** are architects who tackle norms and conventions in their daily work and teaching. As they stress in their interview, this does not imply leaving reality, but to question the rules that define it. Since architecture should also be unpredictable and fun, this includes the method of copying, with all its inadequacies and chaotic side effects. In teaching, they introduced the concept of *Voluptas*—literally, pleasure or delight—to show students how to overcome expectations and norms, or to go beyond them. For educational use, as an architectural "sandbox," they are developing a game platform that helps to convey the dynamic energy of fantastic and imaginary worlds. In the same way that their architecture is not a retreat into virtuality, but another way to confront reality, the game platform trains students to question their work and responsibility for future designs.

Essays

The essays cover three aspects of *Architectonics of Game Spaces*—although this distinction is not meant to be considered exclusive, but rather, overlapping. The three topics are:

1. *Towards a Definition of Game Space,*
2. *Spatial Transitions Between Architecture and Games,* and
3. *The Potential of Game Space for a New Architecture.*

Part 1. Towards a Definition of Game Space

The first section approaches a definition of "space" in video games and architecture. In attempting to include a philosophical dimension of this question, the discussion is aware of the heated debate about the definition of "space" in the history of architecture.

In his essay, **Andri Gerber** presents a range of personalities who, at first sight, seem to be far removed from the context of video games: Reyner

Banham (1922-1988), Immanuel Kant, Humphry Repton (1752-1818), and Le Corbusier (1887-1965). He uses these thinkers to reflect on the understanding of architecture and its space, and how games can be discussed from this perspective as a counterpart. He outlines the concept of "architectonics," and how this term applies even more to landscape architecture than to the architecture of buildings. He suggests how video games could help architects to improve certain skills, such as their spatial ability.

Stefano Gualeni, an architect and philosopher who both teaches game theory and designs games by himself, discusses the experience of virtual spaces and the dissatisfaction that can be induced by their limitations. Games are believed to trigger the experience of "flow," or a sometimes, "sublime emotion"—but Gualeni instead discusses the feeling of "weariness" that also can overcome a player. Through interviews with experts, he identifies strategies delaying what he calls the "experiential erosion of digital environments." He warns against using virtual worlds as an escape from the flaws and incompleteness of the real world; simultaneously, the acceptance of limitations in virtual worlds can be essential to cope with life in the real.

Stephan Günzel, a philosopher, media theorist and expert of the history of space theories, approaches the topic of space by referring to Henri Lefebvre (1901-1991) and the concept of "thirdspace" developed by Edward Soja (1940-2015). In doing so, he is not aligned with other game theorists, who define game space as an allegory or metaphor of "real" space. Günzel shifts the perspective of such spaces from "what or where are they?" to "how are they made"? He successfully demonstrates how mathematical and physical concepts of space are a cultural and subjective expression. From this viewpoint, video games appear to create privileged conditions, which explicate the various means constituting the construction of space over the course of history.

Constantinos Miltiadis, an architect with a broad experience in teaching and researching video games, reflects on spatial concepts from the perspective of mathematics and physics. However, he suggests overcoming these fundamentals through video games and VR devices. While the laws of reality are determined by physical axioms, he questions if it would be possible to experience alternative forms of space, such as in games like *Portal* (2007) or *Antichamber* (2013). Miltiadis points out how such spatial conceptions are determined by the tools used in game productions. Transferring such methods to the context of architecture would introduce a new understanding of space into reality.

Part 2. Spatial Transitions Between Architecture and Games

Constantinos Miltiadis's essay leads to the second section—dedicated to the investigation of the transcending qualities of space, from architecture to game spaces and vice versa. What is the understanding of space in each discipline, and which results can be expected when they connect and exchange?

Ulrich Götz heads the subject area of game design at the Zurich University of the Arts (ZHdK). Trained as an architect, he discusses comparable strategies of spatial design in architecture and game spaces in his research and teaching. In his contribution, he argues that common references between architecture and game design are based on mutual misjudgments of the other discipline. He explains how a lack of deeper understanding of architecture (from the perspective of game designers) and of game spaces (from the perspective of architects) is precisely what leads to the spatial constructions that lack architectural qualities in virtual spaces, and that fail to make proper use of the virtual world's possibilities in real space.

In his essay, **Marc Bonner**, an art historian and media theorist, focuses on the video games *Hitman* (2012) and *Hitman 2* (2016) to illustrate the role of architecture as "medial hinge": he defines architecture as a medium within a medium, influencing our perception and experience in real and in virtual space. The space of games is described as "architectural possibilism" through two overlapping architectonic concepts of space and movement: the *promenade architecturale* by Le Corbusier and the enfilade of the *hôtel particulier*. He claims that architectonic concepts are translated into game space, in which they are adapted and transformed into specific narration and rules.

Sinem Cukurlu is an architect with a passion for video games. In her essay, she reflects upon qualities of architectural space in reality and in games;

she discusses the tools used to convey materiality, light, space, perspective, environment, shape, and form, much like ambassadors between the two disciplines. She emphasizes the proximity of the two disciplines and how architects can profit from both, be it by implementing typical game design methods (such as play testing or simulations), or by implementing qualities of virtual worlds into the real (like emotive spaces). In her eyes, games are powerful tools and environments with which to free the creative potential of architects.

Margarete Jahrmann is a "practical theorist" active in game design and as such she brings in a different perspective on the matter discussed in this book. She playfully investigates the relationship between spatial perception and computer games through games and installations, making reference to a whole set of similar artistic projects that bring together different spatial dimensions, be it on stage, in games or in "reality". Together with Max Moswitzer, she publishes the *Ludic Society Magazine*, a ludic arts research journal on playful methods in artistic research. The center of her article discusses the concept of "flow" as the key to understand the relationship of reality, virtual reality and game space.

Part 3. The Potential of Game Spaces for a New Architecture

The third section is dedicated to the potential video games have for architecture and urban design, to their social and political dimension. All essays agree on the potential of games to not only constitute new communication, but also to open up new ways a community can actively participate in shaping their environment.

After studying and working as an architect, **Ekim Tan** was drawn to serious games through her Ph.D. at the Delft University of Technology—titled *Negotiation and Design for the Self-organizing City: Gaming as a Method for Urban Design*—as well as by establishing her own company, *Play the City*, in 2008. Her essay addresses the advantages of using games in the context of urban design, and what they can teach communities. She suggests that games can be used to facilitate complex urban development processes on all scales (such as quality public space, urban safeties, sustainability, etc.) and in which both the stakeholders as well as other participants can better understand the processes. To enhance better communication and collaboration, Tan refers to the analog game of *Dungeon & Dragons* (1974), and proposes the idea of "hybrid games," combining analog and digital platforms and data.

James Delaney trained as an architect but was also involved in exploiting the architectonical potential of *Minecraft* (2009) early on, with his company *BlockWorks*. He participated in the *Block by Block Foundation*, a partnership between UN-Habitat, Mojang, and Microsoft. His essay explains what makes *Minecraft* so successful as a participatory tool, combining social networks and the interactivity of a virtual environment; and moreover, for teaching CAD basics to laypeople all over the world. From Delaney's perspective, *Minecraft* provides a democratic platform for all stakeholders, particularly those who usually are excluded in planning processes.

Luke Caspar Pearson is an architect investigating the potential of video games and their aesthetics for architecture and urban design, both in teaching and in his practice *You+Pea*. In this, games are understood and researched as didactic tools, as medium, and as cultural artifacts. Linked to examples from architectural history, the use of video games features a more quantitative approach, allowing him to propose alternatives to the current computational trends in architecture. He shows that video games are powerful tools to rethink architecture and to critically assess the future of cities.

INTRODUCTION LEVEL FOUR: LET'S PLAY, SCORES, AND CREDITS

To better understand the logic and making of games, the least you can do is to actually play them (how else would you be able to discuss them?). The libraries of architectural universities should be equipped with gaming computers and consoles; seminars about game design should be included in architectural curricula. But of course, if you want to go beyond the experience of play and fully understand the nature of games, you will need to go a step further and develop games yourself.

In this sense, *Architectonics of Game Spaces* is not about "learning from games," but about "learning by playing." We would agree that the potential of games has not yet received the attention it deserves in academia, where they often remain perceived as a mere amusement. But the impact of games is so powerful precisely because they are so underestimated.

We would like to express our gratitude to the authors who accepted following us in this endeavor, sharing deep insight into their practices in architecture and game design. We would also like to thank those responsible for making this book possible: Oya Atalay Franck, Head of the ZHAW's School of Architecture, Design and Civil Engineering; as well as Stefan Kurath and Regula Iseli, co-heads of the ZHAW's Institute of Urban Landscape (IUL). Furthermore, we would like to express our gratitude to Amadeo Sarbach, Philippe Koch, and Maxime Zaugg for helping us conduct the conference on *The Architectonics of Virtual Spaces*, which evolved into this book. Last but not least, we would like to thank all the colleagues at the ZHAW and the ZHdK for providing us with an environment, in which ideas and controversies about real and virtual spaces can grow. Many thanks also to Lindsay Blair Howe for giving our game-like use of the English language a more serious touch.

Writing this book was a truly playful experience indeed. We hope that our readers will perceive the result as a toy that can be used both for playing and learning!

Andri Gerber and Ulrich Götz, July 2019

Taking Risks!

Andri Gerber in Conversation with Werner Oechslin,
March 19, 2019, Einsiedeln

"Every Citty almost hath it's peculiar Walkes,
Groves, Theaters, Pageants, Games, and fever all
recreations, every country some peculiar Gymni-
cks to exhilarate their minds and exercise their
bodies."
Robert Burton, *Anatomy of Melancholy*, 1621[1]

Werner Oechslin: I would like to begin with an assumption and attempt
to start a discussion about PLAY. If you search Google for the terms "play"
and "game," then the first page of results will direct you to the "top online
games of 2019"—to purchasable and downloadable games. This captures
the fact that "gaming" has come to completely dominate our consciousness when it comes to play. But I object! Due to the sheer number of games
available, our comprehension of play has become much too narrow, and
should therefore be expanded. This is what I will try to do in our discussion.

To "game" seems to be synonymous with an instinct to play. But, even
if there seems to be a theory or a "metatheory" for everything, play remains
anchored to concrete "games." And it seems that these games, enabled by
new advances in technology, have no limit; at least this is the impression
that I get. But Johan Huizinga (1872-1945) and his *Homo Ludens* point at

---

1 | Robert Burton, *Anatomy of Melancholy* [1621] (Amsterdam: Theatrum Orbis
Terrarum, 1971), p. 345.

completely different realities.[2] In this work, it is less about "games" than about the playful as a fundamental *condition humaine*, which therefore concerns our entire culture. We are playful in so many things we do on a daily basis. The flood of gratuitous gaming options we encounter, and their complexity, cannot disguise the fact that what we are talking here is a completely different form of play—and about two completely different perceptions of the world. The deception—and the illusion—of play with which we are confronted, and how appealing this can be, often ends in some sort of insight into, or an "understanding" of the mechanisms behind these kinds of games. They are finite and bound to a concrete case; their appeal is no more, once the game has been played. Obviously, there are also games that can still evoke surprise time and time again, particularly games in which the variations and possibilities are almost endless—chess, for example.

So let us begin here! In a recent interview, Garri Kasparow (*1963) agreed on the fact that "the machine" could win at any chess game, as long as the game is a "closed system," defined by its patterns of movements across the sixty-four fields—with two times sixteen figures—which can be captured in its entirety "mathematically." But why do we still play chess if we know this? Apparently, precisely because of our weakness as human beings: because we can, we must compensate for the endless computational power of the computer in the right moment with our memory, experience, intuition, and creative thinking. To put it more positively: because we can demonstrate our human "intelligence" in this encounter, literally, in "competition." Thus, human beings remain in playful competition according to the terms of their (restricted) capability; this is what triggers their enthusiasm and fascination for this game, despite unequal conditions—even if "the machine" could theoretically do it better. I would claim, therefore, that this is where the *culture* of gaming begins; where the game begins to frame and test our imagination, and our intelligence.

The question remains: To what extent can these observations be extended to other, or even all types of games? We would probably agree that this unfolds in different manners. While chess calls for high standards of mental acuity, recall, combination thinking, etc., playing more simple games can easily lead to boredom. And despite the demonstrated "supe-

2 | Johan Huizinga, *Homo Ludens: A Study of Play-Element in Culture* [1938] (London: Routledge & Kegan Paul, 1949).

riority" of the machine, chess has not disappeared. Apparently, it is about more than the optimization of data; man is playing against himself, and the likes of him with his different capacities—and also with his inevitable flaws. As such, it is fun to play under these conditions! And to the contrary, it is uninteresting to have machines play chess against one another.

In order to understand the high degree of speculation inherent to all forms of *praecognitio* of prior knowledge and anticipation in a janiform correspondence, it would serve us well to compare the game with sixteen figures and sixty-four fields with another—one which is even more spectacular. In his oft-quoted essay "La Biblioteca de Babel" (1941), Jorge Luis Borges (1899-1986) names two axioms that must be followed: first, "la Biblioteca existe ab aeterno," and second—building upon the first— "el número de símbolos ortográficos es veinticinco".[3] The essay is preceded by a quotation from Robert Burton's (1577-1640) *Anatomy of Melancholy*: "By this art, you may contemplate the variation of the twenty-three letters ...".[4] There has hardly ever been a book as chaotic as this one—but of all things, it is here that we find reference to the game and the endless possible variations based on only a few signs. Yet, we can also assume what most of us have already experienced—even without really thinking about it—that almost everything one can think about can be represented by a mere twenty-two or twenty-three or twenty-five signs.

The simultaneous advantage and risk of leaving the protected narrowness of the sixty-four fields behind, and instead dealing with the possibility of infinity, is the absence of a limited and precise system of rules that a set number of fields impose. Based on the fact that we only need twenty-three signs to code language, Burton has pointed to other numerical proportions—such as the possible amount of human beings on the planet—derived from calculating the area each person's footprint requires. Obviously, he soon arrives at the same conclusion as all those who have presented any form of calculations attempting to bring us closer to understanding our magical world, from Roger Bacon (c. 1214-1292) to Galileo Galilei (1564-1642). He puts spherical triangles in relation to melancholia, and is amazed by all the useful means and chin-ups human beings have created—epigrams, anagrams, chronograms, acrostics, etc.—

3 | Jorge Luis Borges, "La biblioteca de Babel" in *El Jardín de senderos que se bifurcan* (Buenos Aires: Editorial Sur, 1941).

4 | Burton, 1971.

culminating in the riddle to beat all riddles, the *Aelia Laelia Cripsis* from Bologna. If any of this still sounds amusing, one could join Robert Burton and Plutarch—who is quoted by the former—in better understanding the "pulchritude": the beauty of mathematics. Referencing his own experience, Burton understood the appeal of card games, models, and sundials. Joseph Scaliger (1540-1609) specifies this idea of a *mathematum pulchritudo,* by further referring to *felicitas demonstrationum*: the moment of happiness inherent to mathematical insight and evidence. This happiness is reserved for those who know how to play this game and are willing to play it: "Cuius scientiae tam certa fides est, ut qui ea non abutatur, numquam opera ludat." It is fun, once you have understood it!

If all this is part of our understanding of play, we should pause a moment in order to realize that the pleasure of play is not due to the elegant rules of the game itself, but rather, in going along with them, in gaining insight and pleasure into them through their mastery. As should be clear by now, an open play arrangement is more fruitful than moving within narrowly framed conditions and predetermined solutions, up a classic standard model. For this reason, when I once had a teacher who assigned us problems with well-known solutions, I abandoned the study of mathematics; I had thought that this kind of teaching was over after competing gymnasium and lyceum, and that the horizon was now open. An illusion! There was no *pulchritude,* and most definitively no *felicitas demonstrationum.* I had looked for these things in the wrong place—although I heard about the combinatorics of Ramon Llull (c. 1232-c. 1315) very early on and had been fascinated by it, as it brings together both the endless possibilities and the economy of means. This idea was so well aligned with life, in all of its imponderability and order; or the other way around, with the life-realities to which *aenigmata* are attributed, mysteries that cannot be solved. Understood as a riddle, reality retreats further and further from the horizon and never ceases to challenge us. Albert Einstein (1879-1955) spoke about this pointedly in his lecture *Geometry and Experience* (1921), when attempting to radically separate mathematics and reality, he realized that, in spite of such a clear and convincing statement, these two, in real life are merged.[5] In his own words: "How is it possible that mathematics, which is a product of human thought and totally independent

---

5 | Albert Einstein, *Geometrie und Erfahrung* (Berlin: Verlag von Julius Springer, 1921), p. 2.

from experience, fits so well on objects from reality?" If we understand geometry as "purely formal"—meaning "detached from any axioms based on assumptions and experiential contents"—then we could reply that one should not bother with such riddles. And we could easily demonstrate how often mathematical concepts have turned to "mystic obscurity". Admittedly, these are considerations coming from outside mathematics that are mixed within them—just as with play, if you consider it to be more than a mere closed body of rules.

Fig. 5: Marcel Duchamp, Formules de l'opposition hétérodoxe dans les domaines principaux [1930]

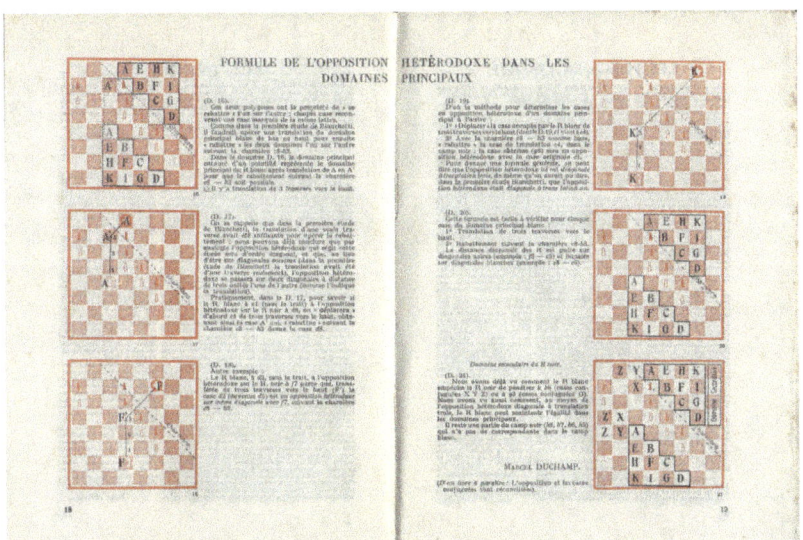

Marcel Duchamp (1887-1968) used the chessboard with its sixty-four fields in reference to the schemes of Llull, in order to present a "formule de l'opposition hétérodoxe". Other worlds? Why then is the "poetical" procedure described so accurately by Raymond Roussel (1877-1933) in his *Comment j'ai écrit certains de mes livres*[6] not "strictly scientific" in the same way as Edmund Husserl's (1859-1938) argues at the very end of his treatise "Philosophy as Rigorous Science" from 1910/11, where he pleads for a scientific

---

6 | Raymond Roussel, *Comment j'ai écrit certains de mes livres* (Paris: Alphonse Lemerre, 1935).

discourse "ohne alle indirekt symbolisierenden und mathematisierenden Methoden, ohne den Apparat der Schlüsse und Beweise."[7]

Fig. 6: Paul Éluard, Poésie involontaire & poésie intentionnelle, 1942

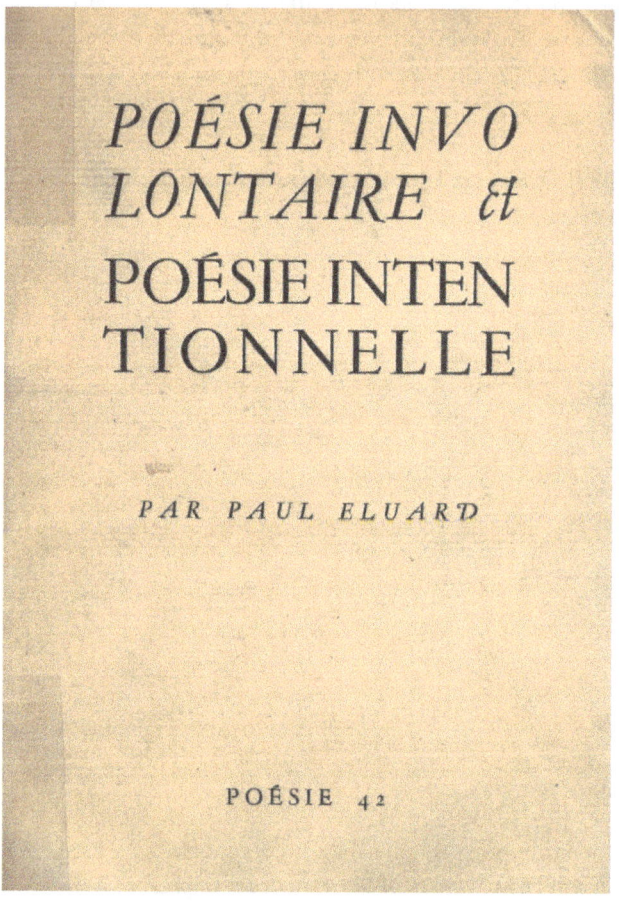

Thus, we quickly slide from the realm of science into the realm of poetry and poetics—the latter, as is well-known, meaning "creation." To this, there is a wonderful sentence by poet Paul Éluard (1895-1952): "Tout hom-

---

7 | Edmund Husserl, "Philosophy as Rigorous Science," in *Phenomenology and the Crisis of Philosophy*, ed. Quentin Lauer (New York: Harper & Row, 1965[1910]).

me est frère de Prométhée".[8] That's it! When I have the possibility of free-dom, then I will be Prometheus; then I will be a creator, and I will have the world for myself, to play freely. That "apparatus of inferences," includ-ing footnotes and evidence, that Husserl ideally would have renounced to use, should not occlude the playful freedom of the scientist the same way as Prometheus, the "creator and artist."

It is a mistake to separate science and play—but also science and rid-dle, science and probability, they all belong together. And if this isn't proof enough, then we should consider Horace. He provides us with the most multifaceted variations on the topic of poetry and reality: "Ex noto fictum carmen sequar"[9] and also "Ficta voluptatis causa sint proxima veris" dis-cussed extensivelsy by Alexander Gottlieb Baumgarten (1714-1762) in Äs-thetik.[10] Fiction has not detached, it has not decoupled itself—and thus it has not been "formalized"—but yet, it remains bound and tied to reality, and enters into a relationship with it.

However, *induction*, a constantly moving and shifting open process, has been discredited by Karl Popper (1902-1994); everything that can be concluded, he argued, is necessarily a *deduction*. He fails to recognize the advantages of a process in which understanding gained step-by-step is developed further and transformed through new experiences and in-sights—and this obviously also includes oscillation and irritation. *De facto*, one always proceeds this way; one might describe the opposite of pure empiricism; a detached, pure deduction as the *idealiter* experimental arrangement ... yet, just as Einstein, one is nevertheless confronted with all possible riddles. This contains a glimpse of the world of *Verisimilia*. Reality does not automatically imply a secure tenure of knowledge; we deal with probability, start from assumptions, form an opinion on everything, and "speculate" in the manner familiar from the philosophical traditions. And finally everything is connected through poetry and play.

---

8 | Cf. Werner Oechslin, "'Poetando'; 'nous poétisons'. TEXTE - wissenschaftliche und andere: TEXTE!" *SCHOLION* Vol. 9 (2012), pp. 5-23.

9 | Quintus Horatius Flaccus, *His Art of Poetry*, trans. Ben Johnson (Amsterdam: Theatrum Orbis Terrarum, 1974).

10 | Alexander Gottlieb Baumgarten, *Aesthetica* (Traiecti cis Viadrum: Impens. Ioannis Christiani Kleyb, 1750).

Fig. 7: R. P. Bohuslao Aloysio Balbino, Verisimilia Humaniorum Disciplinarum, 1666

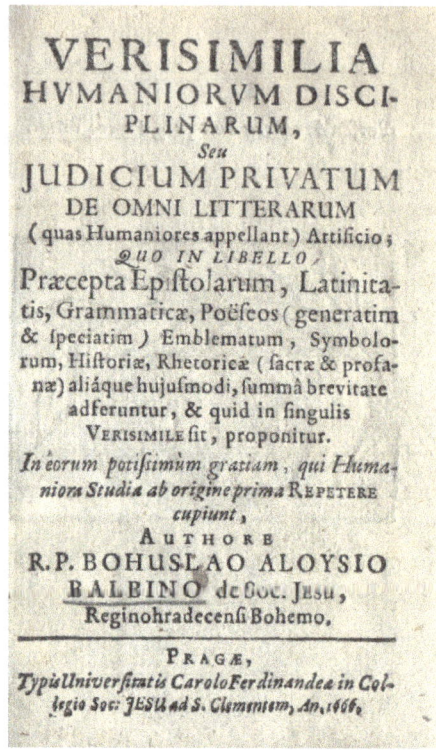

To quote Éluard: "Tout homme est frère de Prométhée". Why should this not apply to "science"? It is from this point of view that we can, we must approach probability. At the beginning of his *Essai philosophique sur les probabilités*, Pierre-Simon Laplace (1749-1827) determined only a few conditions related to probability: namely that everything, whether known or unknown, in one way or another belongs to a "système de l'univers."[11]

There should always be reasons against "hasard aveugle"—blind coincidence—at least according to the "principe de la raison suffisante" (the direct difference between causality and accident, for which Laplace refers to Leibnitz; it was already specified at the beginning of Aristotle's *Metaphys-*

---

11 | Pierre-Simon Laplace, *Essai philosophique sur les probabilités* (Paris: Mme Ve Courcier, 1814).

ics). Laplace assigns his probabilities an "espérance mathématique"; the more the latter is given, the higher the probability. Such mathematically furnished assumption then read approximately like this: "La valeur relative d'une somme infiniment petite, est égale à sa valeur absolue divisée par le bien total de la personne intéressé." In the German posthumous translation by the ingenious Friedrich Wilhelm Tönnies (1855-1936), this tenth axiom reads like this "Der relative Werth einer unendlich kleinen Summe ist gleich ihrem absoluten Werthe, dividiert durch das Totalvermögen des dabei interessirten Individuums".[12] We therefore remain with a mathematical equation; this equation is the riddle. Science and play! And don't forget that game theory has become an important branch of mathematics, and not only as part of mathematics related to the insurance industry.

I hope you will forgive me for my long monologue, but I wanted to at least indicate the direction of my thoughts in regard to the topic of PLAY, as there is a risk that they spiral out of control.

Andri Gerber: Definitely! This was, so to speak, your "opening"—and now it is up to me to counter, even though this is not so easy. But let's start with Huizinga. Among many others, in his publication *Homo Ludens*, he references Giambattista Vico (1668-1744) and his *Scienzia Nuova* (1725), as he was among the first to acknowledge the importance of play as the origin of culture.[13] But what we find equally present in Vico is the idea of a universal language, which he describes as "[...] Lingua mentale, comune a tutte le Nazioni [...]".[14] The topic of a universal language obviously has a long tradition, and has primarily been discussed in relation to mathematics. Could we assume that play is also such a universal language?

---

12 | "The relative value of an infinitely small sum is equal to its absolute value, divided by the total wealth of the concerned party." Friedrich Wilhelm Tönnies, *Des Grafen Laplace Philosophischer Versuch über Wahrscheinlichkeiten, nach der dritten Pariser Auflage* (Heidelberg: Neue akademische Buchhandlung von Karl Groos, 1819).

13 | "Nobody has grasped, or expressed, the primordial nature of poetry and its relation to pure play more clearly than Vico, more than two hundred years ago." Huizinga, 1948 [1938], p. 119.

14 | Giambattista Vico, *Cinque Libri de'Principj d'Una Scienza Nuova* (Napoli: Felice Mosca, 1730) pp. 97.

Oechslin: After "play vs. science," another equally significant topic! This question is unavoidable, and for once we can leave the question of communication by means of language vs. by non verbal means aside. There was and there will always be a kind of "linguistic turn." And why should this not also concern play? In recent times, architecture, too, has been considered a language—not in the sense of a superimposed inscription or the like, but as a specifically strong expression of an *architecture parlante*. In Italy, at a certain point in time, it was all about language: "linguaggio, linguaggio"!

Fig. 8: Giambattista Vico, Cinque Libri de'Principj d'Una Scienza Nuova [1725], 1730

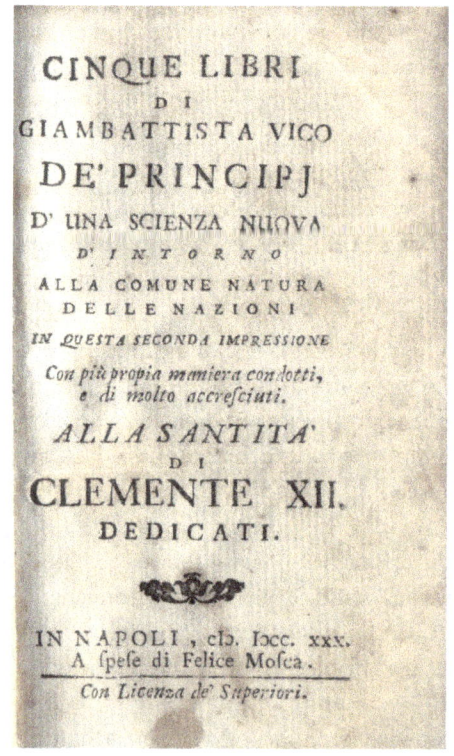

I prefer the more generic term *auxilia*, as it was used, for example, by Francis Bacon (1561-1626). It has always been about instruments, or the various tools we need to assist our heads in the process of comprehension and communication. And these typically possess a distinctly "medial" character, just as the *medietas* of mathematics were emphasized for a long period of time. As such, we have once again returned to play, and also to "play-things": to chess figures, and the sixty-four fields, and the manifold arrangements that result from it.

Our head remains an effective instrument, despite some defaults, such as lack of memory, distraction, etc. But we normally prefer these human weaknesses, the "humanity," rather than the total control of every situation. If one puts everything on a checklist and then systematically works through it, the freshness of ideas and thought suffers. A good game is similar to a good idea, and uses surprise and spontaneity; it surrenders to the illusion of absolute freedom and accepts the risks. Openness and risk are fundamental parts of play and come always together to formulate an open end. As a child, we played an endless amount of games, and they almost ever ended in disputes.

Gerber: Always!

Oechslin: These are what make a game, too. And then there is the corresponding analysis ... because maybe you realized that the other player did not stick to the rules, or did not understand them. The conditions and the system of rules, these are what make a game.

Gerber: I would like to come back to language. It is interesting because, in game theory, there are strong references to language. With Vico, we have this conception of a protolanguage, a language that still has an immediate connection to things. He describes this as "un parlare fantastico per sostanze animate".[15] There is always some degree of separation in the end, which, however, opens also the space for language to become.

Oechslin: This discussion has to be contextualized in the larger frame of the derivation of human culture from things such as the invention of writing. Vico's position, in regard to ideas about the "caratteri fantastici di sostanze humane" is about a "sapienza *poetica*." It is all about a world which is not abstract, but rather, sensed and vividly imagined. One has to "di meditarvi ben sopra" and learn to understand the "Principi di tutto l'umano, e divin saper".[16] The reference is then Aristotle's *Peri hermeneias*, as well as Plato and his *Kratylos*. As such, we are in the midst of questions about things and their representations, about signs and symbols, and of

---

15 | Ibid., p. 153
16 | Ibid., p. 162.

the idea in general that they could free themselves, becoming independent ... risking separation and distance.

Gerber: ... a distance, which in the context of game theory, when talking about the language of games, seems to be regrettable. Here, we have a missing link, because play is supposed to be a language, in a non-metaphorical sense.

Oechslin: Still, I think that the fact that language plays such an important role—at least in the formulation of a theory—is very positive. But are we talking about a theory of those making games, or about a meta-theory?

Gerber: It is kind of both. There is hardly a game theorist who does not design games for themselves. This is evidently a characteristic of this theory. In architecture, you are either a theorist or a designer—rarely both.

Oechslin: Yet there is an ancient tradition and the corresponding expectation, that only one who does things by themselves (as an architect does) can also talk about it competently. Everything lies in the *poiesis*, in the making.

Gerber: Vico too, said that you can only recognize what you yourself have created.

Oechslin: Well, this is how the old concept of culture is constructed—and we still consider it a desirable condition. Culture is that which we make out of our capacity and our determination, as Johann Gottfried Herder (1744-1803) specifies when talking about the "history of humanity": for example, "der Mensch ist zu feinern Sinnen, zur Kunst und zur Sprache organisiert" and "zu feinern Trieben mithin zur Freiheit".[17] And again, we are back to instruments (and thus also to play), which in Italian is described so nicely and precisely as *artificio*. We are the creators of these instruments, yet we have not come so far from this "Verum et factum convertuntur," in which the human being achieves *verum humanum*—having the background of divine knowledge—by agreeing to a pact, and bringing knowledge about things and insight together with doing ("quod homo dum novit, componit item ac facit"). In the marginalia, Vico remarks: "Scientia est cognitio modi, quo res fiat". And before he reveals the path one must follow: "intelligere, ac perfecte legere, & aperte cognoscere." Moreover, he then translates the *cogitare* for a better understanding

---

17 | Johann Gottfried Herder, *Ideen zur Philosophie der Geschichte der Menschheit* (Riga: Hartknoch, 1774), pp. 216-236.

of it into *volgare*: "pensare, & andar raccogliendo".[18] So close to reality, Vico describes this "intellectual" process: no intellectualism and chimaeras!

The architect should be flattered by the fact that architectural metaphors are used so often by the philosopher, to illustrate such correlations—probably because this relationship of thinking and doing seemed to be so evident in architecture. With Immanuel Kant (1724-1804), we find again and again architectural metaphors, in the *Prolegomena* (1783) for example, published between the first and the second edition of the *Critique of pure reason* (1781 and 1787). There he makes the distinction between primary buildings and secondary "much more ample" side buildings "welches er [=der Verstand] mit lauter Gedankenwesen anfüllt, ohne es einmal zu merken, daß er sich mit seinen sonst richtigen Begriffen über die Grenzen ihres Gebrauchs verstiegen habe." Here we have it again, the need—with Kant, the necessity—of connection and the increasing risk that comes with detachment ...

Gerber: Let's talk about a very precise example, and about architecture, by using Le Corbusier (1887-1965). His writings contain many analogies between architecture and games, primarily in the sense of a combinatory system. This appears to me to be a novelty, as this kind of understanding of architecture as process has a long tradition indeed, however, mainly associated with language. This was the case, for example, with Jean-Nicolas-Louis Durand (1760-1834).

Oechslin: Combinatorics is the right reference, and I think it should be clear why this is once again closely related to play. In Le Corbusier's *Modulor*, there are pages containing all possible variations of the subdivision of a square.[19] As is well known, Durand was derogatorily labeled a "chessboard-provost" ["Schachbrettkanzler"] by Gottfried Semper (1803-1879). In reality, his game is much more refined, because it has a goal. He does not content himself with a simple position, nor with a simple geometrical figure-construction; at the end of his series, there are—sufficiently recognizable—schemes of concrete architectural floor plan-figures. I refer

---

18 | Giovanni Battista Vico, *De Antiquissima Italorum Sapientia, Ex Linguae Latinae Originibus eruenda Libri Tres* (Napoli; Felice Mosca, 1705), pp. 14-16.

19 | Le Corbusier, *Le Modulor [I], Essai sur une mesure harmonique à l'échelle humaine applicable universellement à l'architecture et à la mécanique* (Boulogne: Edition de l'Architecture [1950]).

to the corresponding table in the first edition (2e partie; planche 20) of his *Précis des leçons d'architecture données à l'École royale polytechnique* (1802).

Apparently, these images were (still) too abstract; in later editions, the corresponding geometrical forms are collated to newly added architectural bodies, in a way such that the whole "game"—or at least, the individual moves—are laid bare. Yet we miss out on the "joke" of the whole game dispositif, which proposes the all-encompassing, limitless combinatorics of architectural floor plans. In the first edition, this mechanism started with pure geometrical basic forms such as the square; or a square divided by two, three, and four; circles; circles divided by two, and the combination of circles and square-figures. This forms a kind of grammar, which could lead, according to the axiom of "few principles = as many applications as possible," to manifold concrete architectural solutions. It then suffices to specify few representative patterns. One introduces the artifice, typifies the first steps and adds "etc., etc." the same way as a mathematical series—and in a corresponding game.

When the discussion of "typology" came into fashion in the 1960s, one had to realize quickly that most architects preferred this playful approach to the more direct access to a suitable solution—with "their Neufert" at hand. To much risk?! We should be able to better convey the appeal of the game. This would widen their gaze on the allure of combination and variation, the control of which is indispensable to architects when encountering concrete—and often "irregular"—situations. To transform irregular situations into regular floor plans was, for example, part of Sebastiano Serlio's (1475-1554) standard task in composition. In Serlio, who was the first—still using the medium of woodcarving—to demonstrate the early design *all'antica*, we could find additional advices. This included, for example, the detailed analysis and representation of "a parte per parte" and "a membro per membro," in case of more complex situations.[20] Built upon few rules and conventions, one could deal with the most complex building program; combinatory, play! And obviously, this most simple form of combinatorics and systematics was perfectly coordinated with building and building technique: not only design, but also construction was based on this principle.

---

20 | Werner Oechslin, "'A parte per parte - a membro per membro'. Die Konkretisierung der architektonischen Form," *Archithese* Vol. 26, No. 2 (March/April 1996), pp. 15-18.

Gerber: Thus it was not only about a theory!

Let's return to modernism. Modernist architects had a specific relationship to play, through building sets and the influence of play-theorists such as Friedrich Fröbel (1782-1852). It is widely known that Frank Lloyd Wright (1867-1959) references the influence of "Fröbel gifts," when he was a child; with Le Corbusier this influence has been only assumed. Other architects, such as Bruno Taut (1880-1938), have designed building sets themselves. Is this symptomatic of the modernist attitude towards play?

Oechslin: I would say that Fröbel and Durand are not far from each other. These were times when didactical models and systematical pedagogies were particularly valued. Must we remind ourselves that, in this context, play was extremely important? "Fröbel-books," applying the theory of Fröbel, are often in effect building sets, as in this late copy of the second edition of the book *Manuel Pratique des Jardins d'Enfants*. Published in 1874 in Brussels, this book contains sentences such as: "Donnez à l'enfant n'importe quel joujou, confectionné, si vous voulez, avec art, cet objet ne l'amusera véritablement que lorsqu'il sera parvenu à la mettre en pièces."

Fig. 9: J. F. Jacobs, Manuel Pratique des jardins d'enfants de Fréderic Froebel, 1874

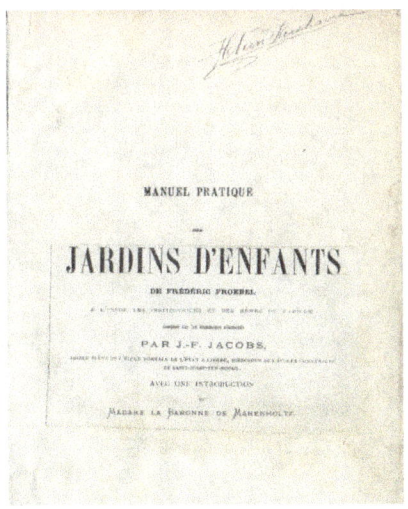

This is then explained through Fröbels' "cube divisé," in the same way that the architect references and reconstructs his composition based on basic forms and bodies. The *Jardins d'Enfants* follows the insight incisively: "L'enfant n'a pu voir ces propriétés à différentes grandeurs, que par la réunion de plusieurs cubes." We are already in the midst of block-play; we have disassembled, compared and set together again ... Quasi the archetype of play! And architecture is defined by Leon Battista Alberti (1404-1472), in the prologue of his *De Re Aedificatoria*, using the concepts of *compactio* and *coagmentatio*.

Fig. 10: Fröbel Gifts, 1874

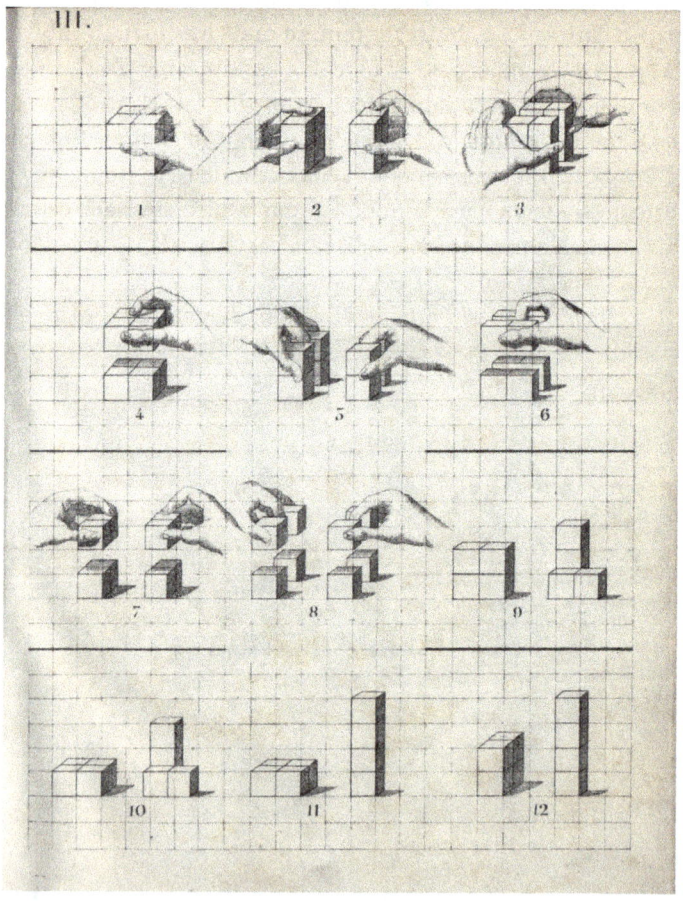

In this, there is not a big difference for architects in relation to the drawing, even though the line is more "abstract" and more difficult to "handle."

Le Corbusier talks about geometry "qui est le seul langage que nous sachions parler" and defines it as follows: "Géométrie: esprit clair et mystère infini des combinaisons." He, too, cites "Prométhée," in order to illustrate creativity and the creation of organisms that are lively because they are moving.[21] To him, it is crystal clear that architecture is founded in a competence with geometry, and that it is form-generating. More specifically, it is not about form, but about figure. In respect to figure, in principle, it is about the concretization of possible forms: Euclid defines them as "closed forms," and thus, it is comparable to the small blocks that result in the Fröbel cube. Thus, game, combination, variation—but all are contained "in rules."

Gerber: You are talking about variations; before, we were discussing instruments. This leads us to a fundamental metaphor: that of architecture as music, as music practice. In the past, it was common for architects to master a musical instrument. Theodor Fischer (1862-1938), for example, was an excellent cello player. We can find an application of this metaphor in the theory of proportions, when Le Corbusier compares proportions to a piano—which does not yet make a good player!

Oechslin: Yes, one has to master the piano, and only then one can play, play! Make music! I always had a weakness for variations. Goldberg, Diabelli, Paganini, and the variation movement of Mozart's *Sonata in D major*: these are all masterpieces, in which the richness of the composition inside a narrow boundary is demonstrated. Maximum freedom with maximal (musical and harmonic) order.

Gerber: At the same time, music can also stand for this nostalgia: for the theory and set of rules you previously mentioned. I would say that music is based on a very strong set of rules.

Oechslin: At least this is how architect Giacomo Barozzi da Vignola (1507-1573) saw it! In the short text preceding his bestseller *La Regola*, he describes how he would arrive at a rule through the comparison of the different perceptions of the "ornamenti" among them and with ancient works. He would then, beyond all observed differences, stop at the point where our eye judges something as beautiful, which is organized through "certa corrispondenza et proportione de numeri" between the whole and its parts, and complements and explains it by noting "come ben provano li

---

21 | Le Corbusier, *Une Maison – Un Palais* (Paris: G. Crès, [1928]), pp. 4, 12, 14.

Musici nella lor scienza".[22] He derives his "regola facile, et spedita" from this: not a complicated system of rules, but rather one which is as simple as possible, ready-at-hand, with the broadest possible applicability and, naturally an effect of perfect harmony.

Gerber: In principle, music appears—to me—to be less playful. Indeed, every interpretation is different, but it is created inside a very regulated world. This constraint is expressed very nicely in the metaphor of architecture as "frozen music." Friedrich Schelling (1775-1854) appears to be the first one to have used this metaphor in his *Vorlesungen über die Philosophie der Kunst* (1802-3) in his famous expression "Architektura ist erstarrte Musik."

Oechslin: These metaphors make me shiver! I'm also not enthusiastic about the "gravity" [Schwere], which Arthur Schopenhauer (1788-1860) attributes to architecture. Too many memorial statues! And the same can be said of the expression "Der Stein ist mehr Stein als früher" from Friedrich Nietzsche's (1844-1900) circle. The poetry of Éluard and his "tout homme est frère de Prométhée" seems more appropriate to me. Other cultures!

Gerber: *Kommende Baukunst* or *Vers une architecture*—that sounds completely different!

Oechslin: Yes indeed! And what should "come" here, what are we waiting for? Promises ...? No, we open ourselves up and walk towards something, with an open end; *vers* an architecture with a projected *durée*—and lot of hopes, a game!

Gerber: Since we are talking about time and the freezing of time, we could also talk about boredom. Beyond the game, time sometimes stands still, seems frozen. And talking about playing, we also play to overcome boredom ...

Oechslin: The game for all circumstances! It always helps—also in case of boredom! And, if we put it a bit more pointedly, the sublimation of boredom is the *Classical*! If something is boring to the point of being valid, then we have reached the Classical. It looks like we can endure certain forms, even if repeated a thousand times! And architecture strives for validity! Not everything has to be exciting; "boring"—because of uniformity—and repeating architecture is particularly apt for urban design.

---

22 | Giacomo Barozzi da Vignola, *I cinque ordini d'architettura* (Firenze: Giuseppe Molini, 1834 [1562]), p. 2.

Gerber: Boredom has also a positive reverse: we know how important boredom can be, since we no longer have the time to get bored these days.
Oechslin: ... and one must fear that all the people constantly fixating on their cellphone and going hectically through the world could lose hold on reality entirely.
Andri: ... and nobody would even realize it!
Oechslin: Nevertheless, I am still confident that human beings will always find a way back to reality. There is always the risk of exaggerating a game. Every game has a reverse; we are both supporter of the *ars oppositorum*, and also well-aware that if there is something thrilling, there will always also be boredom. What matters is to put everything in relation to one another. There will never be one thing without the other.
Gerber: You are talking about exceeding a game. Playing is often destructive, *per se*: you take something away, overcome obstacles, and try to defeat your opponent. Architecture always had a hard time reckoning with its own temporality. One of the few exceptions to this is Japanese architect Arata Isozaki (*1931), who, in the 1980s, would also show his projects as ruins.

Fig. 11: *The knight's castle in Machern, Leipzig, ar. 1795-1796*

Oechslin: Ruins are a sublimation and beautification of destruction. We should never forget that there is also real destruction. A destructive game would be fatal. But when you start a game, you will never have a guarantee that everything will remain safe. Fear of risk? Today, we live in our privileged world, in a fearful society that would like to secure everything. And the outcome of this is rules upon rules. There is a permanent call for new regulations, committees, new procedural forms. This might be the most important message for our time: We should learn to accept risk and to understand again the deep meaning of play. The best rules are those with exceptions, not those that exclude all possibilities and dangers.

Gerber: Without risk, no play! But this calls for consequences, whatever they may be.

Oechslin: Yes, but in the end, we both still have a very positive stance towards play!

Invisible (Game) Cities

Andri Gerber in Conversation with Paolo Pedercini,
January 25, 2019 (E-mail)

Andri Gerber: Let's start with an "easy" question: how do you become a "subversive game designer" (assuming you agree with this definition of your activities). What did you study? And to what extent was this planned, or did it happen by accident?

Paolo Pedercini: It was a bit of an accident. I made my first game for a political campaign. It was an extension of the rather traditional activist work I was doing at the time: making fanzines, setting up websites, designing flyers, and so on. Fifteen years later, I still do that kind of work for political organizations, but *Molleindustria* spun off into a more personal project.

Gerber: Religion, politics, economics ... you tackle big issues with your games. To our understanding, video games are "world constructions." This is what we are particularly interested in: the fact that the game world appears to be a simplified version of the actual world, which enables a better understanding of all the norms, actors, and framework that control this reality. Simultaneously, they break down this complex system into something simpler. Would you agree to this definition?

Pedercini: You can see games as models, meant to capture certain aspects of the real world. Scientific simulations have a specific purpose: they are meant to investigate and predict a phenomenon, and have to be constantly tweaked and evaluated according to the collected data. Game simulations are much more open-ended: their purpose is to entertain or achieve an aesthetic effect. Basically, they represent the real world, just like other artistic forms. The main difference is that games employ rules and interactivity along with audio-visual and narrative strategies. It's dangerous to think that, by virtue of being dynamic and interactive, games can produce a better understanding of real-world system. As Ian Bogost (*1976) claims, games make rhetorical arguments in a procedural form. You can accept their portrayals as truthful, or reject them when they clash with your own mental models. To me, the most valuable part of playing a game like *SimCity* (1989) is not that it explains how a city works, but rather, that it forces you to examine your own mental model of a city.

Fig. 12: Paolo Pedercini/Molleindustria, Leaky World, a Playable Theory, Screenshot, 2010

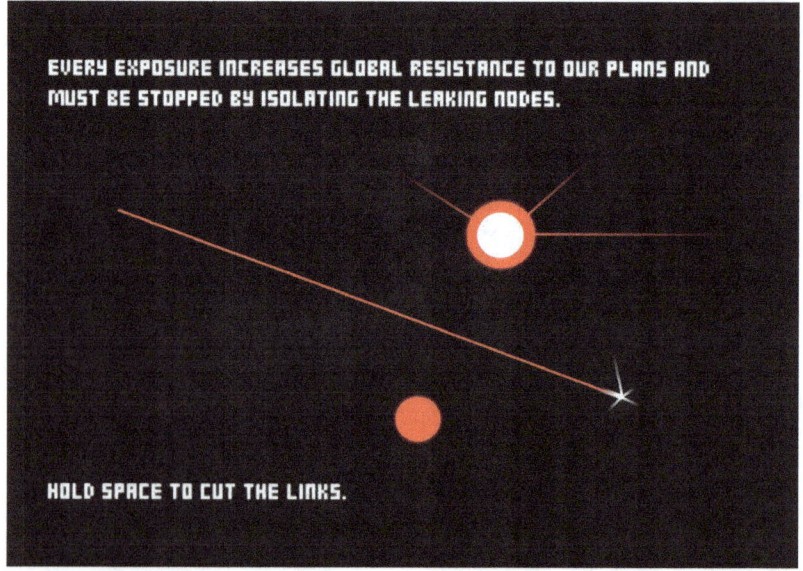

Gerber: If we consider contemporary video games, I would argue that we are faced with a great deal of irony—not sarcasm, as for example in *Fortnite* (2017)—but irony, as something that creates an ambiguous relationship between object and subject, while also leaving room for bitterness and understanding problems. Your work, I would say, is often very ironic in precisely this way. One is left with a sense of *amaro in bocca*, a sour taste. Is this something particular to video games, compared to other media such as film or literature?

Pedercini: Computers are quite literally technologies of control and measurement. Video games are constructed with these technologies and retain a certain cybernetic bias in their tropes, genres, and engines. If the goal is to articulate a critique of power or of capitalism through video games, then the most obvious strategy is to subvert or problematize these phenomena. So I can give you power in the game, but I also try to point out how you may be subject to this kind of power in your everyday life. I can give you a system that is compelling to master and optimize, but also show you how that this ruthless instrumental thinking is destroying our world. If I want to avoid a preachy, moralistic tone, irony can be a valuable rhetorical device.

Gerber: This calls for a question about participation. In a video game you are actively playing, you have to make decisions, you commit yourself to it, which cannot be done with books or while watching a movie, at least not to the same degree. On the other hand, with *Black Mirror: Bandersnatch*, Netflix is trying something in this direction; I remember similar experiments in the television programming of the 1990s. How would you describe the specific form of "personal investment" when playing video games?

Pedercini: I think *Bandersnatch* didn't put any effort in making you care about the fate of the characters. It wants you to explore the limits of this agency, to break its structure, while pulling all sorts of meta-fictional tricks to avoid the problem of branching stories. The result is somewhat cynical and sadistic: you are playing God with the life of the protagonist, fiddling with this new (in the context of television) technology, but maybe it's YOU—the viewer—who is being duped. All of which is in line with the techno-dystopian themes of the series.

Gerber: I find it very interesting that you also design board games. As a player, you have a completely different level of engagement. Where do you see the differences between these two types of game media?

Pedercini: I often come up with small, non-digital games, and I talk a lot about board games in my classes, but I haven't designed, nor published anything significant. From a design perspective, tabletop or card games require a kind of mathematical intuition that very few people have—I certainly don't. From a player perspective, they require substantial commitment and emotional investment: you have to find the right game for the context, invite people over, explain the rules, etc. For political purposes, the social situation surrounding board games has the potential to create and deepen bonds within existing organizations. However, I don't think they work as well as other media: they are not agile and malleable enough to spread new ideas.

Gerber: This reminds me of *Le Jeu de la Guerre* (1965), by Guy Debord (1931-1994), the most prominent member of the Situationists, and Alice Becker-Ho (*1941). It is interesting, because the Situationists were primarily material, on site, yet this game is very abstract and is intended to teach strategic thinking to the players. Does it appeal to you?

Pedercini: The only notable thing about *A Game of War* is that Guy Debord made it. It's a rather old-style, Napoleonic Wars chess variant with one interesting design idea: you have to defend communications and logistical lines radiating out from certain units. Overall, it's rather awkward and old-fashioned, but Debord delusionally thought it was his ultimate masterpiece, and that it synthetized all conflicts ever to occur, so his academic fanboys took it quite seriously.

Gerber: You are working on a well-known reference to architects, the beautiful book *Le città invisibili* (1972) by Italo Calvino (1923-1985). You are planning a whole set frame of game cities, the first one being *Nova Alea* (2016). What is your inspiration from this book?

Pedercini: I always wanted to make an alternative, critical *SimCity*; after several failed attempts, I realized that the idea of a single, all-encompassing city simulation was problematic in and of itself. Cities are historical strata, socio-economic processes, or states of mind as much as they are built environments. That's the reason why Calvino uses them as a starting point to talk about a memory, space and time, or semiotics. I definitely want to talk about cities and urban processes, but I'm inspired by Calvino's magical realism and the limited scope of each short story. Each invisible city is a nice read, but the work really makes sense because it is serial and has its internal relationships and resonances.

Gerber: Playing the game, the message you want to convey becomes very clear. Nevertheless, I was unsure how to play the game itself. I was missing some critical piece of information and got quite frustrated. Is this intentional or am I just a bad player?

Pedercini: I wanted it to be under-explained. Figuring out how it works was supposed to be part of the experience. Unfortunately, that approach clashes with the current design orthodoxy: the player is supposed to be told exactly what to do; all the components should have a clearly communicated function, and so on. I realize the process of rule discovery can be frustrating if you are not in the right mindset. There are a few games that can be cryptic in an engaging way: *Starseed Pilgrim* (2013), *Cinco Paus*

(2017) or many works by Stephen Lavelle, such as *Increpare (2010)*, but they are perhaps an acquired taste.

Gerber: Returning to Italo Calvino: the first lecture of his unfinished series, entitled *Lezioni Americane*, was dedicated to *leggerezza* (lightness). There he writes: "After writing *fiction* for forty years and after several experiments, it is about time for me to define my work; I would propose the following one: my procedure was mostly one of subtracting weight; I tried to subtract weight both from human characters, from celestial bodies, or from cities; I tried mainly to subtract weight to the structure of narration and to language".[1] To a certain extent, I would argue that designing video games is also about subtracting weight from reality. Would you agree to that? And to what extent do you think that lightness is an appropriate attribute with which to describe working in terms of video games?

Fig. 13: Paolo Pedercini/Molleindustria, Nova Alea, Screenshot, 2016

Spaces were collectively acquired and sheltered from the fury of the market.

---

1 | "Dopo quarant'anni che scrivo *fiction*, dopo aver esplorato varie strade e compiuto esperimenti diversi, è venuta l'ora che io cerchi una definizione complessiva per il mio lavoro; proporrei questa: la mia operazione è stata il più delle volte una sottrazione di peso; ho cercato di togliere peso ora alle figure umane, ora ai corpi celesti, ora alle città; soprattutto ho cercato di togliere peso alla struttura del racconto e al linguaggio." Italo Calvino, *Lezioni americane. Sei proposte per il prossimo millennio* [1988] (Milan: Arnoldo Mondadori Editore, 1993), p. 7.

Pedercini: I don't know. When I look at the code of a game in progress on my other window, it's more like a Rube Goldberg machine made of space shuttle pieces duct-taped together. I see nothing lightweight and subtractive in video game development. A game can present itself as clean and minimalistic, but there is likely to be a messy misuse of technology behind the surface.

Fig. 14: Paolo Pedercini/Molleindustria, Dogness. Breed the Perfect Dog, Screenshot, 2018

Gerber: As an extension of this, you frequently speak of your games—maybe also as a form of understatement—as "tiny games". In architecture and urbanism, scale is a fundamental issue, particularly in relation to the scale of human beings. What is the difference between "tiny" and "big" games? Is it only a question of money, or also of content?

Pedercini: Perhaps architecture's relationship with the human scale is similar to video games' relationship with human time. Making "big" virtual spaces is trivial. Making virtual spaces worth spending time in is the real challenge.

Mainstream games developed a perverse relationship with scale and content. In order to please a core audience of teens with a lot of time and little money, they got bigger and bigger in terms of content. Today, if you want to sell a game in the triple-A bracket, you have to guarantee dozens of hours of gameplay. This inevitably alienates young adults and people with less free time, who in turn are pushed toward more "Consumption-oriented" experiences like smartphone games. In order to be highly profitable, phone games need to be addictive and exploitative. An entire "dark science" has been created to keep players hooked into some idiotic match-three game. That is not good either. My simple proposition is to make games that are respectful of people's time and intelligence.

Gerber: Architecture and urban design are very much based on the experience of space. Virtual reality (VR) and extended reality devices are introduced in games, yet obviously the haptic dimension of the spatial experience gets lost. This is very problematic for us architects. You, too, have been very critical of VR, for example in your game *A Short History of the Gaze* (2016). Yet at the same time, one retains a fascination with the possibility of this medium. What are your thoughts on this?

Fig. 15: Paolo Pedercini/Molleindustria, A Short History of the Gaze, Screenshot, 2018

Pedercini: My thoughts on VR can be briefly summarized.[2] The first wave of VR was visionary and utopian, but the technology was not ad-

---

2 | An expanded version of these thoughts is available online: http://molleindustria.org/StrangerPlaythings/

vanced enough. Today's VR is somewhat functional, but it's being developed by morally and creatively bankrupt Silicon Valley bros. These startups are already abandoning proper VR in favor of the next dystopian capitalist fantasy—augmented reality (AR), or whatever. We need to get over the idea that we will all work, socialize, and play inside immersive worlds in the near future, and instead reclaim this technology for rare, strange, niche, site-specific, context-specific experiences.

Fig. 16: Paolo Pedercini/Molleindustria, A Short History of the Gaze, Screenshot, 2018

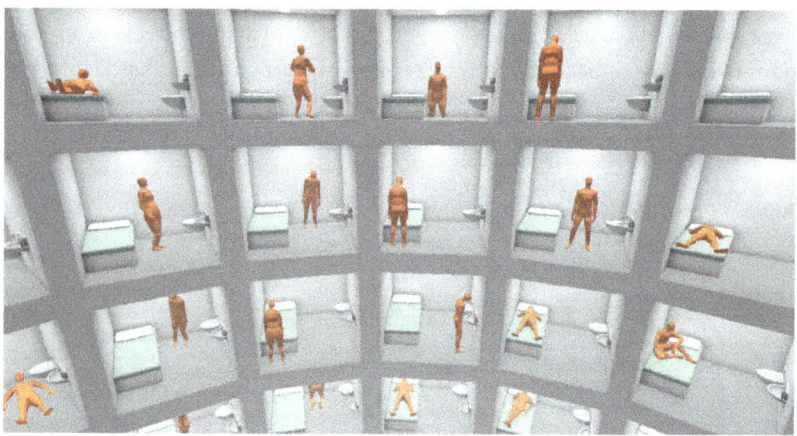

Gerber: What kind of theoretical basis, in literature, would you suggest for a young scholar interested in becoming a game designer? Or is it more about being open to what happens around you and less about being able to run a specific program?

Pedercini: *Rules of Play*, although quite dated, is still a good primer.[3] A few recently published textbooks, such as *A Game Design Vocabulary*[4]

---

3 | Katie Salen and Eric Zimmermann, *Rules of Play: Game Design Fundamentals* (Cambridge, MA: MIT Press, 2004).

4 | Anna Anthropy and Naomi Clark, *A Game Design Vocabulary. Exploring the foundational Principles behind good Game Design* (Upper Saddle River, NJ: Addison-Wesley, 2014).

or *Games, Design and Play*[5], are appropriate for undergraduate students. Computer science is a possible entry point for game design, but there has been a tendency to dissociate the work of game design from game development, which is the technical implementation of game ideas. In my experience, the most interesting game designers come from adjacent backgrounds such as math, film studies, or art. A new wave of young designers is definitely emerging from game design programs, but I'm not sure we are effectively teaching how to not remake existing games.

Gerber: Do you read books on architecture, or where do you find inspiration for the buildings and urban spaces of your games? For example, when you include a panopticon in your games, where do you source the forms and spaces for it?

Pedercini: I don't typically use immersive spaces in my games, but I do teach courses about level and environment design, in which I use a variety of architectural examples.

I tell my students to read *101 Things I Learned In Architecture School*[6] and incorporate some of these principles in a level design assignment (greyboxing). Some concepts don't map at all on games, but others can be extremely generative, such as the notions of "implied spaces" or "denial and reward."

Engineering limitations aside, what makes virtual architecture fundamentally different from actual architecture is the non-utilitarian use. You don't really live or work inside a game. Rather you tend to use, abuse, or traverse the built environment with a specific purpose. We are more in the realm of Marc Augé's (*1935) non-places.[7] The gamer's relationship with architecture is closer to that of a skateboarder or a parkour athlete. In my game design classes, I also talk about "expressive" architecture: memorials, museums, monuments, churches, world expo pavilions, as well as playgrounds and immersive installation art (such as Tomas Saraceno

---

5 | Colleen Macklin and John Sharp, *Games, Design and Play: A detailed Approach to iterative Game Design* (Upper Saddle River, NJ: Addison-Wesley, 2016).

6 | Matthew Frederick, *101 Things I Learned In Architecture School* (Cambridge MA: MIT Press, 2007).

7 | Marc Augé, *Non-lieux: introduction à une anthropologie de la surmodernité* (Paris: Éditions du Seuil, 1992).

(*1973), Yayoi Kusama (*1929), or James Turrell (*1943)). To me, these typologies are more useful for thinking about game spaces.

Gerber: This book is primarily written for architects who are interested in video games. We have actually realized that a lot of architects also work in this industry. Could you confirm this impression? Do you think they contribute any specific qualities to the design of video games?

Pedercini: I don't know about the private sector, but Eric Zimmerman (a game designer) and Nathalie Pozzi (an architect) have been collaborating for years on installation games that don't look and feel quite like anything else.

Gerber: Similarly, *Unity* has become very popular, also among architects, because the program environment is very close to that of 3D programs. To what extent has *Unity* enhanced the accessibility of designing games for laypeople?

Pedercini: It's an integrated environment, with a lot of ready-made components that just work. It's free, flexible, easy to pick up, and it has a robust community and ecosystem. *Unity's* acquisition of *ProBuilder* suggests that they are interested in providing more asset creation tools within the editor. The ability to draft spaces without going back and forth between 3D-modeling software and an engine such as *Unity* can be a real game changer.

Gerber: The gender gap is a big issue in architecture and town planning these days and there are several ongoing attempts to reconstitute the curricula and education of architects. Are there parallels in the game industry? Is it still a strongly "nerdy," male-dominated environment and are there discussions about better integrating women into the field?

Pedercini: Yes, this conversation has been happening for decades, and things have been improving significantly. *Gamergate* was a direct backlash against this trend of inclusion and diversification. Unfortunately, the industry is characterized by a high level of path dependency, as games and computers were marketed as toys for boys from the early 1980s through the late 1990s. Basically, we are missing a generation of women in leadership positions in the gaming industry, and in tech in general.

Gerber: Finally, I want to ask one last "nasty" question: Do you yourself play "commercial" video games? If so, what are your favorites?

Pedercini: I mostly play commercial games, if you mean games that are sold for a price. I rarely play the so-called "triple-A games," or free-to-play fads like *Fortnite* or *Candy Crush* (2012). They have little to offer and they require a great deal in terms of time. However, the remake of *Doom*

(2016), *Alien: Isolation* (2014), and *The Last Guardian* (2016) are excellent high-budget "commercial" games.

In-World Realism

Andri Gerber in Conversation with Konstantinos
Dimopoulos, May 22, 2019 (E-mail)

Andri Gerber: You recently finished writing an atlas on virtual cities. Could you tell me a bit more about this project? How did you come across this subject, and what was the project's ambition?

Konstantinos Dimopoulos: The *Virtual Cities* atlas is a book I had been thinking about for quite some time. I had been long fascinated by the format of the atlas, ever since I took cartography during my university studies. I was in love with the idea of the video game city since playing Dynamix's *Rise of the Dragon* (1990), when I realized that it could simultaneously feel real and utterly whimsical. Moreover, since I work as what I tend to call a "game urbanist," I knew I would thoroughly enjoy such a book. I realized that writing it would be an excellent research opportunity, as well as a deeply creative endeavor.

Back in 2017, I started vaguely imagining what *Virtual Cities* could look like, and which of gaming's urban centers it should include. I even started discussing the project with visual artist and friend Maria Kallikaki, but it wasn't until I was approached by the publishing house *Unbound* that work began in earnest. The unexpected popularity of the proposed book was what finally pushed me to expand, and—crucially—finish it.

As for the ambition behind it, I will be really happy if the first atlas of gaming's virtual cities lives up to its promise. I want *Virtual Cities* to stand the test of time, inspire creators and people who play video games, and act as a showcase of the medium's creativity.

Gerber: What are the qualities you are looking for in these cities? Are there virtual cities you had to leave out because they did not fit into your narrative?

Fig. 17: Konstantino Dimopoulos, Maria Kallikaki, Virtual Cities Atlas, 2019

Dimopoulos: Even though I am convinced that criticism is necessary in the evolution of any form, I do tend to favor its more positive expressions. I thus tend to celebrate the brilliant rather than criticize the mediocre—so in order to pick the cities for my book, I simply had to chose from those I deeply admire. I also tried to pick places from which useful design lessons could be taught, and through which fascinating urban stories could be told, while simultaneously trying to cover as much ground as possible. I wanted the atlas to be as representative of the medium's amazing variety as possible. To feature cities across genres, and of wildly different types, to cover thirty-five years of digital gaming on a multitude of different formats.

From the isometric ruins of *Antescher* (1983) and the text-only civic dystopia of *A Mind Forever Voyaging* (1985), to *Novigrad's* fantasy "open world" (2016) and the sci-fi metropolis of the *Citadel*: I tried to cover this ground while leaving room for less well-known cities. Part of the fun of reading through an atlas, after all, is imagining places you never knew existed, and planning excursions that may never happen.

Obviously, several cities I would have loved to revisit or explore for the first time had to be left out. However, I was happy to discover that there is a much broader range of game cities we should consider important than one might suspect.

Gerber: You also work in the field of video game level design. How do you proceed when you are asked to design a virtual city? Where do you get your information? Do you read books on the history of architecture, for example?

Fig. 18: Maria Kallikaki, 8-bit city of Antescher from the classic ZX Spectrum game Ant Attack, 2019

Dimopoulos: Just like real-life urbanism, game urbanism is an incredibly diverse field. Designing cities is only part of what I do, but admittedly, it's the most intriguing part. In addition to planning for an imaginary city, gaming's interactivity introduces numerous new factors that have to be accounted for, such as a game's genre, narrative needs, and actual level design priorities. A city for a stealth game, to give you an example, will very obviously have to provide numerous hiding places and alternate routes. One thus has to come up with a design that is believable, occasionally phantasmagoric, while allowing for particular gameplay situations and running on specific hardware.

Obviously, creating a city for a 3D-open-world action game is vastly different from designing for a 2D point-and-click adventure, even if both benefit from the very same urban and geographic pool of knowledge. This same pool can also shape a city-building game or provide players in a Massively Multiplayer Online Game with the tools to create their communities in a physical form.

Reading and researching the history of cities, planning, and architecture, as well as striving to refine my understanding of what makes actual and imaginary urban centers work, never really ends. Even though both my Ph.D. and M.Sc. are in urban planning and geography, and I have been researching actual cities since the late 1990s, I find myself constantly reading through books, articles, and even newsbits. Nevertheless, each project requires new and more focused research.

Fig. 19: Maria Kallikaki, The Port of the Dead: Famous Rubacava (Grim Fandango), 2019

Gerber: In an article on *Gamasutra*, you note that one of the main qualities of virtual cities is to create "realism." In an interview you say: "[R]ealism, you see, leads to believability, which in turn leads to immersion. A feeling of presence. Of being there in space".[1] How does one create this "realism" in virtual environments?

Dimopoulos: When I say realism, I do mean in-world realism. That is, a sense of cohesiveness within any given setting, even if such a setting is a magical castle-town, floating alone in deep space. Such a place would also have rules, and should therefore make sense, in order to help the people playing it suspend their disbelief. So, if we create a world where gravity exists, physics should behave accordingly; if our city is crafted by a society, certain societal rules should apply.

What I am advocating is essentially similar to Tolkien's idea of a second, coherent reality, where the imaginary should be almost as detailed and layered as actual reality. I have to admit, achieving such a feat can be very difficult in gaming, where creators often lack the crucial tools of framing and pacing. On the other hand, unlike literature, video games do allow for interaction and agency, which always helps foster immersion and empathy.

As to how one creates realism in virtual urban environments, the answer necessarily varies as wildly as these environments can. Generally speaking, though, for a city to have any chance of feeling real, at the very least it would have to supply the basic functions of urbanism. Assuming we are talking about human inhabitants, this means it would have to provide access to food and water, offer some sort of shelter, and allow for at least a rudimentary sort of economy. Without such absolute basics, a place would only make sense as a former city or a vast, brutal jail.

Gerber: What other qualities are you looking for when designing a virtual city?

Dimopoulos: Imagination, character, and believability are always crucial to me, but I must admit I am often impressed at how well games like *Assassin's Creed Syndicate* (2015) can abstract and recreate historical cities. It managed to fit a more than decent representation of Victorian London, the first metropolis, into a relatively small map, and capture a pop-influenced but thoroughly enjoyable sense of this era's atmosphere.

---

1 | Konstantinos Dimopoulos, "Urban Design and the Creation of Videogame Cities," *Gamsutra* (March 3 2017), https://www.gamasutra.com/blogs/ KonstantinosDimopoulos/20170831/304756/Urban_Design_and_the_ Creation_of_Videogame_Cities.php (accessed July 2, 2019).

There are, of course, far too many ways in which game cities can be wonderful. They can show little and imply much; they can be packed with detail and interactivity; they can hide countless details; they can evolve; they can do environmental storytelling on a historical level; they can support engrossing stories and set the stage for larger than life characters; they can be impressively dynamic and feature constantly changing systems, or even look outlandishly beautiful and unexpected. To be truly successful, above all, a city constructed for a game must ensure it properly supports and facilitates any and all gameplay.

Fig. 20: Konstantinos Dimopoulos, Sketch on a version of Zelda's Clock Town that would feel slightly more realistic than the one presented in Majora's Mask, 2019

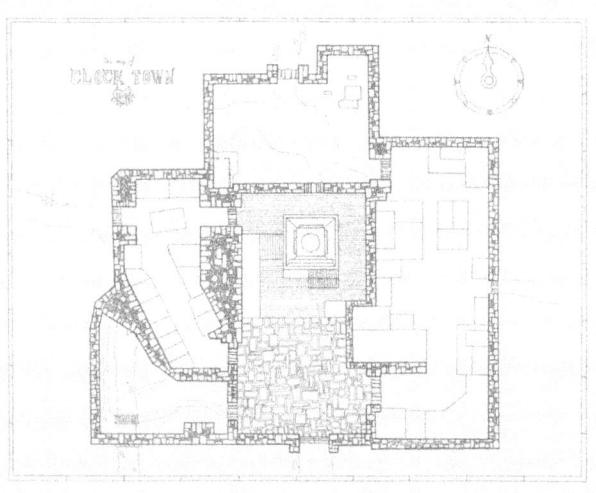

Gerber: We share a passion for H. P. Lovecraft (1890-1937). I remember how frightened I was when reading his stories for the first time; at the same time, I remember how disappointed I was with the various movie-adaptations of his *Cthulhu Mythos* universe, as it is very difficult to convey the specific qualities of Lovecraft's writing. One of my fondest memories was playing the *Call of Cthulhu* role-playing game (RPG) with my friends in the 1980s.

You are now working on a video game based on Lovecraft, which will be released in the summer of 2019, entitled *The Sinking City*. Do you think the game will be successful in conveying Lovecraft's specific sense of terror of?

Fig. 21: Konstantinos Dimopoulos, Maps and sketches for an untitled City RPG project, and forthcoming freeware entitled Nékromegà, 2019

Dimopoulos: To clarify things: I am not currently working on *The Sinking City*, although I am closely following its development. I did work on the game's city for a few months during its pre-production, and I do believe that the team had, and still has, a crystal clear understanding of what makes cosmic horror work. I also believe that they will be implementing unique civic solutions to their world-building, and will provide us with a city that will finally do Lovecraftian horror justice.

As a side note, I have to admit that I still occasionally play the *Call of Cthulhu* pen and paper RPG myself, and am slowly working on creating a nice city for it, as a sort of passion project.

Gerber: One aspect of virtual games you criticize is the absence of the dimension of time, in the sense that we don't see buildings being constructed. The only game I know that does this is *Mafia* (2002). At the same time—as has also been noted during other interviews in this book—this appears to be a problem of architecture and urban design, too, in which one does not adequately consider the temporality of projects, and what could occur after the project is completed.

Dimopoulos: It is true that most people tend to think in an ahistorical manner; this is often the case with both world-builders of imaginary settings and professionals of the material world. We commonly (and incorrectly) perceive the past as something static, and the present as perpetual; this leads us to forget all about history, its traces and processes, and tends to spawn worlds that can feel lifeless or like a theme park.

Thankfully though, as I recently rediscovered while writing *Virtual Cities*, many of the best designers have managed to imbue their urban centers with a sense of history. The *Mafia* games are indeed fine examples, but thankfully, they are not the only ones. Kamurocho can be seen evolving throughout the *Yakuza* series (2005-2017). Shanghai in *Kane and Lynch 2* (2010) is on the verge of a total transformation. The history of *City 17* (2004) is evident in its many co-existing architectural styles.

I would absolutely love to see a great landmark (a cathedral in particular) being constructed during a game's narrative, and I do advocate for giving history and its mechanisms a more prominent role. But I believe we are slowly getting there.

Gerber: Friends sometimes make fun of me, claiming that as a historian, it seems I would rather live in Renaissance Florence or eighteenth century Paris than in our time. The virtual worlds we visit in games obviously have this potential: serving as a comfort from the struggles of our everyday. Yet at the same time, they also have the potential to critically asses our "reality."

Dimopoulos: I completely agree with you. Games and their intricate worlds enable our daydreaming, while consistently remaining political. Even when they do not aim to be! This is especially true when it comes to their cities. I am constantly amazed to see the strong class-based approach even mainstream, AAA titles go for. On the other hand, Paris during the eighteenth century must have been breathtakingly beautiful.

Gerber: If we assume that our everyday is as "virtual" as the environment of virtual cities—because we are dependent on our senses, on our culture, our experiences, and so forth—isn't this a fantastic paradox? Aren't virtual cities sometimes more real than the actual ones?

Dimopoulos: I'd argue that, yes, for a certain period of time virtual cities can feel more real than actual ones. Beyond this, they can even make us think differently about real cities, too, and they absolutely feel palpable to their creators. I find that, when working on a city, I actually think of it in the same terms I would think of one that exists. I think of the citizens, the classes, the trends, what people might feel, and how local society would react to changes, et cetera. But, objectively, virtual cities are not real, nor were they designed to be. At best, they are artful, beautiful, immersive, and evocative illusions that can only partially simulate the way actual urban formations work.

Gerber: To what extent does your background as a rural and surveying engineer, as an urban and regional planner, and as a geography student influence the way you perceive and design games?

Dimopoulos: I spent too many years researching, studying, and appreciating cities, and thinking in a spatial, engineering-influenced manner. As a result, most of my thinking has been deeply influenced by my studies. On the plus side, both urbanism and geography have always been very broad disciplines, which thankfully meant I also dabbled in philosophy, history, design, statistics, math, literature, the visual arts, architecture, and even a bit of coding. This prepared me for the many hats someone working in gaming has to wear, and eventually led me to the field of game urbanism.

Gerber: And has the opposite also occurred? To what extent does your work in game design influence your practice, in urban planning and geographical research? Do you think there is a specific knowledge from designing virtual cities that could be transferred back to "reality," be it research or design?

Dimopoulos: A truly interesting question, but one I do not really feel fit to answer. For the past few years, I've been working exclusively on game cities, and I have returned neither to planning the real world nor to academia. My feeling, though, is that games can essentially influence reality in the ways all art forms can—by inspiring, critiquing, and so on—but also by providing simulation, modeling, visualizing, and useful procedural generation tools.

Gerber: As an extension of this, could you imagine to go back to practicing urban planning? How would an ideal "real" city be planned?

Dimopoulos: Not really, no. I honestly can't see myself attempting to tackle corruption, red tape, and maddening officials anymore. But I will always have very strong ideas regarding the ideal planned city. You see, I am confident that an ideal city cannot exist outside an ideal society, and what would an ideal society actually consist of is a deeply political discussion. Nevertheless, even if we agreed on the definition of perfection in urbanism, I could not accept the idea that one can solve societal, political, or economic problems with a clever plan and a few innovative design choices.

Even simple, almost obvious matters such as restricting the use of the automobile are hotly debated, and no plan has ever managed to even slightly ameliorate poverty.

Gerber: In the article cited above, you say that one of the main pieces of advice you give to urban planning students is: "[P]lease do not think like architects. That's the wrong scale when approaching settlements. Think like urban planners. Even better, think like geographers and planners".[2] I absolutely love this quote, as it refers to a long-standing historical controversy about the true nature of urban design and within whose competency this scale lies. Architects traditionally consider the urban scale as their exclusive playground, yet always in relation to architectural objects. Could you expand on that?

Dimopoulos: Oh, absolutely. I am convinced that the difference between architecture and planning is a matter of scale and function. A city is, quite simply, not a large building. It is an entirely different beast with vastly different functions. It must support vehicular flows, encompass pre-existing patterns and systems, is essentially (when truly abstracted) a construct of economy and geography; it is infinitely more complex than any building. This, of course, does not in any way mean that architects cannot be excellent urban planners, nor does it mean that planning can ignore architecture. Far from it. What we actually have to understand is that those are two different disciplines that simply happen to share a few similar traits, and definitely intersect when it comes down to the scale of urban design.

Gerber: What would be your advice to architects and urban designers wishing to work in the field of video games? How can one best approach it?

Dimopoulos: I suggest they definitely give gaming some thought, provided of course they are already interested in its worlds and systems. As researchers, academics, and creators, people who have been trained to understand and utilize space are—in my experience—very good at both game and level design. Of course, some research into games themselves would also be very useful, as would broad exposure to art, history, philosophy, and science.

Gerber: An obligatory last question: What are your all-time favorite games and what you are currently playing?

Dimopoulos: I'll answer the easy part of the question first: I am currently re-playing the original *Diablo* (1996), and really enjoying my time in *Alien:*

---

2 | Ibid.

Isolation (2014). As for my all-time favorite games, these would have to include *Monkey Island 2* (1991), *Sensible Soccer* (1992), *A Mind Forever Voyaging* (1985), *Space Quest IV* (1991), *Fallout* (1997), *TIE Fighter* (1994), *Manic Miner* (1983), *The Hobbit* (1982), *The Sea Will Claim Everything* (2012), *Witcher 3* (2015), and many, many more. But coming up with a stable, definitive list of them all seems utterly impossible!

Gerber: Most of the games you make reference to are relatively old. Is this because of nostalgia, as you used to play them as a child, or because their representation of the world was much more simple and left more space for imagination?

Dimopoulos: I believe this has less to do with nostalgia and more with the enthusiasm I had for all things digital as a teenager. Admittedly, the older I grow and the longer I work on games, the more I tend to appreciate them in a technical and artistic way, and less as a wide-eyed kid. To be honest, I do miss that feeling.

Video/Game

Andri Gerber in Conversation with Johannes Binotto,

Winterthur, February 1, 2019

Andri Gerber: Let's begin with the end. I know that you have a weakness for the proverbial "happy ending." What if for this book, we would replace it with "game over"?

Johannes Binotto: What interests me about the happy ending in cinema is that it represents a suspended condition: there is a postulated, assumed end; at the same time, it remains a fragile situation. In contrast, the "game over" of a computer game is, interestingly enough, both more arbitrary and more absolute. It obviously also depends on the type of game. There are games that have a strong dramaturgy and are more prone to a happy-ending type of game over.

I think that this doesn't apply to games that you really end, that you truly finish, but to those in which the game over can occur normally, at anytime. Think about when you suddenly have to turn off the computer. Time is over; this is totally arbitrary but also absolute, because the game is not continuing. Maybe extreme gamers would contradict me on this, and claim that they keep on thinking about the game even when not playing it, but I would say this is not the case for the average gamer. One can restart anytime, but it's a new start.

In the case of the happy ending in film, as well as in literature, there is a cut but the text goes on writing itself in the minds of the observers. This is not the case with a game, or at least not in the same way.

Gerber: The real drama is when you haven't saved the game—and your parents walk-in and pull the plug! That's an absolute cut! But would a happy ending also be possible in a game? To be honest, I don't remember ever playing a game until the very end, and this is quite frustrating.

Binotto: That is an interesting thought. I am interested in happy endings that are considered cheap, *deux ex machina* happy endings. But I am interested in these because they make a categorical jump, or what Søren Kierkegaard (1813-1855) calls a "qualitative leap".[1] Something happens that overthrows the entire set of rules that were valid before. I cannot imagine how this would be the case in a video game. Perhaps we can envision it like this: while the end of a game usually implies that all levels have been completed, that all coins and tokens have been collected, in our new game, this reward could happen at any moment instead of only at the end. This would be interesting, very Brechtian, but I have never heard of that.

Gerber: In video games this *deux ex machina* does not exist, as you are subjected to all sorts of rules and constraints. This is precisely where many subversive game designers intervene, questioning the game itself by subverting its rules.

Binotto: You need to develop a hacker-mentality, refusing to play the game the way you should. I think there are similar situations, in particular as related to the spatiality of video games. So for example in GTA—*Grand Theft Auto* (1997)—this would imply that suddenly you leave the car, go for a walk, and simply watch the leaves on a tree. And this could then be the happy ending, because you have left the game, while the game itself goes on endlessly.

Gerber: One is still in the game, but at the same, one has left it ...

Binotto: Exactly!

Gerber: You work in the field of media and cultural studies, and so you move between different disciplines: primarily literary studies, film studies, psychoanalysis, and architecture. It is my understanding that space is what combines all these disciplines in your work. And space, as you know, is an obsession for us architects, as it is both fundamental yet eludes a fixed definition. What is your definition of space, considering how all these disciplines converge in space?

Binotto: My definition of space would be: making a difference. I love the beginning of *Espèces d'espaces* (1974) by Georges Perec (1936-1982), where he says: at the beginning there is a line. A line immediately fabricates a coordinate system; through this, one understands that space is produced

---

1 | Compare: M. Jamie Ferreira: "Faith and the Kierkegaardien Leap," in *The Cambridge Companion to Kierkegaard*, ed. Alastair Hannay, Daniel Marino Gordon (Cambridge: Cambridge University Press, 1998), pp. 207–235.

and can be transformed constantly. This is why I am so interested in media studies: they imply the possibility of transforming space. At the same time, this represents the "lust" of architecture, a lust that is constantly frustrated because of the problem of the building. You cannot create stability while constantly transforming space. In architecture, if you want to build, you have to obey certain physical laws. Mediated space and space in media, however, is a non-Euclidian, topological space, an ever-fluid space. I think this is something that makes architects jealous—whereas media artists might be jealous of the architects' actual buildings.

Gerber: Here I recognize the psychoanalyst talking [laughs] ... I would assert that architecture has lost its role as a metaphor for construction and stability. Since the introduction of new media, the references we typically use are "networks" or "fluids." So this confirms, somehow, the pretended and long-lost "spatial innocence" of architecture ...

I often accidentally write video-game with a hyphen, instead of separating the two words. We know both how important language is, and that this kind of separation is not casual. What would be the prerequisite for binding the two words, video and game, with a hyphen, in order to bring them closer together?

Binotto: This is a very interesting question. "Video game" is, in and of itself, an extremely loaded term, in a way that fascinates me. First, we need to be aware that the medium "video" is a completely different medium than "film." Video is not a photographic medium, and perhaps not even necessarily an optical medium. Rather, it is a medium of writing, and this difference is extremely important. The video signal, as produced in a cathode ray tube, is not projecting actual images onto the screen of your TV set; it consists only of a moving dot of light. The movement of this dot is then mentally constructed into images. In film, one can, of course, say that the movement is an illusion, since movement cannot actually be recorded optically, but can only be simulated through a rapid progression of images. Nonetheless, it is an optical medium, consisting of the individual photograms of the film strip, which are then projected in rapid succession. With video, however, these single images do not exist, and it therefore becomes problematic to define it as an optical medium, unless the definition of what an image is becomes incredibly broad. Video theorist Yvonne Spielmann refers to this when calling video a "reflexive medium": a flexible medium that is defined by constantly folding back its signal onto itself.[2] This also explains why video artists are interested in effects like optical feedback and noise, decaying images, or disturbances. They are precisely because they want to show that these are no longer images, in the traditional sense. Video is a medium that is built on instability; it was not intended as a medium of recording. It is important to remember that video originally consisted of a constant flow of signals without any possibility of storage. Mediums for recording, such as video cassettes, were developed much later. In order to record an early video broadcast, you had in fact film the TV screen, in order to store it. The default mode of video is "send" not "capture." I think this is where the affinity with games exists: the game is a strange activity, one which is not built on a final result, but rather, a process that is self-sufficient. When we play together, we do not actually play in order to win, to win the most marbles, but we play for the sake of playing. There is nothing you take with you from the game once it is over. It is a performative medium that consists only of being played. This makes "video" and "game" so closely related.

Gerber: So in both cases, we have an inscription.

Binotto: Yes exactly. It is all about a constant overwriting process.

Gerber: Like a palimpsest ...

Binotto: Correct.

Gerber: Let's move from one connecting line to the other, from the hyphen to the slash. You have used the slash extensively in your publications—*Tat/Ort* or *Film/Architektur*—what would be required to relate video and game with a slash, and what would the slash imply for the two connected items?

Binotto: In my work, it implies that it is not clear which element is primary, and the two items could exchange positions. Normally, you use the slash to indicate an alternative name, like a.k.a [also known as]. If video and game—written as video/game—could exchange positions, seeing video from a video-art perspective becomes possible; a playful, experimental position, aware of the fact that a video showing images is only one of its many possibilities. This explains the "messy" work of video-artists; they do this, in order to make the medium's own messiness clear. As Marshall McLuhan (1911-1980) points out, every new medium is generally misunderstood, since it is first believed to be merely a continuation of an old medium. For example, everyone believed that TV was just a continuation of film, only

2 | Yvonne Spielmann, *Video: The Reflexive Medium* (Cambridge, MA: MIT Press, 2010).

to realize that it is something else much later on. The video signals in TV can, of course, simulate film, but actually, it is something completely different. You can also plug a sound synthesizer instead of a camera into the TV monitor and you'll start to "see" sound. Expecting video to comprise "images" is thus a very limited and naive understanding of this medium. Instead, we must adopt a playful or experimental attitude towards this medium, one which is less oriented towards a result and more towards a pure process. Once you comprehend this, it would be a "game-attitude" towards video. Then you have video-slash-game, and they become interchangeable.

On the other hand, when the game gets exhausted by its own process, then it comes close to being video. If, for example, you no longer want to arrive at the finish line in a car racing game—when you no longer collect and "store" all the coins and treasures on your way, but rather, you get out of the car to have a stroll, or you just drive endlessly—then you would have a video-attitude in game. That would be video/game, which deserves its name.

Gerber: On a related note, there are several artists creating images based on video game aesthetics, Matthias Zimmermann (*1981) for example. But you would find the video component lacking in such attempts.

Binotto: The late work by filmmaker Harun Farocki (1944-2014) and his four-part video cycle *Parallel* is particularly instructive. Farocki was interested, very concretely, in how video-game makers do games, how they create elements such as wind or plants, and how one could explore these virtual words differently. The videos themselves seem almost utopian, at least to me: they reveal what a different kind of game could look like. Take the television series *Halt and Catch Fire* (2014-17), for example, about the revolution of the computer industry in the 1980s and early 1990s. In this show, a game designer has created a game called *Pilgrim*, of which she is very proud, but people do not understand it. To her, it is the ultimate game, because it is just an endless exploration, with no final destination. Sadly, consumers are not interested in that.

Gerber: The slash both separates and connects. Through the cutting and the connection, this space in between becomes tangible. This leads me to another aspect of games I think is worth discussing: weight. By this I mean the "weight" one loses by editing down and the weight of a new, almost solid connection. There is a weight between video games and reality: as much as video games attempt to copy reality, they will always remain a "lighter" variant. I would argue that architecture in gaming is even lighter than in other mediums, such as photography or film.

Fig. 22: Harun Farocki, Parallel, Germany 2012, Digital Frame Enlargement

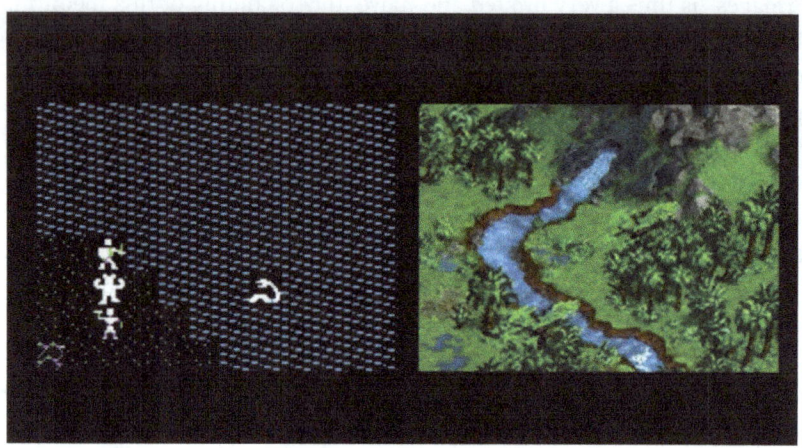

Fig. 23: Juan Campanella, Halt and Catch Fire, episode 4.1 "So It Goes," USA 2017, Digital Frame Enlargement

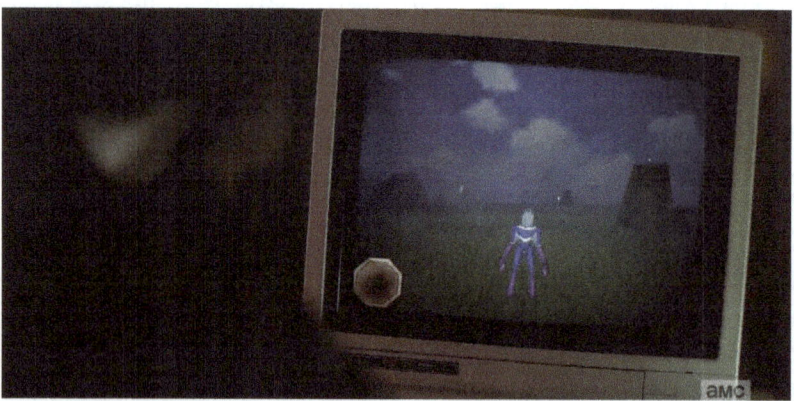

Binotto: I would agree with you, that architecture is "lighter" in image than in reality, also because the former can be so easily manipulated. The medium of video implies that something is in a constant state of change, that everything is a continuous permutation. In photography and in film, this exists in grains and noise, for example. If I had to compare them, I would say that a photographic image is a thick soup, while video is fog. You clearly feel this, because buildings in computer games are made of this fog, and can be exchanged easily and quickly. They have almost no substance.

Gerber: Well, in video games you can do almost anything, and the challenge is to make this architecture look like real architecture ...

Binotto: Exactly.

Gerber: This brings us to the matter of technique. You are currently researching the role of technique in film, not only as a corollary, but rather, as the subject of film itself. I would argue that in video games, technique is almost invisible and has no real influence on the game. What about digital filmmaking? Has technique ceased playing this role?

Binotto: On the contrary! I would argue that the influence of the technique has become even stronger. If you consider the fact that a digital movie is no longer made of images, but instead of pixels that the beholder has to assemble themselves, this is very plausible.

An example of this is films shot in high-definition digital images telling stories that are "pixelated"—fractured and discontinuous narratives without a teleological story arch. Films like *Miami Vice* (2006) by Michael Mann (*1943), for example, or the recent movies of David Fincher (*1962), such as *Gone Girl* (2014). Here, it seems there is no longer any frame of reference, no "hard" reality, just a constant flux of information, endless movement without a goal. And it's not by accident that we find shots of radar and television screens, prototypes of electronic images in such movies. I would argue that something originating with the technique inscribes itself into the film and its stories.[3] While Mann and Fincher seem to be very conscious of that, it also happens in other cases. Even if you use filters and try to make digital video look like an analog film, as soon you stream these movies online, buffering effects will inevitably occur, glitch-

---

3 | See: Johannes Binotto, "Closed Circuits. Immanence as Disturbance in High Definition Cinema," *Disruption in the Arts*, ed. Lars Koch (Berlin/Boston: De Gruyter, 2018), pp. 171-185.

es and data corruption. Moments like this reveal something that actually pertains to the new medium. You witness a deconstruction, in which the digital technique inscribes itself into the movie. This cannot be escaped easily.

As for games, I once had an interesting experience with a simple car racing game, in which I was projected out of the course in a turn, yet I could then keep driving. I was literally driving on the border of the game! On the left, the screen was grey; on the right, there was the game. I was driving along this threshold, and suddenly, I could see the true nature of the game. That was a great experience! This is exactly why some games don't allow you to exit the car and walk around, because this "outside" has not been programmed. But this is exactly where the computer game becomes interesting to me. When you walk towards this invisible border, you recognize the mediality of the games.

Fig. 24: Michael Mann, Miami Vice, 2006, Digital Frame Enlargement

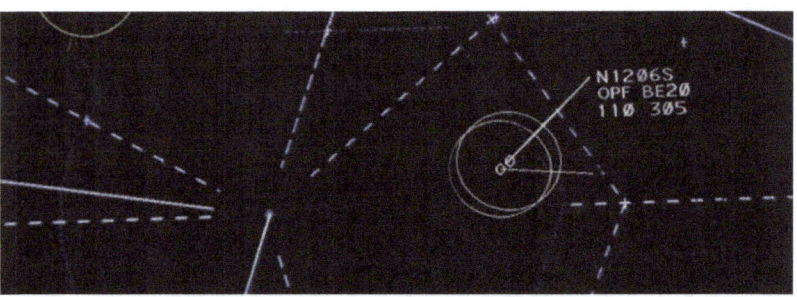

Fig. 25: David Fincher, The Girl with the Dragon Tattoo, 2011, Digital Frame Enlargement

Gerber: One could thus read the development of games in time as a constant attempt to make this border smaller and more inaccessible, both as space and as narrative. In this sense, I think there is a big difference between a movie and a game: in movies, space is constructed and is all about limits and borders, while games are all about the illusion of boundless space.

Binotto: You shall have the illusion that you can go anywhere!

Gerber: The frame is part of the movie, because without borders, you have no space. In games, the opposite is true: you would have, let's call it a landscape, and then we would have to start discussing the sublime and the picturesque as possible conditions of the beholder. But considering your previous work, it might make more sense to talk about the uncanny as a condition of these game landscapes. I would argue that there are no uncanny games, precisely because gaming happens against borders. Thus, there is nothing to turn the *heimlich* (the familiar), into the *unheimlich* (the uncanny), also because you literally inhabit them.

Binotto: I wouldn't agree with you. What characterizes the uncanny is a sudden moment of impossibility or disorientation. The moment where you leave through a door and realize that, through this very door, you actually entered the room you wanted to leave. So this concerns topologies; it is about spatial impossibilities—this is at least how Sigmund Freud (1856-1939) characterizes it. In this sense, the video game has a lot of potential. You never know if people will react to something uncanny, if it triggers an emotion in them. *Monument Valley* (2014) is a good example for this, and I would call it a perfect case study of the uncanny. It corresponds a great deal with what I would call uncanny, even if one does not perceive it as disturbing. Maybe this is because you can feel at home in the uncanny, and you don't feel a rupture between the two conditions of the familiar and the uncanny. This seems to be peculiar to the uncanny of the video game.

When I think about it, another such example would be *Portal* (2007) and the question of where I am.

Gerber: This brings us back to the issue of "game over." Because a game is played over and over, you are more likely to feel at home in the uncanny in a video game than in another medium. I would say that there are few movies that are uncanny when watched a second or third time, once this moment of surprise is lost.

Binotto: … because you know that there is a rupture coming, but you don't experience it as a rupture anymore, as it has become part of a dramaturgy.

Here is a very good example of this: I have not experienced this person-ally, but Danish filmmaker Johan Knattrup Jensen (*1979) has created such a situation with virtual reality (VR). He set up the following: In a theater, the public is seated and each person wears a VR-device. He then calls one person in front to join him; the audience's VR-sets are linked to this person, so everybody in the audience can see what the person sees. Then, he inserts movable walls around himself and this one person so the public is no longer visible. Then, he takes the wall away and the public is gone. He walks through the seats. In reality the public is still there, but through the eyes of the person on stage, they see empty spaces where they are sitting. They see themselves as not being physically there. This must feel extremely uncanny!

Fig. 26: Johan Knattrup Jensen, The Shared Individual, 2016

Gerber: We definitely cannot avoid thinking about the possibilities of aug-mented and virtual reality, especially in the context of video games. I had a very uncanny experience on a rollercoaster in *Legoland*. While waiting in the queue, you see that after the first hill, the track drops down to the right dramatically. When you get on, and you have a VR-headset on, that puts you in a virtual Lego race. The disturbing thing is that the virtual race gives you the illusion of moving forward after the rise, while your body drops down to the right. So even if you know what will come, you are completely immersed in the virtuality displayed through the device.

Binotto: And this is why we should consider one more thing: The uncanny as Freud defines it, is something that has to do with minimal shifts, with subtlety. It is this small suffix, the "un," that mediates between the familiar and the strange. The smaller the difference is, the stronger its effect will be. It would not be able to be about the total collapse of the world. So, in talking about virtual reality, the uncanny is about small changes, about a detail, not something so evident or all-encompassing, such as in *Pokemon Go* or your rollercoaster, even if you experienced it to be uncanny.

Gerber: A good example I have from you is the head of the murder reflected in a mirror in Dario Argento's (*1940) *Profondo Rosso* (1975). At first you do not notice it, even though your head registers that there is something strange. That's really uncanny.

Binotto: Yes, that is a very good example.

Gerber: Let's discuss another issue. You work with the concept of "heterotopia." Do you think we could apply this also to video games? In general we tend to talk about game spaces in terms of utopia or dystopia, because you have other worlds or destroyed worlds, but not necessarily in terms of heterotopia.

Binotto: We must first distinguish between the two ways in which Michel Foucault (1926-1984) has used this term. Foucault's first use of heterotopia comes from *Les Mots et les choses. Une archéologie des sciences humaines* (1966). There, this notion is used to describe a world, in which the common classification system is suspended and another, yet unthinkable system is possible. He explains this by referencing the work of Jorge Luis Borges (1899-1986). So, if we want to apply this to video games, we have to look for games that do not simply consolidate existing systems, but create new systems of order. We would have to examine this more deeply, but it is interesting to consider that games are often advertised as introducing completely new worlds and new rule-systems. The question is, then, whether or not this is true, in the sense of heterotopia. This would be the true challenge for game designers.

In architecture, we are primarily confronted with his second use, which he discussed in a 1967 radio program entitled *Des éspace autres*. According to his definition, these other spaces—he mentions, for example, brothels, colonies and cemeteries—are concrete places that you can find on a map, yet that function in a different way. Applying this to video games would imply shifting the focus from the game itself to the whole dispositive of the person who is playing: What is the relation of the room in which the computer is to the desk, to the chair, and what are the dispositives one is arranging. If you work with a joystick, that makes it even more interesting, because you have lots of feedback from the body, table, room, chair and game worlds. Then, the notion of heterotopia would be very fruitful and precise in this context. So when a child sits at the desk in front of the computer on a chair, and is making certain movements, at the same time, the child is somewhere else. And the chair is the same one it sits on when doing homework, yet at the same time, it is not the same chair and these are not the same movements.

Gerber: It is indeed very difficult to create something completely different. You see this very well in all historical examples of utopia, when it comes to thinking of a new and different architecture and urban environment: at the end everything is just bigger or richer, but not really different. Furthermore, when it comes to the narratives beyond games, almost everything can be brought back to Greek tragedies and comedies ...

Binotto: Yes, indeed. Or could we possibly have "Jorge Louis Borges" type of games?

Gerber: In games, you always need a certain degree of recognizability. Probably, the game you are dreaming about could not be played, and would be too far removed from reality. Games oscillate between two conditions: the "normal" and the truly "impossible," and both cannot be achieved as pure conditions.

Binotto: We should then refer to the incredible success of *GTA*. What is it that makes this game so successful? In reality, it is made up of copies of film-like images; it is a constant citation of pictures we recognize from movies. So what makes it so attractive?

Gerber: Maybe the sense of freedom and its realistic setting?

If we take a step back, referring to the concept of heterotopia, it is interesting to consider how we used to play arcade games in the 1980s and compare this to today, where we move on the street with mobile phones hunting Pokémons superimposed onto the backdrop of "reality."

Before, you really were in another space. I remember playing *Double Dragon* (1987) after school or going to the mythical *Astra Games* in Milan, with its cacophony of sounds coming from the different arcade machines, where I would mostly play *Street Fighter* (1987). These were total heterotopias, in which you delved into another space and time with a fascinating kind of nerd-counter culture. We constantly got robbed by drug addicts that where hanging around there, waiting for little kids with tons of coins …

Binotto: We can read it in both ways: the fact that you can carry your console with you means that you can turn any place into an arcade. This would be the optimistic interpretation. A more pessimistic interpretation, and this has also been discussed in film theory, is that you have reduced infinite possibilities to a pocket size and thus "castrated" game or movie. My stance is ambivalent. I am definitively fascinated by these possibilities, in particular when you can observe how people act while playing and how this changes the space we occupy. At the same time, I am irritated by the possibility of taming not only the scale of reality, but also the game itself, by spending money or looking for shortcuts to overcome its challenges.

Gerber: Again, this is about continuous flux and resistance, tension and flow.

Binotto: The whole gaming industry revolves around these paradoxes: if there is too much tension it is disturbing, yet it cannot be too self-contained. This is why I am so fascinated by the idea of playing a "game against the game," for example, by exiting the car in *GTA* and walking around aimlessly, without any limitations. That's not in the industry's interest, because they don't want you to be satisfied with just one game that you can explore endlessly. They want to sell you another game. From a purely economic point of view, in a game you would need only a corridor to quickly lead you to the end, so that you can buy the next game. But a mere corridor would be far too boring—you need more freedom. So they have to find a compromise.

Gerber: We could say that in games, subversion must be part of the system. However, this obviously cannot be …

Finally, I ask all of my interlocutors a concluding question: Do you regularly play games? If so, which ones?

Binotto: I must admit, I play computer games rarely, and if I do, I often play the most boring game of them all: *Patience*. As you know, I'm obsessed with minimal differences; as such, most games are far to active for me. My preferred games are movies. And movies are much more passive, particularly when you watch the same movie over and over again, which I like the most. However, this passivity permits subtle activities, for example, discovering small details. Similarly, my ideal game would be an extremely complex and at the same "boring" world, in which there's nothing to do but simply to remain—no run against the clock, no coins to gather, simply things to observe. Designing such a game would be rather expensive and I would probably be the only one playing it, so I don't think it will ever be made. This game would, actually, be very similar to how I experience the real world anyways. So, why bother?

Games as Provinces of Meaning

Andri Gerber in Conversation with Silke Steets,

March 20, 2019 (Skype)

Andri Gerber: You are a sociologist working on a wide array of topics, ranging from architecture to urban design, and more recently, on religion. It seems that the subject of video games is still not heavily researched in sociology, or at least many bemoan the scarce literature in this field.

Silke Steets: There have been some interesting insights into how "games" in general can be described sociologically. This was done, for example, by Canadian-American sociologist Erving Goffman (1922-1982) in his book *Encounters. Two Studies in the Sociology of Interaction* (1961). Goffman, among others, reflects upon the difference between the sphere of everyday life and the sphere of games. Both are characterized by a specific state of mind: Whereas we have a pragmatic interest in "surviving" in the sphere of everyday life, we can strip off that "seriousness" in the sphere of games. Still, and somehow paradoxically, games need to be taken seriously, in order to create their own immersive world. Another example from the sociology of games is the notion of "gamification," which presents investigations into how games and competitions have been applied as neoliberal strategies within the framework of our economic system and structures.

Gerber: You recently published a great book, *Der sinnhafte Aufbau der gebauten Welt* (2015), in which you consider architectural objects as "social realities," following and seemingly inverting the theories of Peter Ludwig Berger (1929-2017), Thomas Luckmann (1927-2016), and George Herbert Mead (1863-1931), among others. When we consider architecture in video games, it is supposed to mimic reality, but in doing so, it is obviously a construction. My first question is in relation to this topic is: How would you describe the nature of architecture in games? By games I mean not only video games but also board games or simulation games.

Fig. 27: Silke Steets, Der sinnhafte Aufbau der gebauten Welt, 2015

Steets: I think that when we speak about architecture in the context of these games, we are discussing their emblematic and symbolic character, rather than their material nature. The function of architecture in gaming landscapes is to provide orientation within the game, and to allow to act according to its rules. The function of architecture is thus to steer the process of orientation, and if we translate this back to our reality, then we reduce it to its sign-nature. This reminds me of Kevin Lynch's (1918-1984) book *The Image of the City* (1960). He describes the way one deciphers orientation in space through landmarks, which are designated by objects, architecture, and buildings. In video games, it seems to me that architecture is largely reduced to this function.

Gerber: Speaking to how we perceive architecture in our every day life, Walter Benjamin (1892-1940) described this as a *Zustand der Zerstreuung* (a condition of distraction)[1], because we use architecture without consciously looking at it. I have the feeling that, in video games, architecture is perceived more consciously, precisely because of its central role in providing orientation, and because one has to find a path through it.

Steets: I'm not quite sure. The experience of architecture in video games seems to be similar to the experience of architecture in Disney theme parks. What accounts for this relationship is the fact that games and theme parks are both about telling a story, leading you through its spaces. This is not new; the garden of Wörlitz, for example, which was the first English landscape garden in Germany, started doing the same thing in 1769. Visitors are—in a very Benjamin-esque condition of distraction—smoothly guided through the garden by its spatial and architectural organization. While walking from one visual axis to another, a story is being told. This seems to be very similar to video games. Going through the story is at the same time the act of telling the story. In both cases, as one is moving through a story, the dimension of time is eminent.

Gerber: This reference to landscape gardens is significant. When you mentioned about Wörlitz, I was reminded of the *Manière de montrer les jardins de Versailles*, which was a set of instructions Louis XIV (1638-1715) had prepared for his son—and worked over many times between 1661-1668—about where to walk and where to look in the Versailles gardens.

Steets: At the same time, this is only implicitly communicated in games. You do not get instructions: move from point A to point B, then turn left, and so on and so forth. Games give you the impression of freedom, even though you are obviously strongly bound to a limited space. There are very "hard" algorithms behind the supposed freedom of movement.

Gerber: It would obviously be very interesting if in such a game, you were suddenly and constantly confronted with verbal instructions telling you what to do and what to avoid. Imagine that in *Mario Bros.* (1983). That

---

1 | Walter Benjamin, "L'œuvre d'art à l'époque de sa reproduction mécanisée," *Zeitschrift für Sozialforschung* 5 (1936): pp. 40-66.

would be very revealing about the freedom you have—and also quite disturbing [laughs]!

Fig. 28: Connecting bridge in the garden of Prince George, Dessau

My impression is that games do not so much restrict space but rather open a landscape. Even if you are inside a closed room, you have the feeling because of this constant flow of movement, that you are in a field, in a landscape.

Steets: There is a very similar experience in real space: the bodily practices of skateboarding or parkour. There is a really good book by Iain Borden, *Skateboarding, Space and the City* (2001)[2], in which he describes the skateboarder's experience of urban spaces as a landscape of obstacles that need to be "handled." Even more impressive is the documentary film *Dogtown and Z-Boys* (2001), by Stacy Peralta, about the invention of vertical skateboarding in California in the 1970s. The film shows how skateboarding de-

---

2 | Iain Borden, *Skateboarding and the City: Architecture and the Body* (Oxford: Berg 2001).

veloped from surfing: the landscape of ocean waves becomes a landscape of concrete obstacles, yet the imagination of a parkour-like experience remains the same. This seems to be aligned with what you experience in video games, where you move from obstacle to obstacle. In gaming and in skateboarding, it is all about learning how to overcome obstacles and develop a specific flow. In my eyes, this is one way of creating a connection between the experience of space in the real world and that of video games.

Gerber: This reminds me of the music video for *Californication* by Red Hot Chili Peppers, released in 1999. Here, the elements of the band move, or rather, fly through a typically video-game world reminiscent of California. One line of this song even says: "Space may be the final frontier but it's made in a Hollywood basement." Space is a container; it has to have boundaries, otherwise it is a continuous landscape. Although their landscape sometimes appears to be infinite, games have boundaries, which normally remain invisible. Even the space of one of the most "open" games, *Minecraft* (2009), eventually ends; it is not infinite. At the same time, there are a lot of thresholds and crossings in games that structure this landscape.

Steets: Well, the earth is a globe [laughs], and at least theoretically it is without borders. One could turn endlessly in a circle. It is probably possible to design a game—and perhaps it exists already—in which space just goes on and on endlessly. This exists on some webpages today; as you scroll down, new content is constantly appearing. One never reaches the end of the webpage.

Gerber: Yet if space was endless, there wouldn't be a game anymore! Games have to end somewhere, don't they? And wouldn't this be extremely boring?

Steets: Borders are interesting. I would not define them as the end of space, but rather, as a mode of relating two spaces with each another. One space ends as another one begins. Borders structure space. In games, you often move from one space to the next, when you go from one level to another. In games, the dimension of time is crucial and bound to space.

Gerber: Time is a very important issue, both in games and in architecture. Architecture is the creation of space, but the dimension of time is often neglected.

Steets: "Give me a gun and I will make all buildings move." This is a famous quote from Bruno Latour (*1947) and Albena Yaneva[3] about the application of actor-network theory to architecture. This is an attempt to underscore the process-like nature of the building. Architecture is always part of networks of meaning and action, part of associations, and consequently, its meanings constantly shift. This includes the life cycle of a building and its changes in use over time. I would agree with you, that this is not an explicit focus of most professional architects, who typically focus their attention on the making of the objects themselves. From my point of view, it would be fruitful to more thoroughly consider the "aging" process—the use of a building over time—and to try to include this perspective in the design process.

Gerber: Space is always political; or at least in the architectural discourse, this possibility is strongly emphasized. Yet there are different positions between those who believe that space needs borders in order to have difference—and thus a political dimension—and those who believe that borders epitomize the absence of such a political dimension. When we transpose this to game spaces, there are games designed with strong political content and a political message. Yet, at the same time, there are games that remain devoid of social conflicts, even when Massively Multiplayer Online Role-Playing Games. While these games imply the virtual exchange of many people, they nonetheless cannot be defined as political spaces in the Greek sense of the word "politic," from *poleis*.

Steets: Perhaps it is helpful to consider a game as a "finite province of meaning," as defined by Austrian philosopher Alfred Schütz (1899-1959). With this concept, he distinguishes between the reality of everyday life we are living and different "provinces of meaning," such as the theater, a dream, or a game. Each of these "provinces" suspends a specific aspect of everyday life. In a game, for example, the seriousness of life is suspended. You can do things without consequences; you can play with different identities and try out all kinds of crazy things. Moreover, in games, we die all the time without having to die in real life. This makes the game a non-political sphere; on the other hand, if we think of the game in its

---

3 | Bruno Latour and Albena Yaneva, "Give me a Gun and I will make all Buildings move: an ANT's View of Architecture," *Explorations in Architecture: Teaching, Design and Research*, ed. Reto Geiser (Basel: Birkhäuser, 2008), pp. 80–89.

relationship with the reality of everyday life, it can also be read as a sphere in which we visualize utopias, make them intelligible and even tangible, which can then have an influence on reality. Take *Second Life* (2003), which emerged very early; it was all about creating a harmonic utopia. As such, it could release fantasies that might possibly have an influence on "reality." I would define the political, instead, as a relationship between a game and reality, and how the former can influence the imagination of the latter to act upon it.

Gerber: The history of architecture is full of utopias; in almost all cases, the difficulty of conceiving another kind of architecture or urban environment for a different society is evident. In the end, everything just becomes bigger, or the houses are built in gold, but they are not really different formally, because it is so very difficult to escape our conventions. If we look at games, while there is a desire to reinvent the world, the players also need to have something they will recognize, something that creates a relationship to reality. So, there is a tension between utopia as something completely free of any reference, and the necessity of relating to reality.

Steets: A utopia is a very radical form with which to critique the everyday. Pragmatically, I would examine the motifs that are suspended in reality and realized in utopia, and what can then be learned from these motifs. There is never a one-to-one relationship between reality and utopia.

Gerber: You mentioned the death of the player. If we look at the theory of Jean Baudrillard (1929-2007), stating that reality is a fiction constructed through media and communication, this presents an interesting chiasmus with which to consider games spaces: games try to simulate a reality, which, according to Baudrillard, is nothing but a system of simulations, or a *simulacra*. If we read Baudrillard's early theories, he postulates that one of the few ways to escape the system of simulation that surrounds us is death.

Steets: Dying is very interesting in the context of video games. First of all, it is a metaphor for the "game over." It limits a game in terms of time, and in relation to its boundlessness, in terms of space. We could once again quote Schütz: the passage from everyday life to this finite province of meaning and back is always a very hard cut, a shock. In theater or the movies, it is the moment when the curtain falls and the lights go on. All of a sudden, you're immersed in real life again. Death is obviously the hardest form of a passage from one world to another, and probably the hardest possible confrontation with reality. I do not know if Baudrillard had this in mind when he wrote about the ways to escape the system of simulation. My own work is based on Schützian phenomenology and social constructivism—an approach that considers a world made of things that we as humans can manipulate and which at the same time manipulate us. As I prefer to rely on social facts, my work does not typically reference Baudrillard. I do not think we are operating in a vacuum of pure language-based communication; we are all human beings, with a physical body and a specific history in the material world. From my point of view, Baudrillard focuses too strongly on narratives and fiction where the world is dissolved. From a sociological perspective, it is interesting to see how people deal with reality, and what forms of use or manipulation develop as a result of this relationship.

Gerber: We talked about the cut, the end of the game. The possibility of such an end implies a mediation between these two worlds, a mediation which is governed by many instruments, such as a joystick, a console, and so forth. If we examine the architecture of games, one of its major flaws compared to reality is the fact that it is completely devoid of a bodily, haptic experience. To what extent does this interface, which is also made of body-dependent techniques, provide us with a different means of accessing architecture, for example, by touching the doorknob of a house?

Steets: It would indeed be fun to invert the perspective of the screen and look at people playing through the screen. What we would see would be very reduced, or—to put it more eloquently—very nuanced and fine-tuned body-techniques: the movements of their fingers, of their heads, following the movement of their eyes, et cetera. However, I remember playing tennis on a Wii with a friend of mine, and the day after, I had muscle soreness even though no real ball was played [laughs]! But in general, one can say that these devices and interfaces transform and digitalize materiality into signs and symbols. We are then in a digitalized world. So, once again, we have returned to the symbolic nature of architecture. Body-dependent techniques in games work as a manipulation of symbols, not of matter— although the buttons that we press are still material.

Gerber: We could say that, in architecture, there is a direct link between body and the experience of architecture, while in the game there is a transformation of the body into signs. Along these lines, the next development worth discussing would be the experience of virtual reality, in which the illusion of being immersed in the world of virtual reality is quite extreme.

Steets: Indeed! And we should also consider the affectivity of games. When we play games, we develop feelings: we hate, we love, we kill and get killed, and so on. There is not only a cognitive, but also an affective dimension at work when we are playing a video game. This affective or emotional dimension also affects our body. It is all about feelings, and a total immersion into virtual reality enhances these feelings. In a video game, we are confronted with signs and we have to deal with them cognitively. Yet at the same time, we are also involved emotionally! And this involvement is much stronger with virtual reality.

Gerber: At the moment you are researching religion. You mentioned *Second Life*—it is interesting that these kinds of alternative realities are often accompanied by a predilection for the quasi-religious. Furthermore, a lot of games build upon religious motifs: the "sacred geometry" of *Monument Valley* (2014), or the religious narrative in *God of War* (2005). How can we relate this to traditional forms of religion?

Steets: In the 1960s, the dominant trend in the sociology of religion was secularization theory. The core argument was that the more modern a society becomes, the less religious its members will be. According to this theory, religion had been pushed aside and reduced to something people would only discuss within the four walls of their home. As a consequence, religion would lose social acceptance. Today, this position has been relativized: it is true that traditional churches continue to lose both their significance in society and their members. At the same time, a strong parallel has arisen in alternative forms of religion, forms of spirituality such as television preachers or New Age philosophies, even yoga. Video games as a form of religion, are nothing special—they are just another mode of these new forms of popular spirituality.

Gerber: At the end of these interviews, I always ask whether my interview partner plays video games. You mentioned having played with a *wii*. Are there any other games you play?

Steets: Normally I don't play at all [laughs]. Most of my knowledge about video games comes from my nephew, who regularly plays video games— but I am definitely not a gamer!

Free your Imagination!

Andri Gerber in Conversation with Philipp Schaerer,

March 26, 2019 (Skype)

Andri Gerber: Let's start *in medias res* with a *modus operandi* that you mention very frequently: composition. This is surprising, as in architecture, we normally associate composition with the venerable *École des Beaux Arts* in Paris—and consequently, with a boring and static design procedure based on symmetry, plans, and elevations.
Philipp Schaerer: You are right: there is that tradition on one hand—think of Jean-Nicolas-Louis-Durand (1760-1834), with his building components and the way he would bring these together. It was a *leçon à faire*—principle of addition—in order to ensure order and proportionality in an overall structure. On the other hand, I understand "composition" in a much more liberated and less rigid way. In my work and in my teaching, composition is mostly used to rearrange supposedly incompatible pictorial elements. It's about experimental and visual compositional techniques. My primary interest lies in the optical connecting and rearranging of what are seemingly incompatible image constructions, which have very little to do with reality: utopian in terms of content and mostly composed, in terms of visual vocabulary, of photographs, thus apparently very plausible and realizable. For example, in the teaching module *Cut-Ups,* we created a series of perspective and illusory image compositions based on the rearrangement of found photographic fragments. These montages might still create the impression of a real setting in nature or the built environment, because they respect the laws of photographic representation in respect to its visual appearance. But, at the same time, the content shown by interweaving and stringing these elements together is highly fictitious. Or, instead of using image fragments as source material, we have also worked with found

3D-library components on the internet, in order to compose assemblages based on the free sampling of these individual elements (in modules entitled *Artifacts* and *Architectural Capriccios*).

However, we also compose with words, not just with images. For example, in the module *Compounds—Word and Image,* in which students were asked to make up a series of compound words. They did not correspond to any existing reality and had no fixed denotation (for example stair-bed; mobile-forest ...), and therefore had to be visually encapsulated and interpreted. Through this procedure, students have to begin with their own imagination and are unable to refer to already existing pictures examples. In architecture, more and more frequently, elements are available in databases and students tend to simply make "cocktails" out of these references, without reflecting on what they are doing. It can be nice to look at, but repetitive.

Fig. 29-32: Architectural Capriccio, 3D-Composite, Computer Rendering Course: UE-N, Constructing The View II, Spring 2016, ENAC, EPFL. Students: Laura Porta, Lina Vallander

Fig. 33-4: Cut-Up, Image Montage, Course: UE-L, Constructing The View I, Autumn 2017, ENAC, EPFL. Students: Olmo Viscardi, Cédric Wehrle, Thomas Lutz, Benjamin Bonnard

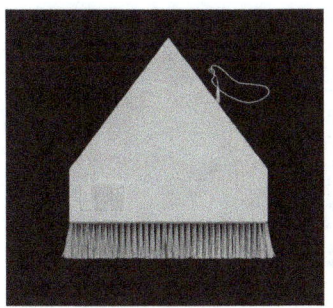

Fig. 35-6 Artifact, 3D-Composite, Computer Rendering, Course: UE-N, Constructing The View II, Spring 2017, ENAC, EPFL. Students: Marcelo Rovira Torres, Diane Stierli

Gerber: Besides composition, you often mention construction. While the first term, according to my understanding, implies a distance between subject and object—reminiscent of the level of abstraction in compositions such as those of École des Beaux Arts, which never considered the urban context—the second seems to imply a closer connection to material things. Things get physically manipulated and constructed.

Schaerer: Despite the fictional nature of my work, there is a strong sense of workmanship, which I associate with this construction of images. You join elements in a way that results in plausible visual arrangements and that has an aesthetic appeal.

Fig. 37-8: Seating-Dock (Word and Image), Axonometric Drawing/ Image Montage, Course: UE-L, Constructing The View I, Autumn 2016, ENAC, EPFL. Student: Dan Relecom

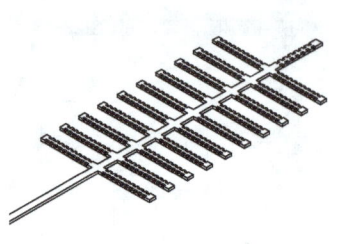

Fig. 39-40: Fluffy-Column (Word and Image), Sketch/ Image Montage, Course: UE-L, Constructing The View I, Autumn 2016, ENAC, EPFL. Student: Michael Casares

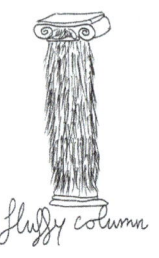

Fig. 41-2: Running-Stair (Word and Image), Axonometric Drawing/ Image Montage, Course: UE-L, Constructing The View I, Autumn 2016, ENAC, EPFL. Student: Eva Herunter

Obviously, I work with "flat" fragments rather than building components. Composition applied to images implies fewer constraints: you can disregard gravity and objects can be morphed, blended, or scaled without any problem. Images are the perfect testing ground, because so many constraints and rules are suspended, and you are not tied to these like you are in reality.

Gerber: Reality is an important keyword. You often speak about utopia when describing your work. What is the relationship between reality and utopia? Would you agree that reality and utopia are always somehow related, and that reality itself is somehow always a construction?

Schaerer: I think I must specify that I use the term utopia mostly in the context of images—without a political or social connotation. Probably this is not the most precise use of the term, but I like to apply it in describing a fictitious setting. If we couple reality and fiction, I think their boundaries will become more and more blurred in the future. For example, consider the fact that, when gaming, you have real outbursts of emotions: you are happy when you get to a next stage or you are frustrated when you constantly fail to overcome an obstacle. Just think about the social interactions that exist in games with multiple players. Emotionality is something that brings reality and fiction together.

Gerber: You talk about emotionality—what kind of emotions do your images trigger in the eye of the beholder? Is seduction a term that could explain this relationship?

Schaerer: The images from my personal work originate from a personal necessity, a desire of mine, and are therefore linked to my past. This began with my education as an architect at the ETH Lausanne (EPFL) in the 1990s, and then my emplyoment at Herzog & de Meuron Architects. These images are not born of some kind of theory, but rather, they are the consequence of my history and the outcome of my practical work at Herzog & de Meuron. My first image series, *Bildbauten* (2007), is a good example for this. I was fed up with all of the overloaded architectural visualizations that I produced for their office between 2001 and 2006—project visualizations that operated on gimmickry and primarily used for competition entries. I felt the need to follow another path: to fundamentally question the fragile relationship between image and architecture, the visual structure of images, and the prevailing practices surrounding images in architecture offices at that time. The *Bildbauten* series deals with the impact and the claim to credibility regarding architectural images that appear to be photographs—yet they are not photographs. Instead, they are completely designed and constructed from scratch. By means of their exaggerated and orchestrated way of representation, they modelled themselves on the object-like appearance and the formal language of contemporary architecture.

Fig. 43: Steps of Development, Bildbau No 5, 2007, From the Bildbauten Series. Author: Philipp Schaerer

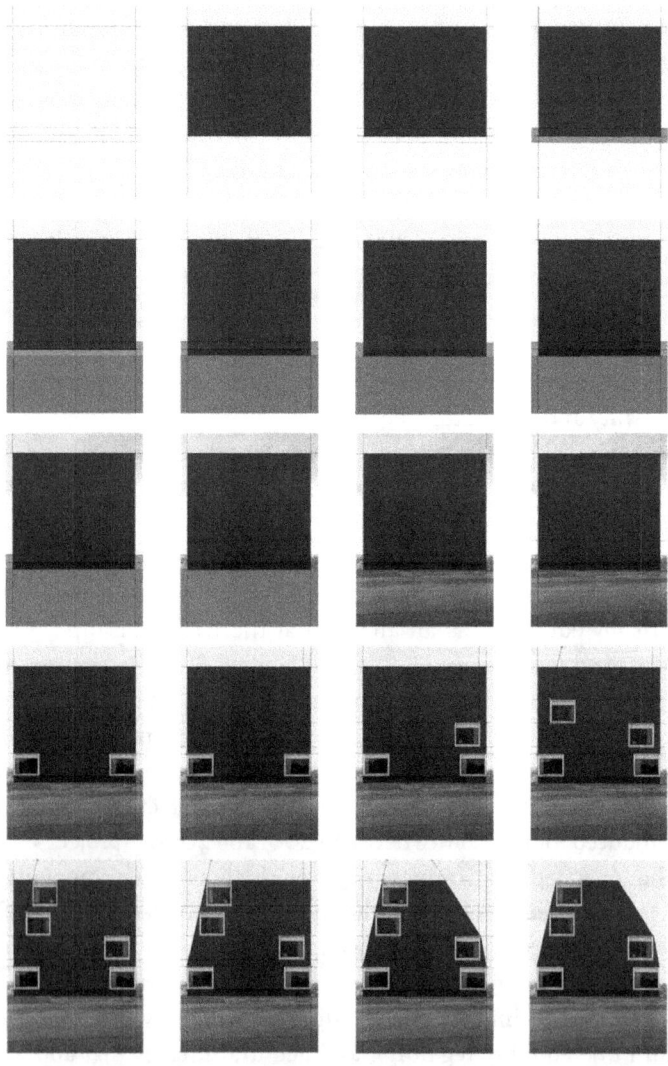

I think the interesting aspect of the *Bildbauten* series—especially in the context of architecture—is that these images bypass and disregard our traditional perception and understanding of graphic material. We still link abstract representation (sketches, schemes, illustrations, and so forth) to an idea. In the context of architecture, for example, this is a vehicle with which to anticipate a possibly built reality. In contrast, a photographic representation is generally still interpreted as proof, linked to a fragment of materialized reality. In the architects' experience, the photograph of a completed construction traditionally represents the culmination of a long process with a large number of different iterations—kind of a visual "trophy." The *Bildbauten* images are now inverting those conditions; despite their highly photorealistic appearance, they are graphically built-up from scratch and do not have any connection to concrete planning and spatial ambition. In this series, a vertical canvas is the background, and two lines of delimitation (ground-façade and façade-sky) define three surfaces (ground, façade, and sky), which then are covered freely and decorated with image textures. There are no floor plans, elevations, or sections—in general, there is no elaborated spatial concept, on which the *Bildbauten* are based. They are like wallpaper with no context—a subtle criticism about the making of architecture in our digital-capitalist era.

I think that the fact that photography and computer image processing—two utterly different imaging methods—can result in images that are no longer visually distinguishable by means of optical features constitutes a milestone in the history of image production. This should not be underestimated: an image derived from a fictitious setting is now in competition with a photographic image taken from the built environment. Fiction mingles more and more with the distortion of our physical reality. Looking back to the first examples of computer renderings or analogue image montages, you still could see the technique, you still could see that the images were constructed.

In an analogue photomontage, individual image fragments are tied to their surface material—most commonly paper or sometimes photographic film—which makes weaving or blending them together difficult: unless the montage is carried out with great skill, it is almost always possible to discern a cut or tear line, and it takes a great deal of experience, time, and effort to eliminate all traces of where one fragment ends and another begins. Since digital images do not have any surface material, but consist purely of pixel-based data, seamlessly blending fragments of all types and sizes is comparatively easy in a digital collage. The worst consequence of this process is that you don't even need all that laborious spatial planning anymore; you can skip that, and instead produce a series of photorealistic images, post it on the internet, and make people believe that they depict a completed construction.

Gerber: How would you describe the type of knowledge that you contribute to your images as a trained architect? Does it make sense to distinguish between pictorial and spatial knowledge in this context? **Schaerer:** I think these two types of knowledge are completely different. When you are in a space, you are there with your body; you have a bodily experience based on all of your senses, and this experience is very hard to translate into a purely visual and two-dimensional language. Human beings are constantly moving, and experience their own presence in space; this intimate kind of spatial knowledge is built on these experiences, and is therefore extremely difficult to communicate and to someone else. You can develop a theory of space, of course, but it will always remain abstract and removed from spatial experience.

Pictorial knowledge, on the other hand, is something quite independent from your body and instead related to the medium of the image—which has doubtlessly become the most powerful medium for the distribution of visual content today, regardless of location. Unfettered by any particular carrier, it can be multiplied at will and transported anywhere. Images only function on a visual level, and we only require a limited set of sensory tools to perceive and judge them. This primarily occurs on two levels: on one hand, we can interpret an image in an iconographic way—evaluating the content, which elements are depicted—and on the other, we can look at an image and ask ourselves how it's made, what its visual language is, and consider its stylistic approach. With images, there are fewer perceptual stimuli, yet this creates many more possibilities than actually being in present in space, because you can project more into an image. If we take my *Bildbauten* series as an example, it is clear they only work as images. If built, they would not be nearly as interesting! Because they free your imagination! **Gerber:** When I look at *Bildbauten*, I ask myself what these buildings look like beyond the front façade, when you turn a corner. So, I try to execute a change from image to space, which is of course frustrating because I cannot transport myself into the image—unless I suffered from the *Stendhal syndrome* depicted by director Dario Argento (*1940) in his eponymous movie from 1996.

Fig. 44-5: Bildbau No 2/ Bildbau No 6, Image Montage, 2007, From the Bildbauten Series. Author: Philipp Schaerer

I agree with you that it would probably be disappointing to see them in person; yet, at the same time, they probably would retain something mysterious and intriguing. This is the main difference between space and image, and the corresponding knowledge that they provide. It is all about retaining information, and the possibility to fill this gap with your curiosity and imagination.

Schaerer: I totally agree with you. Despite their realistic style of visual representation, the *Bildbauten* images remain quite intangible and elusive, refusing to be embedded in a context, whether spatially or on in regard to their meaning. They are self-contained like satellites traveling around the world, the same way "normal" architectural images are exchanged through the Internet.

Gerber: You live in this world of images—but have your ever felt the desire to build?

Schaerer: Right after I finished my studies in 2000, I worked at Herzog & deMeuron Architects on the construction phase of a project extending the Aargauer Kunsthaus (1996-2003). So, I do have an idea of what it means to be part of a project, with all the difficulties and problems that come along with it—in particular, the contact with so many different kinds of trades and people. After this experience, I knew that I was not interested in doing something similar on my own. I found all of the financial and organizational aspects of running an office quite unappealing.

Gerber: Would it then be accurate to say that your work is a kind of escape into the world of images?

Schaerer: Probably, yes. But they also tell that I'm still interested in architecture. In my leisure time, I regularly develop small projects, let's call them "paper architecture," or fictional buildings that exist only as a floor plan and an elevation. I do this primarily for my own satisfaction. Elaborating the projects on paper is enjoyment enough; I don't need to go one step further and jump into the fray construction and detailing, et cetera [laughs].

Fig: 46-7: Cigar House, 6-Courtyard House, fictional projects, 2012, Exterior Views and Floor Plans. Author: Philipp Schaerer

 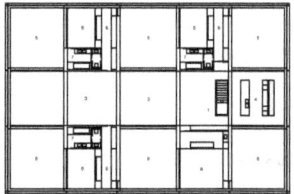

Gerber: When we look at your images, a paradox is evident: you criticize the availability of images, yet you also produce images. How do you resolve this dichotomy?

Schaerer: It's probably important to specify the type of images to which you refer. In my early work, between 2000 and 2010, I did quite a lot of commissioned images—architectural visualizations for offices—but I stopped as soon as I realized that this is nothing but a huge "image - washing" machine [laughs]. I was oversaturated with these exaggeratedly staged image-constructs. I had enough of the constant concern for the image's visual impact, the will to maximize the project's pictorial resonance with ever-more spectacular renderings. To return to your question, I am not criticizing the availability of images in general, but rather, the stylistic means with which architectural visualizations are executed, the image strategies that strongly refer to the marketing and advertising industry. I didn't feel comfortable with that anymore.

That's why I've been concentrating on my own artistic work over the past ten years—without a client—working on series of images at the intersection of architecture, photography, and graphics, experimenting with the pictorial representation techniques of the built and natural environments. These images work with references and allusions and try to address the increasingly blurred boundary between the digital world of images and the material world of objects. They do not scream for attention, and do not feature spectacular perspectives—the *Chicago Series* (2017) serves as a good example. The project begins with aerial views of built architecture—the fifth façade, an architectural element so often neglected—and tries to poeticize and translate it into an independent and "refined" abstract pictorial figure. The work thus focuses on ordinary and common architecture, features the hidden, makes the invisible visible, and seeks the unobtrusive beauty in the banality of our built environment. The pictorial figures may undoubtedly recall the genre of abstract painting, although the work is exclusively based on photographic material.

Fig: 48-9: V19-01/V23-01, From the Chicago Series, 2017. Author: Philipp Schaerer

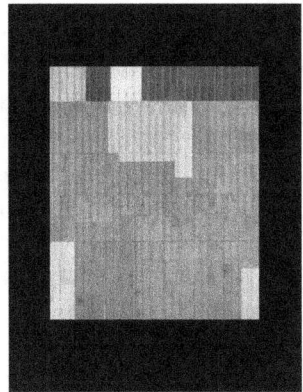 

Gerber: Obviously your images are implicitly a critique of these phenomena. Being both affirmative and critical is probably something one can only do with images. In architecture, this is almost impossible, because you either build, or you are a critic. Was this one reason you turned to images rather than to built architecture?

Schaerer: One reason why I have turned more and more to pictures is certainly their dimension of time and their elasticity. In the production of architecture, it takes years from the first conceptual sketch to a finished construction. Images, in contrast, are more agile; they are fabricated faster and are rarely subject to external constraints for their completion. I do not need to build in order to test ideas and concepts, when I'm primarily interested in visual relationships. On the contrary, the medium of "image" gives me much greater freedom to experiment with visual configurations.

Gerber: What about the current uncontrolled growth of digital images in architecture, both in practice and in teaching?

Schaerer: It's obvious that today, at least on our latitude, architects are developing, visualizing, and communicating their designs by means of digital tools. This binds them to the functionality, the expressiveness, and the processing possibilities of the programs they operate. Of course, as in many other fields of activity, the use of the computer provides great convenience: the work becomes more efficient, and content can be handled more easily. However, I think we are also seeing a dissatisfactory side effect, mostly in design fields: stereotypical aesthetics have become practically interchangeable. We can observe the tendency of global architecture to become more and more similar in appearance.

This is evident not only in built structures, but also in the imagery of the projected and digitally rendered design concepts. One of my central concerns in teaching is to convey an extended vocabulary of digital image techniques, developing more specific and individual forms of expression with computers, which involves a more creative approach to computer-based technologies. For example: In the architectural context, computer renderings are predominately used to emulate pseudo-photographs, but no one mandates that the rendering can only be used for producing photorealistic images. A tool does not do the work by itself; more decisive is the way in which a person uses it. A computer rendering can also be used for more abstract representation. For example, mapping 3D-models with non-photographic texture maps, as we did in the course module called *Virtual Reconstruction*, or in my work *Mines du Jardins*—a series of 3D-plant arrangements—were one-hundred percept rendered, yet they do not follow a straightforward photographic representation technique, and do not use texture maps at all.

Fig. 50-1: Virtual Reconstruction, Screenshot 3D Scene/ Final Computer Rendering Course: UE-L, Constructing The View I, Autumn 2014, ENAC, EPFL. Student: Antonios Prokos

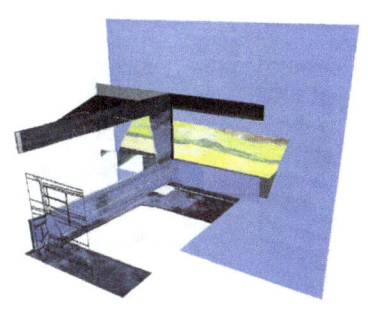
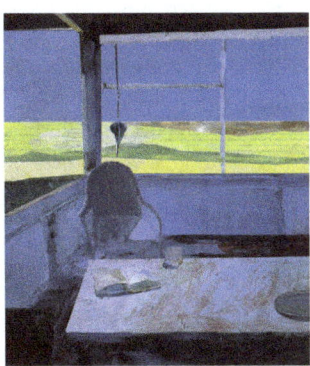

Fig. 52-3: Screenshot 3D Scene, (Mines du Jardin No 2)/ Computer Rendering, 2012. Author: Philipp Schaerer

Gerber: Did it affect you that your images have been transported onto the Internet, and are suddenly available anytime? This implies a commercialization of your subversive stance ...

Schaerer: Yes, the *Bildbauten* images travel the internet with particular frequence, and are still regularly re-linked and posted on virtual pinnwalls. Two Ph.D. students who also run an architectural office also reused a *Bildbau* image, proposing it as their own contribution to the exhibition *Ways of Life, Experimenta Urbana in Kassel*—a complementary event to the *Documenta* exhibition in 2017. Stefan Kurath intervened by writing a letter of protest to the organizers, and the participants ended up having to withdraw their contribution.

Fig. 54-7: Morten Rockford Ravn, From the Fear and Loathing in GTA V Series, In-game photographs, 2017

Gerber: Let's address another important topic: Do you yourself enjoy gaming?
Schaerer: I am not really a video-game maniac. But I do remember that I played *Winter Games* (1985) and *Summer Games* (1984) with great fervor, which ran on my 8-bit Commodore 64 computer in the early 1990s. Maybe I played too much at the time. I just came back to video games upon acquiring a Playstation in 2015—a completely different world in regard to performance, graphics, and interactivity. Today, I am most interested in the types of video games that provide a territory to explore, with different types of natural landscapes and built environments. I have to confess that I'm most attracted to game environments in which the graphics are highly photorealistic, with a high degree of detail, and supported by an accurate simulation of weather and different qualities of light. An example of such a game, is *World of Tanks* (2010). It's a free multiplayer online game featuring mid-twentieth century tank battles. The gameplay is secondary to me, but the pictorial representation of the various landscapes is amazing and

very rich in detail. For example, there are dancing butterflies between the leaves in the air, or you can watch the grass swaying in the wind. Therefore, it's not surprising that several contemporary artists have begun to use these virtual playgrounds as their sets for taking photographs: exploring different environments, waiting for a particular moment, and shooting a still of the real-time rendering by means of the in-game camera. An example of this is the Danish artist Morten Rockford Ravn (*1987). His in-game photography project, called *Fear and Loathing in GTA V* (2017), uses the video game scenery of the fifth edition of Grand Theft Auto.

Gerber: What about virtual reality (VR) devices? Is this something that interests you as well?

Schaerer: I think it's important to watch the development. Think about the first cellphones on the market—they were massive devices which only bankers could afford [laughs]! We have all experienced how these devices have become smaller over time. Although it would be possible to shrink the components of the mobile phone further and further, after a certain point it wouldn't make sense anymore; as long as we use our fingers to operate the cell, it will remain more or less the current size. Now, turning to VR-devices, especially the headset: they are still large and cumbersome, similar to the first cell phones. But I'm sure that these VR components will undergo an intensive "miniaturization" process in the future. The relevant organ to record visual information is the eye, and there are already transparent membranes able to display visual information. It is not a big step to develop VR-contact lenses, which could be worn at any time. I'm quite sure nearly everyone will wear them in the future, and probably sooner than we expect, comparable to the impressive spread of mobile phones throughout our societies. Of course, this will have significant ramifications in the way we perceive and shape our environment. We can't ignore that.

If we assume everyone will year VR-lenses in thirty years, any physical object that can be experienced solely by the eye—with no impact on our body—could become obsolete, simulated perfectly with VR-lenses. For example, all flat, ornamental architectural elements would no longer need to be materialized. This is also true for the color tones of façades and interiors, which could be replaced by a customizable color setting for each individual lens projection. Even the existing traffic signs and billboards could completely disappear physically. Signs and advertising would, instead, be projected onto your lenses, tied to your precise geographical position—and so on.

Gerber: Do you think this would result in a loss of reality, or that "reality" will be exchanged for another type of "reality?"

Schaerer: First of all, I think the term "reality" needs to be refined, particularly in our era, in which we are confronted with an ever-increasing amount of digital content. We still link the term to something with a physical presence, something that we can touch and experience with our body—we still primarily associate the term with the material environment. Being increasingly confronted with intangible digital content, our understanding of "reality" becomes troubled. As mentioned before, when you play a video game and have real outbursts of emotions, it's absolutely real—proven by the intensity of your emotional reaction—despite the fact that the game is a pure intangible, virtual simulation of action. I'm deeply convinced that we will not "lose" reality, but that the term and his significance will change, blurring the boundaries between the physical and the virtual more and more.

Gerber: You frequently refer to bodily experience. In architecture, this topic is definitely underrated, even though there are some scholars who have discussed the topic extensively, such as Herman Sörgel (1885-1952).[1]

Schaerer: I love Camillo Sitte (1843-1903) and his book *Der Städtebau nach seinen künstlerischen Grundsätzen* (1889)! The whole notion of urban space one has to "unravel" through the movement of the body is simply fantastic, and greatly impressed me during my architectural studies. I think all architects should read his book!

---

1 | Rainer Schützeichel, *Die „Theorie der Baukunst" von Herman Sörgel: Entwürfe einer Architekturwissenschaft* (Berlin: Reimer, 2019).

A Fascination for Empty Rooms

Andri Gerber and Ulrich Götz in Conversation
with Francine Rotzetter, April 9, 2019, Zurich

Andri Gerber: Prior to studying game design, you studied architecture. What was this experience like for you?

Francine Rotzetter: During my studies in architecture I was taught how to react to a certain place, to a specific need with a designed space. For me both aspects are equivalent in architecture. It is similar in game design but with a stronger focus on the user's needs.

Gerber: Do you think designing a game allows for greater freedom than designing architecture? Or is it just about different types of restrictions?

Rotzetter: When designing architecture, you face many norms and standards. There are far fewer such constraints in game design. Of course, games are also restricted by rules and guidelines, but they reference the player's representation and behavior. When you design a room, the player needs to understand how to move around within in. These kind of general questions and conditions must be respected. At the same time, you basically start with an empty space, which will slowly be shaped by the conditions you create.

Gerber: The initial emptiness—is it that what fascinates you about designing games?

Rotzetter: Absolutely! But also the fact that you need to create constraints in order to make the game understandable and playable.

Gerber: We know that games need rules in order to provide freedom and choice. Paradoxically, you can hardly be free outside of a defined frame. It is interesting to hear you speak about emptiness, because there is a *topos* of fearing the blank page in creative professions.

Rotzetter: You need to have an idea when you start to fill the empty room. You have to limit the player in ways that support the game. After that, you can start removing some constraints, up to the point that the game doesn't work anymore. Then you add new constraints again.

Gerber: So, you would describe the design process as a kind of subtractive procedure?

Rotzetter: Yes, absolutely. At least this is how I do it.

Ulrich Götz: You spoke about filling the empty room. According to my observations, architects are not likely to fill this empty room with a narrative. They shy away from imagining what might happen within these rooms once they are inhabited. In game design, the absolute opposite is the case. To slightly exaggerate things: it is all about anticipating actions and narratives within a game. Almost every cubic centimeter of space needs to be considered in anticipation of what might happen there, which stories might unfold. In contrast, architectural space is oriented by its subjection to strong formal and legislative limitations—nobody dares to ask what kind of narratives the occupants will bring into such a space once they are there.

Rotzetter: In this context, I realized that today's market asks for flexible plans and the possibility to change the function of buildings. It seems to be all about providing maximum flexibility. When I think back to my architectural studies, this was never the case, as we always were given a task with a pre-determined function. But to be honest, we never had to think about the kind of narratives you just mentioned.

Gerber: When you design a video game, do you have people to test your game during development?

Rotzetter: Admittedly, I don't have this much experience yet, and that's why the reference has always been me.

Götz: You need a clear idea and hypothesis about how your game should work. It was really impressive when we visited the offices of Ubisoft in Paris with students, where they showed us a two-hundred page catalog from their research department. Ubisoft had visited Washington, D.C. for several weeks, taking thousands of photos, and meeting and interviewing as many people as possible. They talked to representatives from politics, as well as members of the subculture, in order to get a realistic picture of the city. All of this resulted in the game *The Division 2* (2019). Behind the development of such a dense narrative lies a huge amount of work. And this effort is even integrated in the promotion of the game: Ubisoft wants to let people know how realistic the game is.

Gerber: The relationship between reality and its copy in games—between "real" and "virtual" architecture—is a fundamental issue we address in this book. How would you describe the relationship between these two counterparts?

Rotzetter: I would say that they are very close, maybe even too close. Very often, game designers stick to what they know and translate it into games. There are obviously exceptions, particularly in indie games, but in "AAA" games, they really try to copy reality.

Götz: One main difference between the real world and open-world games is that the former is the result of many authors, while the latter is the product of very few.

Fig. 58: The Legend of Zelda: Breath of the Wild, 2017

Rotzetter: At the same time, when a game has only one author, you can feel his or her personality within the game, and you also can identify with it in a way you mostly cannot with open worlds—precisely because they lack this sort of personality.

Götz: That's an interesting point. The "reality" outside has been shaped over centuries and by many architects, urban designers, administrators, politicians ...

Rotzetter: Absolutely. And if you look at Le Corbusier's (1887-1965) urban design concepts, they all failed—which was because he imposed them top-down, without negotiating. The same would happen if one designer would create an open world game alone. That simply could not work!

Gerber: But how do you deal with history? Games do not simulate history. They represent a current state. One exception: In a game like *Mafia* (2002), the course of time is simulated: Buildings get erected throughout the duration of play.

Götz: I think we should address the question as to how participation could be possible in the design of game spaces. I do not mean participation in form of later modifications, since then, once again only one author defines the space of the game, in a god-like fashion.

Rotzetter: I assume this is really difficult. One possibility I could imagine is rather undesirable: when a game references or copies another game—because it works well and people like it—then you get some kind of layering, in which someone else uses the principles of your world and develops them further.

Götz: I think that the factor of coincidence is very important in the making of "real" cities. So many people participate in different ways in shaping these spaces. In this sense, I think it would be interesting to let architects participate in competitions for the design of buildings in game spaces. This would be a way to introduce a different level of authorship in game spaces and make it more "real." The editors of games use catalogs of buildings—we should open that up, and fill the virtual cities of games with the contributions of architectural competitions!

Gerber: That is an excellent idea!

Götz: We just came up with an example of what we could import from architecture—now let's talk about the differences between architecture and game design. Is there something particular to game design that cannot be found in architecture?

Rotzetter: I find that architecture is less interested in the user of the created space, and the way events and interactions will unfold there. In contrast, this is a fundamental aspect of game design.

Gerber: If we accept the definition of architecture as the design of space, where do you see the main difference between "real" space and game space?

Rotzetter: I would say the main difference is the limited sensory perception of game spaces. You can use many tricks to overcome such limits, for example, using sound; however, you will never be able to convey the sensation of touching a stone and feeling that it is cold. You can use the sound of gravel when your avatar walks on it and the player understands what goes along with it, but it is not the same. Here, architecture has a huge advantage: it is real [laughs].

Gerber: Is this sensual design specific to architectural knowledge? Or is it knowledge that comes from game design?

Rotzetter: This clearly comes from architectural knowledge! Another example: architects traditionally include natural lighting in their planning. Just think of Louis Kahn (1901-1974), who defined architecture as the interplay of light and shadow.

Gerber: Which other specific aspects of architecture did you learn in your studies that you now apply to game design?

Rotzetter: For example, how to design a plan in such a way that the space feels more exciting or less easy to explore. Architectural studies made me aware of the emotions that can be connected to spatial design.

Götz: In your research, you have worked on "non-verbal guidance systems in open-world games." To what extent was this subject influenced by your education as an architect? Were you interested in such topics during your studies, or did this evolve out of your studies in game design?

Rotzetter: The actual trigger was a game I used to play, *The Elder Scrolls V: Skyrim* (2011). I always try to trick a game, going beyond its borders and getting to somewhere the game designer would not expect me to go. In this game, I had the feeling I managed to do so—but then I realized that the game designer had envisioned this possibility, leaving an "easter egg" there. This was a eureka effect! I started to ask myself: how could they know I would try to get there?

Götz: You examined guidance systems in very large open worlds. Do you think the same principles could be applied to small-scale worlds, such as buildings?

Rotzetter: It definitively also works in architecture. When you enter a house, you usually follow the light; you will be attracted to brightness, or you will look out a window onto an open space. This works exactly the same way in video games, in which game designers use light to guide one's movements. On the contrary, if they want to scare you, they will situate you in a dimly lit place. Having said that, I have to state that in comparison to the possibilities of video games and virtual reality, architecture is still in the Stone Age.

Fig. 59: The Elder Scrolls V: Skyrim, 2011

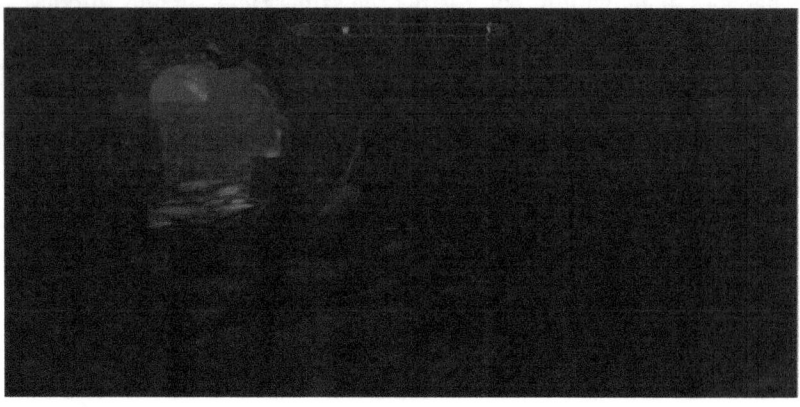

Fig. 60, F.E.A.R, 2005

Gerber: Do you think this difference in possibilities is specific to the discipline of architecture, or does it have to do with games *per se*?

Rotzetter: I think it is both. Games often remain looked upon purely as entertainment products. Some people even consider games a waste of time, even though they can be very productive. Architects, on the other hand, have been debating the same issues, over and over again, for centuries. I think it will take more time to understand the potential of games.

Gerber: I have the impression that few architecture students play video games. At least, this was the result of a survey we did for a research project.

Götz: I don't fully agree. Established architects probably don't play games—and wouldn't admit if they did—but I am pretty sure that architecture students do.

Gerber: Interesting—because years ago, talking about soccer was an absolute no-go in the architectural community, until several soccer stadium competitions were launched, and star architects such as Peter Eisenman (*1931) or Jacques Herzog (*1950) and Pierre de Meuron (*1950) turned out to be absolute soccer fanatics! [laughs]. Now you just need Peter Zumthor (*1943) to declare his passion for video games....

Götz: Which is quite unlikely.... [laughs]. Francine, do you think that other established forms of fictional spaces have been more successful in influencing architecture? What about film architecture, stage design, or even comics? All of them feature elaborated spatial design strategies.

Rotzetter: Film definitely had a lot of influence, and more recently, comics too—especially since the recent Marvel film adaptations.

Götz: How do you think architects are inspired by film?

Rotzzetter: Think about *Inception* (2010), and how urban space was depicted: this had quite a strong influence on architects and urban designers. I do not mean the structure itself but more the atmospheric effect which is also very important in architecture.

Gerber: Film is an established and well-respected art form—games haven't yet achieved this status.

Götz: Does your research in game design help you in your current work?

Rotzetter: At the moment, I am working on the creation of VR scenes and I feel definitively sensitized about many aspects of game design, for example the importance of audio, which in architecture usually does not get that huge amount of attention.

Götz: Audio is definitely a very important aspect of games. Are there any other examples?

Rotzetetter: An important aspect I learned from working on video games was the importance of setting a starting point. I was often asked by clients to set a starting point in VR right at the entrance of the apartment. Not in front of the entrance, that one would first have to open the door, which in turn would lead to a completely different arc of tension, after the door. The starting point would be mostly in the corridor. I usually try to make them aware that this is not an appropriate way to get started. Usually, I set the starting point where you get an overview of the scene.

Götz: So, because of your game design experience you chose the establishing shot in a VR architectural setting in an entirely different way. You chose a point from which you can overlook everything, and then decide to approach the scene more closely.

Rotzetter: Indeed. Or maybe in an even more dramatic way: creating an obstacle which must first be overcome in order to enter the scene. This was definitively influenced by my research into games. These are small tricks and you can definitely learn something about them by designing video games!

Towards an Architecture of Desire

Andri Gerber in Conversation with François Charbonnet
and Patrick Heiz, March 19, 2019, Zurich

Andri Gerber: Let's start with a really easy question: How serious is architecture [laughs]?

François Charbonnet: Well, architects are responsible for the largest artifacts produced by mankind. Given the fact that these objects are supposed to last beyond their immediate use, and that they should convey a specific cultural value about any kind of environment—for successive generations—I'd say architecture is a pretty serious matter. It is even more serious, should you consider architecture the main agent of our *political milieu*.

Patrick Heiz: ... I would add that even the performative aspects of architecture go beyond solving a problem, and would even question the ability of the architectural project to be an adequate "mediator" of our lives. Architecture can definitely generate an array of potentialities, but in essence, it is inert, which confines it to the "margins" of life.

Gerber: But shouldn't these potentialities also be fun?

Heiz: They can definitely be fun!

Charbonnet: I suppose one would have to define "fun" before one could consider architecture as a form of "entertainment." But there is, no doubt, a ludic dimension to design: for now, let's say that architecture is a serious game, as your initial question suggests.

Heiz: We should also underscore that the central question of the architectural project is not architecture, *per se*, but life, in all of its complexities. Like any other human beings, architects are driven by contradictory and equivocal intuitions and expectations. To project always means identifying and, secretly, staging intricacies; however, it is more often confrontational than it is strategic—and this friction is definitely a source of energy.

Fig. 61: Made in, Zollstrasse, 2014-2019

Gerber: I would assert that there can be no fun without friction! Out of all the topics in the present book, the relationship between the "real" or "actual" and the "virtual" is of particular significance. Related to this, I am very interested in the way you work. You usually produce amazing collages, bringing together references, materials, and many other things, yet they remain quite abstract; they do not necessarily reveal what the building will look like. You vindicate the autonomy of the design process but how do you deal with the moment when these images become real? What happens during this process with this imagery? Maybe your clients expect you to have it built the way the images appear.

Heiz: Well, we haven't built very much much so far; we are therefore seldom confronted with this issue [laughs].

Charbonnet: Construction is really only about solving problems: facing a well-identified issue and solving it appropriately. I am well-aware, of course, that a lot lies in the specifics of "appropriately" ... nonetheless, I think that designing, or rather, "pro-*ject*-ing," is an alienating process. The architect should consider design as a sort of dispossession, rather than an appropriating procedure. Moreover, as the prefix suggests, it is bound to a dynamic consideration, not only because it requires a certain level of detachment, but because of the very nature of an idea which—metaphorically—travels through time at a certain speed, and should live beyond fulfilling its original function. In this regard, the image can efficiently complement the objectivity of the accurate drawings required to realize an architectural project, addressing issues beyond these incontrovertible prerequisites. But a project is always "yet to come"—at least as far the architect is concerned—it is *en devenir*, aspiring, and shouldn't be reduced to a product. What I mean to say is that to delineate architecture objectively is to deny an image its full evocative—and therefore performative—potential. Images, unlike drawings, must be read and experienced, and there are as many possible interpretations as there are eyes beholding them.

Heiz: Once again, architecture is primarily a process, not a product. An image can essentially suggest the existence of meta-information that can be deciphered, while simultaneously triggering a sort of immediate comprehension. The image—unlike an accurate representation—can be detached from its meaning and accordingly raise questions.

Charbonnet: One of our primary aims is to address issues beyond the quantifiable, to engage in a critical consideration of collective memory that seeks to overcome bias and preconceived notions. "What lies beyond" is really the territory we want to investigate. This led us to *Voluptas*—the studio we are currently leading at the ETH Zurich. In their work entitled *Anti-Oedipus* (1972)[1], Gilles Deleuze (1925-1995) and Félix Guattari (1930-1992) describe *volupté* as a sort of residual energy, that which is left when everything else has been removed. There are many voluptuous moments in the elaboration of an architectural project, even if they remain a secret.

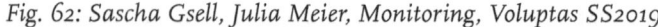

Fig. 62: Sascha Gsell, Julia Meier, Monitoring, Voluptas SS2019

Gerber: Let's discuss this notion of *Voluptas*. Where do we find it, and can this be shared? François, you spoke about the project as something you throw away, and Patrick, you mentioned the relationship that an architect develops with the client. So where do we find *Voluptas*? Is it in the process, in the result, or in both?

Charbonnet: It can take place at any point in the process, for instance, when an unforeseen potential is consciously activated and stands in con-tradiction—or at least in friction with—one or several of the predeter-mined requirements. It can also be a personal exchange with the project's stakeholders: what I mean is that *Voluptas* cannot be reduced to a specific

1 | Gilles Deleuze and Félix Guattari, *L'Anti-Oedipe. Capitalisme et schizophré-nie* (Paris: Minuit, 1972).

feature or narrowed down to a specific point in the process; it is a vague essence and dynamic—in the sense of a "vagabond"—and escapes any definitive categorization. This doesn't mean that it can never be quantified. For example, in our Zollstrasse project—currently under construction—the depth of the primary façade or the sheer monumentality of the public space on its infrastructural side are undeniably voluptuous.

One of the main challenges we face is that, by obsessively multiplying such interpretative "threads," we tend to blur any unequivocal statement. Instead, observers are left with their own (biased) understanding. Our projects demand an interstitial reading, so to speak, and invade programmatic and legislative gaps to critically address a given issue.

Gerber: Regarding the concept of program—there is a nice book by Czech philosopher Vilém Flusser (1920-1991)[2], in which he states that the future is not about being either a master or a slave, but about programming or being programmed. Considering the importance of the program in your work—also in terms of programming games—where would you situate yourselves in relation to this?

Carbonnet: Any architecture is a *rapport de forces*, at any given point in the process, even before any architecture has been conceived. What takes place in the mind of a potential client can only be appropriately described as a *rapport de forces* between expectations, vanity, an economic and political environment, and so forth. It becomes more obvious—almost trivial—when considering the built object itself, which can literally only stand as a reality balanced between substances. The systematic and constant negotiation that comprise the process of designing is also a *rapport de forces*. It is as if architecture was doomed by the constraints necessary for it to exist. The program, as such, is a relevant part of this set of tensions; its potential lies far beyond the simple configuration of square meters. Each piece of a given function is in active negotiation with the others. And most importantly, the program is there to be *re*-programmed and questioned. This is one of the most pressing issues, I think, in the contemporary production of architecture, in which none of the supposed prerequisites are being critically addressed. There is an obvious opportunism—not to say cowardice—coming from the architects who pledge an undiscerning allegiance to any stipulated framework. I do not mean to say that we, as a profession,

---

2 | Vilém Flusser, *Dinge und Undinge, Phänomenologische Skizzen* (Munich: Carl Hanser Verlag, 1993).

should indulge in unnecessary provocations, but rather, that it is imperative we critically engage with program, to ensure more than simply fulfilling its requirements.

Fig. 63: Luca Meyer, Thierry Vuattoux, Parody, Voluptas SS 2019

As a brief example of where we positioned ourselves a few decades ago:
in an interview with the French daily newspaper *Le Monde*, Renzo Piano
(*1937) recalled that, among the nearly 600 competition entries for the
Centre Pompidou in Paris, their proposal was the only one to question the
actual legislative bulk of the Marais...the only one! It is hard to believe, but
what was considered a crucial, critical comment about this situation in
the 1970s would undoubtedly be dismissed as an unnecessary provocation
today. Is it to say that the world has radically changed in the meantime?
Probably not, but our expectations about what comprises the architectural
project have certainly fundamentally evolved.

Heiz: ... let me add that there is always a risk of being stranded among
the systematic and the normative. To prevent this from happening, we
propose embracing life in all of its inadequacies, its chaotic and meaningless details—this constitutes the essential program of architecture, not
the form nor the virtuous assembling of materials. Of course, this does
not deny the relevance of these notions in the process of designing, nor

ban the service-provider imperative linked to the production of any architecture; it simply stakes a claim for a "dark territory of possibilities."

Gerber: This is why we prefer the term "architectonics" instead of "architecture."

Charbonnet: Architecture is one of the very few fields, in which contradiction should be praised as something ...

Gerber: ... necessary.

Charbonnet: ... yes, necessary! You see, architecture as a discipline is devoid of any axiomatic statements: nothing can be claimed as trivial or essential, because of the very absence of syntax and grammar. As a result, everything must be questioned ... this echoes the position of Rem Koolhaas (*1944) in *S, M, L, XL* (1995)[3], when he speaks about the radical insecurity of the architect when making a decision. There are literally so many opportunities to be wrong that the architect's mindset is in a state of constant unrest. Contradiction might well be the fuel of any articulate project.

Gerber: The question is, then: How do you program contradiction?

Heiz: Absolutely! Staging contradictions is what we deal with. This is true not only in our practice, but also in the academic context: to orchestrate contradictions that would reveal what one could call *les failles poétiques du lieu*, the poetical "cracks" of a place, which contain the exhilarating moments of life.

Charbonnet: We also have to admit the difficult time we sometimes have when promoting such an approach with students. The reason might well be that they are unable to formulate a "problem"; in other words, they are only interested in solving one! There is hardly an issue when designing—a program, a legislation, a budget, and so on—that does not constitute a problem *per se*. To properly activate the issue, one needs to leave one's field of expertise behind, in order to engage with the contradictory state of the world, so to speak; in order to stimulate not only greater critical leverage, but also catalyze exogenous forces. To do so, one must acquire specific knowledge—and this quest is everything but complacent.

Heiz: In other words, we ask our students to become generalists, that is, "enemies" of their time, and to obsessively question any type of conven-

---

3 | Rem Koolhaas and Bruce Mau, eds., *S, M, L, XL. Office for Metropolitain Architecture* (Rotterdam: 010 Publisers, 1995).

tions. We are often confronted with colleagues that seem to exactly know what architecture is. Not necessarily in an arrogant way ...

Charbonnet: ... but often in a complacent way. I mean, complacent toward whatever is revolving around the issue of architecture itself.

Gerber: Let's come back to *Voluptas*. In preparation for this interview, I re-read *Le plaisir du texte* (1973) by Roland Barthes (1915-1980).[4] In this book, he discusses the relationship between an author, his text, and a potential reader, as well as the kind of reactions the latter may have, citing either the order of *plaisir*—pleasure—or *jouissance*—pleasure, delight, ecstasy. While the former takes place at a distance, the second implies a *passage à l'acte*, an acting out, in order to achieve pleasure. I wasn't sure how to locate *Voluptas* in relation to these two forms of pleasures, as the term implies a bit of both. What is interesting in Barthes's discussion is the fact that he underscores the need to have a space in order for play to occur, yet while one can talk about *plaisir* in these terms, the notion of *jouissance* eludes any critical or theoretical approach. Considering the latter, how can you teach *Voluptas*, and how can you discuss it with your students?

Fig. 64: Joël Berger, Noé Lanfranchi, Artai Sanchez Keller, Contamination, Voluptas FS 2018

Heiz: You seem to question the outcome of such a methodology—and you are right to suggest that *Voluptas* embraces both sides of the notion of de-

---

4 | Roland Barthes, *Le plaisir du texte* (Paris: Éditions du Seuil, 1973).

light! I would say that *jouissance* evokes a sort of abandonment (come what may!) while *plaisir* still refers to rational comprehension. The beauty of all this is that one doesn't contradict the other. They are not mutually exclusive notions. We just believe that the three Vitruvian ordinances fail to address the concept of "residual energy," in the sense that *Firmitas, Utilitas* and *Venustas* depict architecture in a discerning, categorical, and objective way. *Voluptas* invites us to consider what lies in between or, again, *beyond* these notions. It could well be that *Voluptas* is an emanation of the three ordinances, but we refuse to reduce the concept to this. It investigates an environment driven by more than just political or economic; it depicts a world where *desire* is the prime force behind decision making—a part of the *jouissance* you mentioned.

Gerber: Well, *jouissance* is really a form of *passage à l'acte*, while *voluptas* is more of a yearning for something. So, what happens in this *passage à l'acte* with *Voluptas*?

Heiz: ... as I said before, we neither intend to stifle the concept nor the product at such an early stage in its development ...

Charbonnet: Let's try to identify voluptuous figures of architecture. Once, I said that I believe many *voluptés* lie somewhere else and often in anonymous situations. Examples are Francesco Borromini's (1599-1667) work or projects by Etienne-Louis Boullée (1728-1799)—who raised architecture to cosmic levels—or even more obviously, by Jean-Jacques Lequeu (1757-1826). Similar to these French revolutionary architects, figures like Iwan Iljitsch Leonidow (1902-1959) or, closer to us, the 1989 competition trilogy by OMA (*Terminal Seebrugge* (1988), *ZKM Karlsruhe* (1989) and *Très Grande Bibliothèque Paris* (1989)) apply. Or Aldo Rossi's (1931-1997) social housing project in Berlin, where a sample of the Palazzo Farnese's façade is staged as a radical political statement. All of these works express a jubilatory and excessive use of architectural tools. Of course, these are a few all-too-glorious moments in the history of architecture; they simply have one common feature: something that escapes the rational and the quantifiable.

Gerber: It is funny, because when you look at your projects, there is always some element hovering in mid-air. It is like a signature. These seem to be literally excessive pieces ...

Charbonnet: It is more of a *coquetterie* than anything else. In physics, one distinguishes a laminar flow from a turbulent one, in which the trajectory and dynamic of matter escape any predictability. There is indeed some-

thing similar in some of our projects. Once primary functions are fulfilled, the composition is, so to speak, free from quantifiable imperatives.
Take the portico of the *Erechteion*, for example, noting how the feminine
figures indicate more than the sheer path of the forces: they suggest a very
moving contradiction between permanence and a transient state.

Gerber: Absolutely! There is something that escapes reason, gravity ...

Charbonnet: ... you see, Archimedes' admonition to distance the observer
from its subject has always been a sort of a leitmotiv—not an ideological
stance, but a necessary distancing to witness phenomena in all their complexities. Give me a place to stand, and I will move the earth! One can't
record nor monitor anything, unless one can stand to the side.

Fig. 65: Made in, ZSC Arena, Competition Entry, 2012

Gerber: Returning to the idea of excess, I was reading Jean Baudrillard's
(1929-2007) notion of the "ecstasy of communication." To him, this is
something negative that culminates in the "désert de la communication,"
and is also always self-consuming.[5] Beyond the proximity of "excess" to
"ecstasy," is there not a danger in this approach becoming self-consuming, self-referential?

---

5 | Jean Baudrillard, *Simulacres et simulation* (Paris: Galilée, 1981).

Charbonnet: ... It could well be.

Heiz: What we have discussed really applies to the early stages of projects, during which the idea travels at its greatest speed; the danger would be to maintain the architectural project in this ethereal state. But we never consider the project to be autonomous as such, and any meaningful architecture is bound to confrontation with a pragmatic and non-poetic reality.

In this regard, we very much look forward to the completion of our first large scale project, on Zollstrasse in Zurich, where a "disproportionate" monumentality meets the most stringent requirements of performative infrastructure.

Charbonnet: I recently came across Robert Musil's (1880-1942) seminal work *The Man Without Qualities* (1930), in which the author describes a sixth sense called the *Möglichkeitssinn*—a sense of the possible. This most fully embodies what we are trying to depict: a sense that escapes the actual impossibility of the present in order to activate potentialities within a speculative timeframe or contextual background. It is essential to us for the simple reason that the architectural project is thus embedded into a completely different dynamic. The question then becomes what it could fulfill and imply, rather than what it actually is: it is really a catalytic impetus, which is open to several equivocal readings. Looking back at *Made in*'s projects, we can say without any doubt that most of them have dealt with this issue in one way or another.

Gerber: Let's return to the notion of architecture as a serious game. Interestingly, Roland Barthes also relates *jouissance* to boredom. The same way one cannot plan for *jouissance* in advance, you cannot anticipate or plan boredom. The playful, the fun is then all about not being bored. Architects have perpetually tried to escape boredom and produce spectacular buildings. I was wondering if you have ever considered boredom in your work. How we can put *Voluptas* in relation to this?

Charbonnet: It is a difficult question because boredom—like its counterpart, excitement—is almost exclusively a matter of perception.

Heiz: ... the least we can say is that we have always tried to avoid nostalgia or mere contemplation, in order to legitimize a project. History is indeed a sort jurisprudential array of specific contexts, but it shouldn't be mobilized to validate any architectural stance. It should merely act as a sort of resonance chamber, coloring the project with the traces of the past to trigger active doubt and critical reflection.

But it seems that I just drifted from your question to become evasive.

Fig. 66: Joël Berger, Noé Lanfranchi, Artai Sanchez Keller, Contamination, Voluptas FS 2018

Charbonnet: Another digression, if I may: Are you familiar with the movie *Novembertage* (1989/90) by Marcel Ophüls (*1927)? The BBC asked Ophüls to interview people crossing the Berlin Wall on November 9, 1989, and then again several years later, in order to document transversal changes in the way people comprehended their newly acquired freedom. Surprisingly, not all of these people evaluated these changes positively. Many of them had experienced serious difficulties in adapting to their new political environment, and mourned the downfall of their previous state despite their newfound freedom of movement. It is fascinating and moving—and to certain extent also puzzling—to see how people utilized their imagination to project an illusionary cultural synchronization with the other side of the wall. But when the unified territory was formed, this multiplicity of imaginative potentialities became a concrete reality.

Gerber: In *Novembertage*, there is obviously a very strong temporal component: an extended time frame, and then another time after. In gaming, you have also a very strong temporal dimension: you have a beginning and you have an end, a game over, and then you can start again and move on. How do you treat the aspect of time in architecture?

Charbonnet: It is a dimension which is often neglected. As an architect, you are only asked to fulfill an immediate requirement. A short-term perspective drives most of the decision-making processes. But *what* of the effect of time onto architecture?

If we consider the *Portraits* series we led at the ETH prior to *Voluptas*, the images produced were black and white. They became shades of gray, for they were mourning representations, something that had been lost.

Time is definitely a dimension that we intend to investigate: in our competition entry for the ETH Lausanne (EPFL) pavilions, we intentionally "staged" a general law of physics to contradict the peremptory, and all too transient, dynamic of technology: what can be experienced in the present could remain unchanged over time, not as an architectural feature as such, but as the experience of architecture itself. The resilience and appropriateness of architecture should be measured over time. Any architectural project can fulfill immediate requirements; what is more ambitious, and more difficult to achieve, is the "stamina" of an idea, whether it is on a semiological or purely performative level. I tend to think that nothing can really curb the passage of time, and that therefore nothing really is bound to an end, as William Faulkner (1897-1962) noted: "The past is never dead; it's not even past".[6]

Heiz: I tend to think of the matter slightly differently: Yes! A building in and of itself comes to an end—but only for its original purpose. I mean, this is where it really begins, where a situation is activated and later instrumentalized by people. The urban is the sum of all lived experiences, just as Venice is the sum of all sensuous realities projected unto it—it is not built substance on the "margins," as such, but everything that takes place in its vicinity. Building as an author is therefore not enough: one has to consider the actor's side of it!

Charbonnet: One can easily realize how difficult it is to activate such an understanding of urbanity—now that the *oikos* has taken over the *polis*— *oikos* and *polis* do not evolve along the same timeline, and most importantly, do not have the same requirements. While economic stipulations are always quantifiable—if unpredictable—and enslaved by short-term profitability, the urban is a much more diffuse and complex realm, in which highly subjective, contradictory, almost explosive potentialities are being orchestrated. Any rule or norm (whether soft or hard) is actually

---

6 | William Faulkner, *Requiem for a Nun* (New York: Random House, 1951).

reframing imaginary potentials. It is a very serious matter, just as it is to suggest that any decision can be legitimized through conventions or legal frameworks. A result of this is that one faces non-liable entities more often than responsible political actors. I mean, architecture is simply not being debated, beyond its feasibility or its current appearance.

Gerber: That is odd indeed!

Regarding responsibility, it is interesting that you always present yourselves as an office that does not follow rules. Concerning your planned involvement in video games in your teaching, it is noteworthy that you have decided to turn to a different medium, and one which is highly regulated by rules. Isn't that a paradox, because you cannot avoid rules? If you play chess, for example, you have to respect the rules ...

Charbonnet: Yes, but chess is an interesting, yet tricky example. Algebraically, the first move begins a spiral into multiplicity. After both players have initiated their moves, 400 possible board setups exist. After the second pair of turns, there are 197,742 possible games; after three moves, there are 121 million, and so forth. Therefore, there are more possible scenarios on a chessboard than physicists estimate to be the total number of atoms in the universe! Through a series of extreme constraints, you end up with ...

Gerber: ... more freedom.

Heiz: We are often accused of not playing by the rules in our competition entries; but again, rules are there to be questioned, if not contradicted. We are interested in the conditional, not in the conventional, and consider our practice as *eu*-topian more than *u*-topian!

Gerber: What kind of relationship do *Voluptas* and gaming environments have with the "real"? It seems you are saying that when you are breaking the rules, you remain within a range of possibilities. How "different" will this world be?

Charbonnet: We are not yet far along enough to define, once and for all, where we are going. But what we can say is that we did not initiate *Voluptas* out of frustration with the actual world. *Voluptas* is, instead, a sort of imaginative tool to investigate the condition of the present: students are systematically confronted with a contemporary predicament and are asked to turn these notions into the *agents* of their project. Our aim is to precipitate an accurate understanding of the notion over the years through "combinatory dynamics"—each topic is subsequently perceived through the diffracting lens or active prism of the composition. *Voluptas* is built upon *desire* rather than upon objective provision: its "Euclidian" form is that of an *arborescence*, a directed tree graph.

Gerber: In this sense, the expertise you bring to games is not that of an architect who builds houses, but rather, an architecture of desire.

Heiz: Yes. We should push towards the non-utilitarian, in order to produce new "desirable needs."

Gerber: I have one final question. It is now quite is clear what you can contribute to the work of game spaces. But what do you think you will learn? I could imagine, for example—if you allow me to anticipate your answer—that one thing might be this missing urban dimension you referenced. Do you think this might be something with which you could engage?

Charbonnet: Well, we are definitely interested in learning about the specific frameworks of the gaming industry; we aim to cultivate and develop, a virtual environment for gaming purposes. The *how* is yet to come, but it is also important to state that this studio will be linked to a research program, which aims to model the forces at stake while designing—not as an exclusive and dogmatic series of precepts, such as the *Five Points* by Le Corbusier (1887-1965), but as a dynamic, driven by an array of what Gilles Deleuze would call *précurseurs sombres*: the prerequisites for any event to take place.

Heiz: To me, one of the true delights of being an architect lies in the intensity of our encounters with specialists, with craftsmen, who embody an inherited form of tacit knowledge. *Voluptas* should be an invitation to generate similar encounters, but in the context of an imaginative and open realm.

Gerber: It is a kind of BIM [Building Information Modeling] of imagination and desire [laughs]!

Heiz: Sort of, yes [laughs]!

The Architectonics of Game Spaces

Or, why you should Play and Design Video Games
to become a better Architect

Andri Gerber

REYNER BANHAM PLAYS GTA 5

Architectural historian Reyner Banham (1922-1988) famously began his book *Los Angeles. The Architecture of the Four Ecologies* (1971) with the following comparison: "So, like earlier generations of English intellectuals who taught themselves Italian in order to read Dante in the original, I learned to drive in order to read Los Angeles in the original".[1] Banham argued that, in order to understand the Los Angeles of the 1970s, one had to abandon the classical canons of architectural history and drive a car along the highways and landscapes of the city, considering the cinematic speed of the car and a specific gaze through the windshield.[2]

After publishing his book, Reyner Banham appeared in a whimsical BBC documentary on Los Angeles, entitled *Reyner Banham Loves Los Angeles*, in which he drove around in a car and talked to people: "Los Angeles needs some explaining," he says in the movie. Once again, a change in medium—from archive to car, and now from book to TV—was necessary to cope with the complexity of this post-urban phenomena par excellence. Los Angeles, the city of the future, could no longer be approached by the traditional means of walking around, or studying sources and plans in

---

1 | Reyner Banham, *Los Angeles. The Architecture of Four Ecologies* (London: Allen Lane – Penguin Press, 1971), p. 23.

2 | English novelist James Graham Ballard (1930-2009) also shared this fascination with cars.

dusty archives; it called for a shift in perspective. Consequently, this implied a different understanding of architecture, shifting from singular objects to "ecologies," comprising infrastructure and landscapes.

Los Angeles remains a social and cultural paradigm of our time. As such, I would argue that, in order to understand Los Angeles in 2019, we must get out of the car—and get into a *virtual* car in a video game! We have to shift our attention from Los Angeles to *Los Santos*, L.A.'s game copy in *Grand Theft Auto 5* (2013). Thus, we require not only a change of medium and "reality," but a change in approach, turning from driving and describing to playing. As we emphasize in this book, this holds true for all of the activities one can execute in a video game, from driving a car to running through the manifold spatial landscapes one can act upon. How fun it could have been, to see Banham play *GTA 5* and comment on his playing on his own YouTube channel!

Banham thus expanded the definition of architecture to ecology and shifted the medium of his narrative. He was not the only one to approach post-urban conditions differently at this time: Robert Venturi (1925-2018), Denise Scott Brown (*1931), and Steven Izenour (1940-2001) also brilliantly exposed this lesson one year later, in their book *Learning from Las Vegas* (1972), which was the product of a research project with their students at Yale University in 1968. In this book, they pleaded for an investigation of Las Vegas by car—a place thoroughly ignored by the official architectural discourse of the time. They outfitted a car with a camera to record and understand the sign-landscape of Las Vegas—especially at night. Today, we could adjust this kind of investigation by utilizing in-game photography, which is also available in *GTA 5* (Philipp Schaerer discusses this possibility his interview in this book).

But Venturi, Scott Brown, Izenour and Venturi's former partner, John Rauch, extended their vision even further: in an exhibition held in 1976 at the Renwick Gallery of the National Collection of Fine Arts, the Smithsonian Institution, they depicted all of the invisible signs that define everyday architecture, by giving the buildings speech bubbles. Through this, what is commonly ignored or seldom-noticed information suddenly becomes visible. Moving beyond recording and interpreting, they revealed what is normally invisible.

Perhaps it is not so surprising that the subsequent work of Robert Venturi and Denise Scott Brown was focused on an architecture of façade, understood as system of signs; they inverted the modernist method of designing a building inside-out by designing outside-in. Unsurprisingly, Venturi has often denied the spatial nature of architecture and underscored how this and the urban landscape are composed of signs, and not of forms. Their dematerialized and iconic architecture serves as an important reference for understanding architecture through the medium of the video game, and how this, in turn, can influence "real" architecture.

To delve deeper into this kind of understanding, in the following sections, a philosopher—Immanuel Kant (1724-1804)—a landscape architect—Humphry Repton (1752-1818)—and an architect—Le Corbusier (1887-1965)—play games. Through their ludic activity, we will try to learn something about the relationship between video games and architecture. We will use Kant to reflect on their mediation more generally; then Repton to propose landscape architecture rather than architecture as a reference for game spaces; and Le Corbusier, in order to hint at the many lessons architects can learn from playing video games.

IMMANUEL KANT PLAYS DOOM

Referring to Kant and his concept of *Architektonik* (architectonics)[3] might initially appear far fetched and even presumptuous, yet for many philosophers before and after him—Arthur Schopenhauer (1788-1860) and Friedrich Nietzsche (1844-1900), in particular—architecture was one of the chosen metaphors for describing the "building" of philosophy. What makes the notion of architectonics so suitable for our purposes is the fact that Kant uses it to explain the relationship between philosophy and architecture, in which the latter is not only a metaphorical double, but a *system* going far beyond any formal or simple comparison. Thus we are not talking about a simple *image* of architecture translated to video games, but about the possible *natures* of architecture. This allows us to discuss how "architecture" is translated into games and video games, and what its relationship is to its virtual counterpart. At the same time, we must acknowledge that, even today, we do not yet have a convincing or shared

---

3 | Kant was not the only one to use this concept. For example, Johann Heinrich Lambert (1728-1777) published *Anlage zur Architektonik oder Theorie des Einfachen und Ersten in der philosophischen und mathematischen Erkenntnis* in 1771, only one of his many other works.

definition of what architecture is, which makes it even harder to discuss in the context of video games.

Kant, in his attempt to bridge between empiricism and reason, often returns to the metaphor of architecture as a construction of reason, which must be built upon solid ground and a solid foundation.[4] But he goes further, explaining how one of the main problems with his critique of pure reason in terms of architecture is that it is built through aggregation; the plan, the idea behind this aggregation, can only be intelligible once the building has been completed: "It is, however, a customary fate of human reason in speculation to finish its edifice as early as possible and only then to investigate whether the ground has been adequately prepared for it".[5] The term "architectonics," or "the art of systems," thus encompassed the impossibility of the *a priori* innate to this kind of endeavor.[6] The same reasoning can be found at the beginning of Kant's *The Critique of Judgment* (1790), when he describes the relationship of philosophy to a critique of pure reason as one in which the latter is not part of the former, but is necessary to design and test—*"entwirft und prüfet"*—the former.[7]

Kant's position is one of distance, at the forefront of similar attempts throughout human history, particularly in metaphysics. In this, a second metaphor appears; one which is particularly apt in discussing architecture in these terms: the ruin. On one hand, existing knowledge is described in terms of "scattered ruins," with which the impossible *a priori* building could be constructed.[8] On the other hand—and this seems even more

---

4 | "Now it might seem natural that as soon as one has abandoned the terrain of experience one would not immediately erect an edifice with cognitions that one possess without knowing whence, and on the credit of principles whose origin one does not know, without having first assured oneself of its foundation through careful investigations, thus that one would all the more have long since raised the question how the understanding could come to all these cognitions a priori and what domain, validity, and value they might have." Immanuel Kant, *Critique of pure reason* [1781], translated and edited by Paul Guyer and Allen W. Wood (Cambridge: Cambridge University Press, 1998), p. 139.

5 | Ibid., p. 140.

6 | Ibid., p. 691.

7 | Kant, Immanuel, *The Critique of Judgment* [1790] Translated with Analytical Indexes by James Creed Meredith (Oxford: Clarendon Press, 1989), p. 9.

8 | Kant 1998, pp. 692–3.

pertinent for our discussion—at the end of *Critique*, he dares to gaze upon his own theory-building, and all he can see are ruins: "The title stands here only to designate a place that is left open in the system and must be filled in the future. I will content myself with casting a cursory glance from a merely transcendental point of view, namely that of the nature of pure reason, on the whole of its labors, hitherto, which presents to my view edifices, to be sure, but only in ruins".[9]

If we thus utilize Kant's architectonics to discuss what architecture is, it is because we hope to clearly diverge from an understanding of architecture as something built, solid, concrete, and understandable. On a basic level, this can be interpreted as a reference to the weightlessness of architecture in video games: it can never have a solid foundation, as it has no corporeality. But architectonics is more than that: it is a condition of instability, and a metaphor for the attempt to counteract this instability and the impossibility of the *a priori* plan. Only through making—*der Entwurf*—do architects truly understand their plans. Architecture is always doomed to ruins. The architectonics of Kant therefore mean an understanding of architecture as something impossible and unstable. If we wish to imagine Kant playing *Doom* (1993) or *Quake* (1996)—admittedly suspending more disbelief than imagining Banham playing *GTA 5*—it is because of the gaming logic of constantly moving forward, without a clear plan, of constantly being frustrated in the attempt to gain ground, of fighting against continuously appearing monsters and being in a space which is both open and closed, and therefore ambiguous.

The constant need to destroy without the possibility to construct is a rather fitting spatial metaphor for Kant's concept of architectonics. Video games—and games in general—quite literally celebrate ruin and destruction. Even if this might be an all-too-simple transposition from architecture in "reality" to architecture in video games, beyond the simple lust and pleasure in destroying things—which, as Werner Oechslin points out in his interview in this book, always has a serious and problematic equivalent in reality—this opens architecture up to a dimension, which is normally neglected in the everyday practices of the discipline.[10]

---

9 | Ibid., p. 702.

10 | Andri Gerber and Philippe Koch, "Architektur muss als Ruine gedacht werden (um politisch zu sein)," *Archithese* Vol. 4, (2017), pp. 8–16.

Part of the difficulty of describing architecture—that which makes it architectonics—is based on its "ungraspable" spatial nature.[11] In many in-
stances, the spatial dimension has been recognized as a key component
of video games[12]; this is, obviously, a significant link to architecture when
understood as the "thoughtful making of spaces".[13] At the same time,
there is probably nothing more highly debated than the nature of space
in architecture: the epistemological, cognitive, or phenomenological perspective, among many others.[14] What can be said is that the experience
of space relies on all of our senses, and is tightly bound to our bodily
presence. Research into the notion of "embodiment" and our relationship
to virtual avatars are fundamental in this regard[15]; this concept has been
widely discussed in the context of video games.[16] We can agree that the experience of architectural and urban space requires rest and a slow pace—
you quietly walk into the Pantheon and then rest in the middle, or you
walk along the boulevards of Paris and let your gaze wander—and with
rare exception, these are qualities many games do not offer, when they are
e.g. founded on speed and action.

What works against the sense of architectural space is not only the
speed of the game, but also its extended scale. Even in the space of *Mario
Bros.*, which seems to be contained by the size of the screen, we are always
moving forward anticipating what comes next, and the game's narration is
subordinate to movement. In this sense, in games, the dimension of time

11 | Andri Gerber, *Metageschichte der Architektur. Ein Lehrbuch für angehende Architekten und Architekturhistoriker* (Bielefeld: transcript, 2014).

12 | Espen Aarseth, *Cybertext: Perspectives on Egodic Literature* (Baltimore MA: Johns Hopkins University Press, 2007), p. 44.

13 | Louis Kahn, "Space and the inspirations," [1967] in *Louis Kahn, Essential Texts*, ed. Robert Twombly (New York: W.W. Norton, & Company Inc., 2003), pp. 220-227.

14 | See Jörg Dünne and Stephan Günzel, *Raumtheorie: Grundlagentexte aus Philosophie und Kulturwissenschaften* (Frankfurt am Main: Suhrkamp, 2015).

15 | Isabella Pasqualini, "The Architectonic Avatar – Multisensory Aspects of Architecture," in *Proportions and Cognition in Architecture and Urban Design* [2017], ed. Andri Gerber, Tibor Joanelly, and Oya Atalay Franck (Berlin: Reimer Verlag, 2019), pp. 95-108.

16 | See for example: Gordon Calleja, *In-game: from immersion to incorporation* (Cambridge: MIT Press, 2011).

seems to dominate the spatial dimension. Space here is never as strong as time, unlike in architecture, where time is subordinate to space.

An equivalent to the spaces of DOOM or Quake would more likely be a garden than a building. Even better would be a hybrid of the two, such as the Villa Giulia in Rome, created for Pope Julius III (1487-1555) by several architects, primarily Jacopo Barozzi da Vignola (1507-1573). Here, architecture is in the service of experiencing the garden. In this villa, there are three gardens, all of which are on different levels, and they culminate on the lowest level in the Nymphaeum; the garden was also always considered a threshold to other "faunal" worlds. When moving through the garden of the *Villa Giulia*, one constantly questions the nature of architecture and its relationship to the gardens, and that's why, one has no specific goal but movement itself.

Translated back into game spaces, these ideas are *architectonic* rather than *architectural*; its spaces are clearly connected to the order of landscape gardens, rather than to the order of buildings.

HUMPHREY REPTON PLAYS ZELDA

In Diane Morgan's book on Kant, she describes one of the most appropriate novels on the topic of the landscape garden: the *Elective Affinities* (1809), by Johann Wolfgang von Goethe (1794-1832). In doing so, she utilizes a game metaphor: "In the novels, the owners of the estate, Charlotte and Eduard, are like players of a *Space Invaders* computer game. They hopelessly attempt to parry dangers that come from all directions".[17] There is no higher reference for landscape gardens than that of the English landscape garden. Born out of an anti-urban sentiment, it became the foil of the French garden—a metaphor of absolute power—and came to represent the more democratic English form of government embodied by the *Glorious Revolution* (1688) and the *Bill of Rights* (1689). At the same time, it was as "undemocratic" as the French garden, as it provided a well-guarded and closed enclave for the wealthy, even though it simulated openness. The invention of the *ha-ha wall* illustrates this point particularly well: the terrain in a garden would slope downwards toward a recessed wall, such

---

17 | Diane Morgan, *Kant Trouble. The Obscurities of the Enlightened* (London/New York: Routledge, 2000), p. 22.

that the wall itself did not obscure the line of sight within the landscape. This provided the illusion of openness, while at the same time securing the garden.

One of the main sources of inspiration in laying out gardens came from landscape painting; many garden pioneers, such as William Kent (1685-1748) or William Gilpin (1724-1804), were painters. Probably the most influential artist was French painter Claude Lorrain (1600-1682), who was famous for his picturesque aesthetics. The "Claude glass," or an oval, convex, and darkly-tinted hand-held mirror, was named after him because it reflected an image as an abstracted, idealized landscape. As if reality would not suffice!

Several theories of the sublime and the picturesque were developed through the experience of gardens, yet none subscribed to a unified discourse. On the contrary, this lead to many discussions and quarrels about the true nature of the sublime and the picturesque, particularly in regard to its relationship with beauty.

The English landscape garden emphasized wandering through an organic landscape, without symmetric order, in which the gaze was oriented toward points of view, such as temples or fake ruins. These garden sometimes even contained an "ornamental garden hermit," or a man paid to play this role. The garden represented an enacted fiction, a game to play for the bourgeoisie. Furthermore, its dimension and natural character should evoke the sublime, while the crumbling of fake monuments should make the beholder tremble. As absurd as it may sound, the English landscape garden was often much more expensive in its construction than the French formal garden, as it often implied major groundwork and even the creation of artificial lakes. In one of the main treatises on the picturesque, by William Gilpin, he describes how one should treat a Palladian Villa in order to make it more picturesque:

A piece of Palladian architecture may be elegant in the last degree. The proportion of its parts, the propriety of its ornaments, and the symmetry of the whole may be highly pleasing. But if we introduce it in a picture, it immediately becomes a formal object and ceases to please. Should we wish to give it picturesque beauty, we must use the mallet, instead of the chisel: we must beat down one half of it, deface the other, and throw the mutilated members around in heaps. In short from a smooth building we must turn it into a rough ruin.[18]

Fig. 67: Unknown artist, Claude glass, 1775-1780

One of the main champions of the English landscape garden was Humphrey Repton (1752-1818), who came to the profession after having failed in many other endeavors. It was Repton who introduced the term "landscape gardening" to describe his work.[19] One of his peculiarities was his "red books," in which he would create delightful images of a site before and after his planned intervention, allowing his client to see the advantages and changes his project would engender. In these books, the alternative scenery was evoked either by slipping a languet on the side or by setting aside a page with the existing situation. What made Repton's work so appealing was his thorough understanding of situating build-

18 | William Gilpin, *Three Essays on the Picturesque* (London: R. Blamire, 1792), p. 7.

19 | Humphrey Repton, *The Art of Landscape Gardening. Including his Sketches and Hints on Landscape Gardening and Theory and Practice of Landscape Gardening* [1794], ed. John Nolen (Boston/New York: Houghton Mifflin Company, 1907), p. 3.

ings, shaping the terrain, and his use of vegetation, which he discussed in several publications and represented in a series of well-known diagrams.[20]

Fig. 68: Humphrey Repton, Diagram, 1794

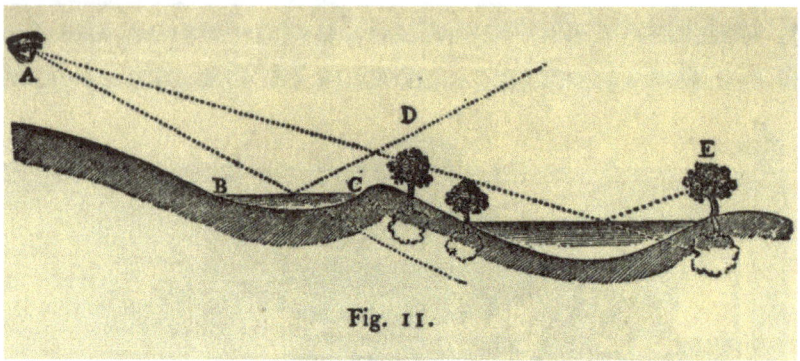

Kant once again becomes relevant, as he discussed the nature of the sublime in its relation to beauty in the landscape garden extensively. Kant would juxtapose architecture against the landscape garden, as the latter has no function or end. Landscape, then, represents a "free play of the imagination in the act of contemplation," and has no other function than to please.[21]

The English landscape garden is therefore a far better reference for game spaces than architecture: it is, in essence, a realization of pictures or paintings, it is strongly artificial, and it is based on a story that unfolds along a path (see the interview with Silke Steets in this book). It is not about bounded spaces; on the contrary, exactly as in video games, it is about concealing the boundaries that are there, yet should not be perceived by the users. It is about time and movement through an "open" landscape, and movement is directed towards selected *point de vues* and architectures. The entire landscape is constructed around a certain atmospheric effect, which should—in the best case scenario—evoke the sublime. Even if just literally, the fake ruins are actually akin to the doomed nature of the architectonic, in which ruins are real—but not actual.

---

20 | Ibid., p. 43.

21 | Morgan, 2000, p. 12.

It is therefore unsurprising that the term "ludic sublime"[22] has been used to describe the aesthetic experience of games such as *The Elder Scrolls IV: Oblivion* (2008) or *Dark souls (2011)*. In reference to the latter, theorist Daniel Vella has emphasized—also by using Kant—how the experience of the game is constructed around "the player's drive towards mastery of the game coming face-to-face with the impossibility of obtaining complete, direct knowledge of the underlying system".[23] This creates a gap, in which a player can locate the very possibility of this "ludic sublime." Repton, as an expert of making the sublime, would have loved to play and design such games!

LE CORBUSIER (REALLY) PLAYS FRÖBEL

It is not by chance that modernist architects developed an obsession with games and play, as they used them to break a static, conservative, and "serious" understanding of architecture. At the same time, their interest in games was tied to the development of innovative pedagogies such as the Bauhaus, and in general, to early childhood development. The best example of these kinds of games were the *Fröbel Gifts*, developed by German pedagogue Friedrich Fröbel (1782-1862). They had a widespread influence in kindergartens in Europe as well as the United States.[24] In his autobiography, American architect Frank Lloyd Wright (1867-1959) recounts the formative impact that these games had on his development and his architecture[25]; the same influence has been assumed in the case of Le Corbusier (1887-1965), as he frequented a kindergarten in Neuchatel where *Fröbel Gifts* were used.[26] One can easily imagine a young Charles-Édouard Jeanneret playing with them, and becoming inspired for his later career

---

22 | Philip Shaw, *The Sublime* (Abingdon: Routledge, 2006).

23 | Daniel Vella, "No Mastery Without Mystery: Dark Souls and the Ludic Sublime," *Game Studies*, Vol. 15, No. 1 (July 2015) http://gamestudies. org/1501/articles/vella (accessed April 22, 2019).

24 | Norman Brosterman, *Inventing Kindergarten* (New York: Harry N. Abrams, 1997); Canadian Centre for Architecture, *Toys that Teach* (Montréal: CCA, 1992).

25 | Frank Lloyd Wright, *An Autobiography* (London: Longmans, 1932).

26 | Marc Solitaire, *Au retour de la Chaux-de-Fonds: Le Corbusier-Froebel* (Martigues: Éditions Wiking, 2016).

as an architect. For to him, architecture would become an endless game: *"Ce jeu est sans limite"*.[27]

Fig. 69: J. F. Jacobs, Manuel Pratique des jardins d'enfants de Fréderic Froebel, 1874

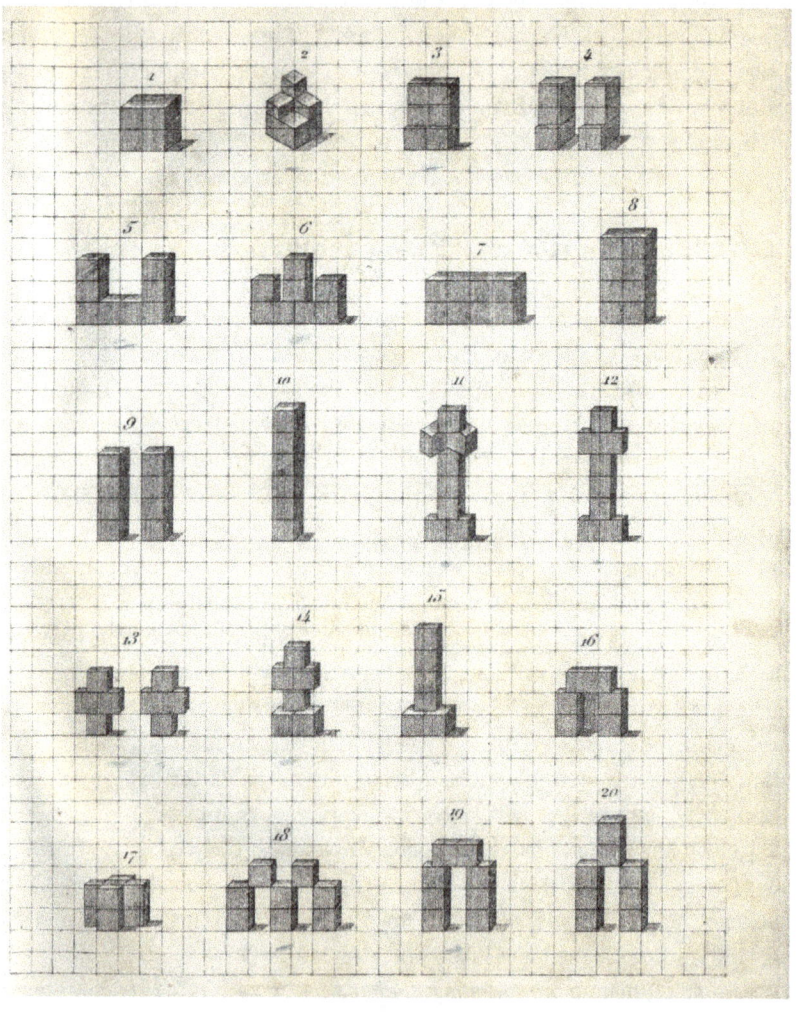

27 | Le Corbusier, *Le Modulor [I], Essai sur une mesure harmonique à l'échelle humaine applicable universellement à l'architecture et à la mécanique* (Boulogne: Edition de l'Architecture d'aujourd'hui, 1950), p. 94.

Simultaneously, modernist architects developed construction-related games, such as the marvelous glass construction set *Dandanahm* (1921) by Bruno Taut (1880-1938), or in an extended version to the scale of reality, as with *Baukasten im Grossen* (1923) by Walter Gropius (1883-1969) and Fred Forbàt (1897-1972). An unrealized design by Walter Gropius and Adolf Meyer (1881-1929) was even made for the *Friedrich Fröbel Haus* in 1924.[28] To stay in the context of the revolutionary pedagogy of the Bauhaus, one has only to consider the "functionalist" chess design by Josef Hartwig (1880-1955): *Bauhaus Schach* from 1924. Here, the pieces were designed so that their form revealed their function, that is, the movements they could make on the board.

Games and play were considered both enriching and a trigger to overcome old-fashioned understandings of architecture. If we extend this logic to the contemporary praxis of architecture—beyond our critique of their belonging to the order of a landscaper garden—what could we learn? The main argument for playing video games, from this perspective, is the fact that they can enhance certain skills: first and foremost, a person's spatial ability!

Video games have long time been associated with a negative bias and with the stereotype of a nerdy, white, male "gamer" spending hours in a basement, instead of doing homework. The addictive nature of games is always one of the main criticisms put forth against games. Furthermore, games are considered simple amusements with no further value. But what if there are also things that can be learned from gaming, particularly for architects?[29] Without romanticizing the potential of positive effects, there is an important point to be made—corresponding with a long tradition of doing so—that games can indeed have also a positive impact. As stated in one of the many psychology papers that have investigated these questions:

---

28 | Canadian Centre for Architecture, *Toys and the Modernist Tradition* (Montréal: CCA, 1993).

29 | One obvious positive aspect, which is closely related to architectural design, is "creative mode": the possibility to design parts of the game world, such as levels, or even the game itself. Minecraft allows one to choose a "world type"; in *Super Mario Maker*, the entire game was about designing the levels for Mario. This kind of adaptation is almost as old as video games themselves, called "modding" (from the "mod-" of modification), and was promoted both by gamers themselves through coding and by game platforms.

"At very least, the research on the negative impact of these games needs to be balanced with evidence for the cognitive benefits of the same games".[30]

The potentially positive impact of (non-digital) games on their players is a long-established insight. Child psychologist Jean Piaget (1896-1980) noted the importance of games in early childhood development, both for the development of spatial ability as well as the ability to locate and relate objects and the self in space. Since then, educational psychology has conducted several investigations into the cognitive and educational effects of video games, emphasizing their benefits, ranging from: cognitive, motivational, emotional, social benefits[31] to autonomy, competence, and relatedness.[32] Gaming, in particular action games, "enhances several aspects of vision",[33] fosters social skills, problem solving skills, spatial skills, and cultivates "a persistent optimistic motivational style".[34]

This idea is not only relevant to developmental theory, but has already been explicated in literature and film. One of the first examples is by American author Orson Scott Card (*1951), with his short story *Ender's Game* (1977) and its subsequent novelization in 1985. He imagined a future conflict between humans and aliens, and a program set up to train the most gifted earthling children through complex war video games. The most talented would become commanders of their war fleets. This idea was adapted into the movie *The Last Starfighter* (1984), by Nick Castle (*1947). Similarly, in the *South Park* episode entitled *Best Friends Forever* (2005), Kenny plays the PlayStation game *Heaven vs. Hell* and reaches level sixty, when he is hit by a car and falls into coma. While the episode revolves around the ethical question of whether or not to turn off his life-support machines, Kenny arrives in heaven to discover that the game *Heaven vs. Hell* was actually designed by God and the angels, in order to find somebody to guide a heavenly army against the army of hell. As Ken-

---

30 | Isabela Granic, Adam Lobel, and Rutger C. M. Engels, "The Benefits of Playing Video Games," *American Psychologist*, (January, 2014), p. 70.

31 | Ibid., p. 66.

32 | Adam Eichenbaum, Daphné Bavelier, and C. Shawn Green, "Video games: play that can do serious good," *American Journal of Play*, Vol. 7, No. 1, (2014): pp. 50-72.

33 | Ibid., p. 56.

34 | Granic, Lobel, and Engels, 2014, p. 71.

ny was the only human ever to have reached level sixty, he had developed the necessary skills to be the chosen leader.

Of all the skills gaming can transmit, spatial skills are the most relevant for architects, as they build on the kind of knowledge that allows them to imagine and design spaces. In the context of a Swiss National Science Foundation-funded research project by the Institute Urban Landscape at the Zurich University of Applied Sciences (ZHAW), in collaboration with the Chair of Cognitive Sciences and the Chair for Research on Learning and Instruction at ETH Zurich, we developed a new psychometric test for assessing the spatial abilities of architects.[35] This test targets specific spatial mental processes expected in architects' work, such as the transition between 2D and 3D perspectives, the manipulation of volumes, the capacity to move back and forth between an allocentric and egocentric perspective, and changes in the scale of objects. The project started in 2016 and was completed in the fall of 2019. We tested approximately 600 architecture students, both on the bachelor and master level. These students filled out a questionnaire and were asked about their gaming habits. Interestingly, more than 40% of the students answered that they never play video games; 24% said they do so rarely; 11% responded that they played regularly in the past; 12% play occasionally; 7% play 2-3 times a week; and only 2% answered that they play daily. If we compare the results of these students in our test, overall, people who reported playing computer games tended to do better on spatial tasks than those who either never or rarely played. Performance was positively correlated with frequency of game playing. Though these correlations were typically small (around .20), the pattern was consistent. One possible explanation for this covariation is that playing certain video games has a positive effect on the development of spatial ability, though we cannot directly infer this causality from the way our study was designed (we did not inquire about the type of game in our survey).

Certainly, playing video games alone does not lead to becoming a successful architect, but it might be an additional means to develop the spa-

---

35 | Andri Gerber, Michal Berkowitz, Beatrix Emo, Stefan Kurath, Christoph Hölscher, and Elsbeth Stern, "Does Space Matter? A Cross-Disciplinary Investigation upon Spatial Abilities of Architects," in *Research Culture in Architecture. Cross-Disciplinary Collaboration*, eds. Cornelie Leopold, Christopher Robeller, and Ulrike Weber (Basel: Birkhäuser Verlag, forthcoming).

tial abilities architects require for their work. It should be noted that studies in spatial ability have consistently found gender differences in some types of spatial ability tests (mental rotation, in particular), with higher scores for men.[36] As a consequence, measures for improving women's performance have been investigated, including the use of the game *Tetris* (1984).[37] Our findings replicated this gender gap, on the level of bachelor students in particular. In addition, we found that playing video games was less common among the women of our sample. When we evaluated if gender and playing video games predicted test performance, we found that both contributed to their score. Interestingly, gender differences in test performance became very small on the master level, indicating that women had a proportionally higher increase of spatial ability compared to men. Therefore, it is not surprising that current literature points to video-game training as a possibility for increasing spatial ability, in particular for women.[38] Although further longitudinal studies are needed to definitively confirm these findings, playing video games might prove useful in improving the spatial ability of architects and reducing the gender gap.

36 | Melissa Terlecki and Nora S. Newcombe, "How Important Is the Digital Divide? The Relation of Computer and Videogame Usage to Gender Differences in Mental Rotation Ability," *Sex Roles*, Vol. 53, No. 5/6, (September 2005): pp. 433–44.
37 | Nora S. Newcombe, "Picture This. Increasing Math and Science Learning by Improving Spatial Thinking," *American Educator*, Vol. 34, No. 2, (2010): pp. 29–35.
38 | "Possibly the most intriguing finding was that when provided with videogame practice, the women in the study improved significantly more on spatial Visualization than the women who were not provided with videogame practice. Similar to the findings of previous research, the males scored significantly higher than the females on both spatial orientation and visualization. Although the women initially scored significantly lower than the males on 'Targ' and Spatial Visualization, they were able to equalize their scores when provided with videogame practice." Diana Gagnon, "Videogames and Spatial Skills: An Exploratory Study," *ECTJ*, Vol. 33, No. 4 (1985): p. 273.

CONCLUSIONS

When discussing architecture in "reality" and in a video-game environment, we cannot simply apply a definition of the former to the latter without first understanding the transformations it underwent in translation. *Architectonics* is the most apt term of comprehending the architecture of game spaces; it is more a condition than an object, and one that conveys the impossibility of the plan and the inescapable condition of ruin. This definition allows us to compare the two conditions, which can only help us better understand what architecture could be when evaluated together and in order to do so, we must expand our definition of architecture to include landscape architecture.

When Reyner Banham described his travelogue through Los Angeles, he not only referenced looking forwards, but also backwards, through the rear window: "But while we drive along the freeways that are its crowning glory or prime headache, and con the rear-view mirror for historical illumination, what shall be the route?"[39] This perspective is reminiscent of the *Angelus novus* figure painted by Paul Klee (1879-1940), and Walter Benjamin's (1892-1940) interpretation thereof as metaphor of history:

A Klee painting named 'Angelus Novus' shows an angel looking as though he is about to move away from something he is fixedly contemplating. His eyes are staring, his mouth is open, his wings are spread. This is how one pictures the angel of history. His face is turned toward the past. Where we perceive a chain of events, he sees one single catastrophe, which keeps piling wreckage upon wreckage and hurls it in front of his feet. The angel would like to stay, awaken the dead, and make whole what has been smashed. But a storm is blowing from Paradise; it has got caught in his wings with such violence that the angel can no longer close them. The storm irresistibly propels him into the future to which his back is turned, while the pile of debris before him grows skyward. This storm is what we call progress.[40]

Video games, in a sense, represent both progress and impossibility, because the pace of the game does not allow to look backwards. When play-

---

39 | Banham, 1971, p. 36.

40 | Walter Benjamin, "Theses on the Philosophy of History", in *Illuminations*, trans. Harry Zohn (New York: Schocken Books, 1969), pp. 257-8.

ing *GTA 5*, images in the rear-view mirror are blurred—due to computing power—and as such, the game—like most games—is predicated on a constant gaze forward. Yet, the landscapes of these games have a history, as they are related to a reality that has been shaped over centuries. We can only hope that games will someday include this view backwards. Architecture—or better yet, architectonics—and landscape architecture, with their rich histories, might just be able to contribute to this endeavor of understanding "reality".[41]

41 | Special thanks are extended to Poul and Constantin, who are much better players than I am, and who gave me much advice about the games we like to play together. I am also indebted to Stefano Gualeni and Rainer Schützeichel for a critical review of the first draft of this essay.

Virtual World Weariness

On Delaying the Experiental Erosion of Digital Environments

Stefano Gualeni

INTRODUCTION

Media and game scholars often approach digital games as artificial systems that disclose specific interactive situations and scenarios to their players. For instance, Ian Bogost[1], Paolo Pedercini[2], and Riccardo Fassone[3] have characterized such situations and scenarios, in respect to the possibilities with which they can be experienced and manipulated, as inherently limited. In their respective works, these three authors frequently focus on the spatial and operational limits afforded by virtual environments. The way those limitations are set, they argue, is one of the most definitive characteristics of this media form—and can even reveal the designers' ideological stances.

Aligned with the philosophical traditions of phenomenology and existentialism, in this chapter I will use the term "world" to indicate a group of beings (along with their individual properties and mutual relationships) understood as a unified set. In order for this set of "somethings" to be rec-

---

1 | Ian Bogost, *Unit Operations: An Approach to Videogame Criticism* (Cambridge, MA: MIT Press, 2006).

2 | Paolo Pedercini, "Invisible walls, puffy clouds, and the unheavenly world behind them," *blog post* (April 1, 2014) http://www.molleindustria.org/blog/invisible-walls-puffy-clouds/ (accessed April 24, 2019).

3 | Riccardo Fassone, *Every Game is an Island: Endings and Extremities in Video Games* (USA: Bloomsbury Publishing, 2017).

ognized as a world by a subject, it is necessary for that subject to be able to establish an interactive and mutually-constitutive relationship with those somethings. Moreover, when worlds are experienced, they must, to a degree, be able to be perceived persistently and they must be consistent behaviorally (that is, the condition in which they are intelligible must be stable).[4] This interpretation of world is not only concise and widely applicable, but it also allows me to establish what I consider to be a useful distinction between being *in* a world and what we *experience* during dreams, hallucinatory states, or dissociative events (such as mild daydreams or when immersed in literary fiction). "Virtual worlds" are thus understood as particular kinds of relationships that can be established with digital environments. These virtual worlds disclose artificial and often extra-ordinary[5] horizons of possibilities for both doing and experiencing.

As described in the first paragraph, the inherent artificiality of virtual environments is also understood as a guarantee of their finitude and limitedness. The qualities and affordances discussed in this chapter are not exclusive to digital game spaces, but characterize practices and interactions that take place in a variety of world-disclosing technologies.[6]

---

4 | Stefano Gualeni, *Virtual Worlds as Philosophical Tools: How to Philosophize with a Digital Hammer* (Basingstoke: Palgrave Macmillan, 2015), p. 6.

5 | In this context, adjective "extra-ordinary" corresponds to its etymological origin, indicating something that transcends the ordinary, an experience that goes beyond one's everyday identity and customary relationship with the actual world.

6 | In his 1990 book *Technology and the Lifeworld: From Garden to Earth* (Bloomington, IN: Indiana University Press), American philosopher of science and technology Don Ihde presented his understanding of the implications of technologies by analyzing the ways in which they contribute to how reality can be experienced and interpreted by human beings. Among the four kinds of human-technology relations he discusses, the third—that of "alterity relations"— is specifically relevant to this discussion. In alterity relations, according to Ihde, technologies do not filter or enhance our capabilities for interaction and perception, but are the very terminus of our experience. These technologies give their users access to artificial contexts for experience and interaction, while the everyday world—not playing an active role in this relationship—remains in the background. Common examples of alterity relations include getting money from an ATM or playing a digital game.

In light of this observation, it becomes relevant to ask why this chapter specifically focuses its attention on digital games and on their inevitable (spatial) boundedness.

First and foremost, the core of my argument as to why video game environments are particularly relevant topics of investigation lies in their being experientially configured and encountered as worlds. The artificial and interactive spaces of digital games—as worlds—allow us to play with (and around) their affordances and their technical limitations, and to extract meaning and pleasure from both of them. It is especially noteworthy that—in several languages, including English—the term "play" does not only signify an enjoyable, non-serious activity, but it also indicates the limited space in which a mechanism can move and perform its operations. From this standpoint, the creators of any kinds of virtual worlds can be recognized as holding a position of power in relation to their audience, as the former largely configure the "possibility space" of "play" for the latter.[7]

---

7 | I consider it necessary to add the adverb "largely" to this sentence, as the possibility space of a virtual world cannot be deemed as uniquely determined by the intentions of programmers, designers, or creative directors. It inevitably involves a degree of compromise with what the players know about the virtual world in question, which beliefs they have about it, and what the players desire to do within it. For developers, it is not always possible to predict, determine, and restrain players' aspirations and actions. Digital game glitch-runs and their "modding" are especially persuasive examples of how our relationship with those virtual worlds is effectively a negotiation, and not an imposition. The same can be said of various approaches to play that overtly rebel against the functional intentions and implicit ideologies that structure game worlds. Transgressive approaches to game rules, game affordances, and game conventions are recognized as forms of social subversion in the works of several authors, notably including Espen Aarseth and Mary Flanagan. From their theoretical standpoint, subversive play is an important cultural tool that stimulates independent critical thought, self-reflection, and promotes social change (Aarseth 2007; Flanagan 2009). To quote Fassone on this same point, the rigid borders of a game's formal structure "do not prevent playing from being an intrinsically transformative, interpretative and ideological act." Riccardo Fassone, *Every Game Is an Island: Borders, Endings, Extremities in Video Games* (Doctoral the-

A common understanding of the role of a game developer involves establishing (or at least partially establishing) what is interactively and perceptually available in (video)game environments: which elements and behaviors those worlds include and allow, and what is—instead—omitted from their "possibility horizon." This term references the ancient Greek origin of the word horizon, ὅρος (*oros*), which denotes a frontier—a spatial limit. Constructed on this etymological foundation, "horizon" is used here to indicate the spatial and operational boundaries that a (video)game environment affords its players.

VIRTUAL WORLD WEARINESS

This chapter presents notions and ideas that originally emerged in the context of my practical involvement with video games, both as a player and as a designer. I will begin by discussing a particular feeling that emerged as a result of my playful encounters with the possibility horizons of video games, as described in the previous section. In doing so, I am referring to the realization that—as a player—a gaming environment can be experientially exhausted and, as such, is ultimately banal. In other words, I examine how our deliberate engagement with the interactive environments of digital games can trigger sensations that are analogous to what Romantic authors referred to as *Weltschmerz*, or "world-weariness."

The Romantic idea of *Weltschmerz* can be understood as being almost exactly antithetical to the concept of the "sublime" embraced during the same period.[8] Much of the Romantic sublime focused on the awe-inspiring vastness of nature, and the impossibility of the human senses and human intellect to ever grasp its size and meaning—yet to someone experiencing the phenomenon of *Weltschmerz*, the world appears to be meaningless and dissatisfactory.[9] Whereas the Romantic poets found themselves inadequate and fragile, in relation to a sense of the sublime that transcended their perceptual and intellective capabilities, this contrasting

sis discussed at the department of humanistic studies of the University of Turin, Turin, Italy, 2013), 30.

8 | See: Philip Shaw, *The Sublime* (Abingdon: Routledge, 2006).

9 | Wilhelm Alfred Braun, *Types of Weltschmerz in German Poetry* (New York, NY: Columbia University Press, 1905).

sense of world-weariness is closely related to the feeling of hopelessness, even boredom; it is the realization that our experiences of a world make us progressively more aware of the impossibility of transcendence.[10] Aligned with these interpretations, this chapter uses *Weltschmerz* to indicate the sensation that a certain world is inadequate to satisfy our intellectual and emotional aspirations.[11]

There are many aspects of our relationships with digital games that can elicit (or be accompanied by) feelings of world-weariness. In analogy with actual-world weariness, a dissatisfaction and the boredom with digital game environments emerges from aspects of their finitude and banality. The most common among these "world-pains" are the players' direct encounters with the game's spatial boundaries (tall walls, invisible barriers, puffy clouds, cliffs, fences, etc.). Other frequent triggers of "virtual" *Weltschmerz* are, for example, recognition of the aesthetic repetitions of game textures and assets (buildings, trees, statues, textures, characters, etc.), and the recurrence of interactive patterns and in-game situations (the dreary routine of "grinding," the ceaseless repetition of the same lines in dialogue with non-player-character, the very un-surprising occurrence of surprise encounters, etc.).[12]

---

10 | Paul Martin provided a similar reflection on the sublimity and the domestication of video game spaces in 2011. In his article "The Pastoral and the Sublime in Elder Scrolls IV: Oblivion" (*Game Studies: The International Journal of Computer Game Research*, Vol. 11, No. 3), Martin identified the "sublime" (a concept involving nuances of immensity, incalculability, and danger) and the "pastoral" (for the familiar and non-threatening) as two successive moments of our experiential relationship with a certain video game space.

11 | In a way that resonates with this interpretation of "world-weariness," Norwegian existential philosopher Peter Wessel Zapffe clarified that "[m]an is a tragic animal. Not because of his smallness, but because he is too well endowed. Man has longings and spiritual demands that reality cannot fulfill. We have expectations of a just and moral world. Man requires meaning in a meaningless world" (*The Philosopher Peter Wessel Zapffe in his 90th Year*, Tromsø: Original Films AS, 1990).

12 | The notion that the world-weariness of artificial environments can be mitigated by pursuing aesthetic variety and breaking the repetition of modules might be interesting to apply to the actual world. For instance, the application of principles and ideas presented in this paper to modular and repetitive

Some of the recent work by game scholar Sebastian Möring focuses on the sense of boredom and meaninglessness that emerges when the challenges that are present in a game world have been overcome or removed, and all enemies have been defeated.[13] Experiencing such a virtual world can, by definition, trigger the feeling of weariness discussed above, as significant parts of its meaning and appeal have already been effectively done-away with (or played-away with). This is especially true regarding what are known as "games of progression",[14] in which a ludic setup affords and in-vites the defeating and removing of challenges and enemies as their *raison d'être*. Accordingly, I have suggested elsewhere that perhaps the only possi-bility for something extra-ordinary (and to a degree, transcendent) to hap-pen within virtual environments is found when we experience glitches. By this, I mean our interactive encounters with non-catastrophic malfunc-tions of computer software or hardware that are recognizably anomalous.[15]

If it is evident to us—as players—that the experience of empty, re-petitive, and bounded environments is a crucial trigger for virtual *Weltschmerz*, then it is equally clear that the designers and developers of digital games have an interest in keeping their audience from experienc-ing this particular kind of dissatisfaction. As a consequence, the most common design techniques aimed at delaying the emergence of virtual world-weariness involve making those triggers as inconspicuous and dif-ficult to encounter as possible. A very obvious example of this design ob-jective is the fact that the literal horizons of digital game environments often appear as aesthetic or thematic illusions of distant lands, buildings, cities, islands, planets, and star systems that exist at the periphery of our

architectural designs, such as those commonly characterizing public housing and rationalist city-planning, is one possibility of doing so.

13 | Sebastian Möring, "On the Relation of Boredom and Care in Computer Game Play from an Existential Ludological Perspective," *Brandenburg Center for Media Studies*, Ludic Boredom Workshop unpublished conference proceedings (Potsdam: Jun 1, 2018).

14 | Jesper Juul, "The Open and the Closed: Games of Emergence and Games of Progression," in *Computer Games and Digital Cultures Conference Proceedings*, ed. F. Mäyrä (Tampere: Tampere University Press, 2002), pp. 323–29.

15 | See: Stefano Gualeni, "On the de-familiarizing and re-framing effects of glitches and glitch-alikes," in *Conference proceedings of the DiGRA International Conference: Game, Play, and the Emergent Ludo Mix* (Kyoto: August 6-10, 2019).

vision, and cannot be reached or examined closely. Similar strategies of unknowability or concealing the spatial boundaries of virtual worlds also include presenting them to the player in ways that make contextual sense within the fictional setting of a certain environment: to represent them as parts of the environment that are intuitively impossible to overcome, inaccessible, or obviously deadly. Among the most common ways to give fictional meaning and to disguise the spatial limits of digital games are precipitous mountain ridges, impassable lakes of magma, cliffs, broken bridges, tall walls, electrified fences, endless stretches of water, and so on and so forth. Other strategies to prevent the experiential encounter with a virtual space's borders and boundaries involve creating game spaces that have "periodic boundary conditions" (worlds that wrap onto themselves, as if they enfolded a sphere). This is the case, for example, in the classic arcade game *Asteroids* (1979). Yet another approach for making the spatial boundaries of a video game impossible to actually be experienced as boundaries is progressively generating new (coherent and playable) content, as the players move beyond spaces that were previously visited. For example, Mojang's *Minecraft* (2009), CCP's *EVE Online* (2003), and Hello Games' *No Man's Sky* (2016) utilize this technique.

As indicated by the title of this book chapter, my objective in this text is to identify and discuss game design approaches and solutions that delay the experiential erosion of digital environments. As such, I will now specifically focus on the spatiality of virtual environments, and on ways designers can deal with their artificiality and their consequent finitude. I will pursue this objective by reflecting upon my own practical experience as a video game designer, as well as in structured discussions with scholars and independent video game developers. Their primary design work lies in combatting the emergence of world-weariness as described above. The interviewees for this essay were (in alphabetical order):

- Mike Cook—Independent video game developer and game researcher (http://www.gamesbyangelina.org)
- Mark R. Johnson—Game studies scholar and independent video game developer of *Ultima Ratio Regum* (https://www.markrjohnsongames. com/games/ultima-ratio-regum)
- Antonios Liapis—Researcher in the field of procedural video game content generation (http://www.antoniosliapis.com)
- Niccolò Tedeschi—Artist and game developer at *Santa Ragione*, inde-

pendent video game development team of *Foto*nica (http://www.foton-ica-game.com) and Mirrormoon EP (http://www.mirrormoongame.com)

On Delaying the Experiential Erosion of Digital Environments

Emphasizing a particular kind of existential dissatisfaction that manifests itself in digital environments, researcher and developer Mike Cook argued in our interview for this essay that "we dream of doing and being a particular thing in a world, and then we find ourselves unable to do it. It is a typical 21st century condition—to be trying our hardest to escape into a digital world and then realize that we cannot act in the way we wanted. It is almost like being in a nightmare where one is unable to move one's arms, or to speak." Interestingly, for Cook, our weariness has less to do with the granularity of the environment in question and more with its regularity: the more familiar we become with a certain world and its logics, the less interesting and surprising this world becomes, progressively losing any sense of the sublime. In our dicussion, Cook focused his attention on the repetition and the modularity of elements in digital environments—aesthetic components of the experience of a game world that are particularly problematic for someone like himself, who aspires to generate interesting, playable environments algorithmically. Over time, he argued, "we become numb to the patterns inherent in the algorithms that constitute the world."

Solutions to this problem in particular were widely shared by all of the developers and researchers I interviewed. Everyone recommended, for example, intentional masking of or creating breaks in computer-generated patterns (through procedural content generation), and authored content (or custom elements directly designed by humans). The rationale behind this stance is that the integration of procedural content through custom-generated assets can trick the human brain into misinterpreting the complexity of a computer generator, and overestimate the aesthetic variety and experiential richness of a digital environment. "The player builds a mental model of how content is generated in a certain world," Cook explained:

[...] and then they encounter something that does not fit that model. Their assumption that the [custom] content comes from the same algorithm that generated the rest of the world prompts them to re-evaluate their initial mental model, and in this way, their respect and interest for that world erodes a little slower.

Additional ways to mask the regularities and the repetitions of procedurally generated content in virtual environments that were discussed by my interviewees include:

- adding "noise" to pre-designed game content; that is, allowing a generator to introduce small aesthetic and functional variations to existing game modules in order to make it harder for the players to recognize them as something already "known" (this is the case, among others, with *Mossmouth*'s video game *Spelunky* (2013);
- giving the players the possibility and tools to modify, destroy, or reconstruct shared virtual environments. In his interview for this essay, Liapsis explained that these tools allow the players to provide additional complexity and experiential richness to interactive, digital spaces that—because of this—inevitably feel less artificial and more "lived";
- using data from the internet to both disguise procedurally generated patterns and to allow a digital environment to increase the feeling of "real-world" by referencing actual current events;
- erasing all the saved states and information about a world when a game session ends. According to what Johnson argued in his interview for this essay, losing information and access to a world as well as the civilizations that inhabited it, its undiscovered religions and tales, and its unvisited lands after a game is over not only makes it harder to reverse-engineer the ways in which that world was generated, but can also trigger a lingering feeling of mystery about it.

In addition to the virtual *Weltschmerz* elicited by experientially encountering the boundaries of virtual worlds, and the stale repetition of spatial as well as interactive patterns, both Tedeschi and Johnson recognized a third trigger for world-weariness that is common in contemporary video games: the fact that events in virtual worlds are often inconsistent with their narrative (or more widely thematic) context. The experience of contextual dissonance emerges from the need that game developers have to constantly negotiate their creative and expressive aspirations with the technical and functional limitations imposed by the technologies with which they design. As players, according to both Tedeschi and Johnson, we are constantly (and painfully) comparing virtual experiences with actual ones (which are considered our "phenomenological bedrock"), and we are also measuring the former against the backdrop of established expressive forms, their genres and canons. Tedeschi clarified this point with a particularly poignant example, stating that:

[...] in *Red Dead Redemption* (2010), a videogame that amply borrows its themes and aesthetics from the Western movie genre, it is possible to walk into various saloons and engage non-player characters in a game of poker. What I am about to discuss resonates with the representations of the American Old West that we are all more or less familiar with: I am in a saloon playing poker in the world of *Red Dead Redemption*. After a few hands, I have almost lost all of my money and so—while the game is still ongoing—I decide to stand up, shoot all of the other players, and walk out with all the money. Once I have killed all of the other players, however, no money is to be found on their bodies or on the table where we were playing. Apparently, *Red Dead Redemption* treats the game at the poker table as a technically separate instance of the world, rather than a part of it. My actions, which were completely consistent with what has been established in the Western genre, are not acknowledged by the game. At that point, that world revealed its artificial constitution and lost its "worldliness" for me...to a point that everything from that point on felt phony and pointless.

In response to the problem of thematic inconsistency, Tedeschi and Johnson each suggested design solutions that the creators of interactive, digital environments could start to employ with today's technologies and tools. Tedeschi argued that the kind of contextual dissonance that he diagnosed could be avoided by setting up worlds that do not reference the actual one. Referring to *Santa Ragione*'s design for *Mirrormoon EP* (2013), they tried:

to propose a very abstract experience in terms of narration, interaction and aesthetics. The world of *Mirrormoon EP* is never wholly defined: it is an open world, a minimal world that is simply 'suggested' to the player. This 'openness' might not be the final solution to the problem of thematic inconsistency, but I think it goes in the right direction; that is, letting the players interpret what they encounter rather than pre-determining for them how a world is to be understood on the basis of previous, common experiences. This could be understood as a Duchampian approach to game design: *ce sont les regardeurs qui font les tableaux.*

Fig. 70: Santa Ragione, screenshot of Mirrormoon EP exemplifying the minimal, procedurally-generated features of their explorable content, 2013

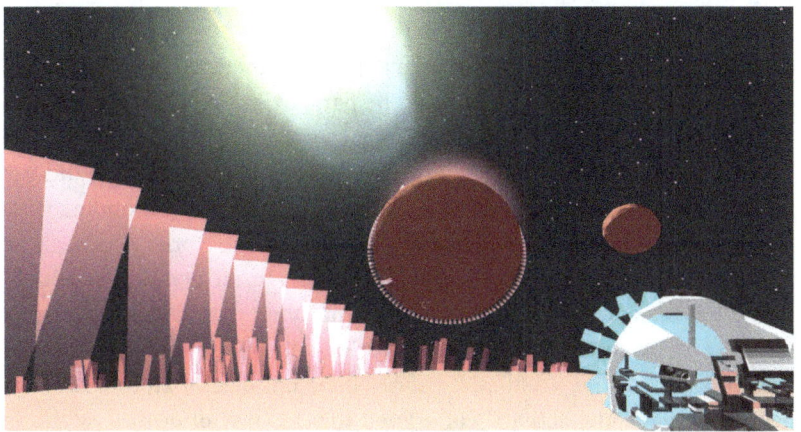

Discussing the same problem, specifically in relation to procedurally generated environments, Johnson foresaw developments and new techniques that could ensure the emergence of more believable and coherent worlds. Johnson, who pioneered some of those techniques himself in his game *Ultima Ratio Regum* (2012), insisted that part of the solution consists in striving to generate all the components of a virtual world in an interconnected fashion, such that each aspect natively relates to every other aspect. It is relatively easy, wrote Johnson:

[...] to make a generator that spits out Game-of-Thrones-esque names for cities like Wolfweald, or Queen's Throne, or Dragonlance, or whatever...But the real challenge is making those generated things ‚percolate‘ through the remainder of that world, reflecting in everything: from how people speak to what they wear, how they act, what their history is, et cetera.

CONCLUSIONS

Beyond contributing fitting comments on the design and procedural generation of less "painful" worlds to this chapter, Liapis mentioned something
that I consider worthy of particular attention in his interview; something
with which—in the cautionary spirit that is typical of the concluding sections of many literary works—I would like to close this essay. In response
to one of my questions—or, rather, as an amendment to it—Liapis called
my attention to the fact that it would be paradoxical to think of our sense
of unease and dissatisfaction in video games as simply meaning that we
would instead prefer to pursue any task in the actual world. He did not
believe that we would, say, rather go do laundry or grocery shopping than
explore enchanted kingdoms in a high-fantasy game world. Although he
admitted having experienced the feeling of virtual world-weariness—
which he considered not only common, but inherent to how we currently
design and experience video game worlds—Liapis pointed out that his
way of coping with virtual *Weltschmerz* does not revolve around the idea
of "returning to the actual." He argued that his way of dealing with the
kind of *Weltschmerz* induced by a digital game usually involve starting to
play a new game: beginning to explore a new environment, experiencing a
new possibility horizon, and a new promise of happiness and satisfaction.
To be sure, Liapis appeared to be well-aware that these ambitions cannot
be fulfilled by the systemic artificiality of contemporary digital technologies—or perhaps even at all. However, he seemed equally dissatisfied with
the prospect of considering actual experiences the answer to our shared
malcontent with virtual ones.

I do not mean to imply—in this essay or elsewhere—that the actual
world can ultimately satisfy and complete us, or that our aspirations can
finally obtain an adequate response through our experiential relationship
with it. Beyond the Romantic era, with its plethora of examples as to why
that might not be the case, ancient Greek tragedies as well as the artistic
and philosophical currents of Existentialism and Absurdism also stand as
historical landmarks for Western culture's awareness of the meaninglessness of our existential struggle in this world. What I propose in this essay
is the idea that *all* worlds (regardless of their virtual or actual constitution)
are ultimately absurd, and that technologies cannot be expected to fix the
inevitably boring, painful, and even tragic dimensions of our existence.
Digital environments are, I argue, better understood as existential tools:

not as contexts in which we pursue complete happiness and satisfaction, but as instruments that allow us to negotiate various aspects of our (individual as well as collective) existence, in new and unexpected guises.

Regarding this standpoint, a human being cannot be understood as existentially "solvable"—nor is it possible to be completed and satisfied—by technological means. This is not simply a problem with current technologies or our mastery of them; we are constitutively bound to dissatisfaction, and inherently driven to explore and experiment with new worlds and unfamiliar possibilities of being. Virtual environments, in their peculiar ways, arguably provide those experiences and possibilities. In doing so, they contribute to our existential struggle, both allowing us to transcend some aspects of our everyday relationship with the actual world, and in disclosing new ways in which our very incompleteness can be experienced and understood.

The Lived Space of Computer Games

Stephan Günzel

HENRI LEFEBVRE AND THE SPATIAL TURN

Since the late 1980s, a "spatial turn" has affected the arts and humanities, and in particular, cultural studies. This also extends to computer game studies—one could even assert they had involved analyzing the spatiality of digital games from the very beginning.[1] To understand this new approach, it is crucial to examine the origin of current debates about the spatial turn. This can be traced back to 1974, with the publication of Henri Lefebvre's (1901-1991) book *La production de l'espace*. It took almost two decades to recognize his spatial account of culture; but once his book was translated into English, neo-Marxist and postmodern theorists began to discover the relevance of a spatial approach to sociology and urban studies.[2]

Lefebvre's thoughts were finally introduced to a broader audience when the geographer Edward Soja (1940-2015) published his reading of *The Production of Space*.[3] The monograph was a follow-up to Soja's publica-

---

1 | Stephan Günzel, "The Spatial Turn in Computer Game Studies," *Exploring the Edges of Gaming: Proceedings of the Vienna Games Conference 2008-2009— Future and Reality of Gaming*, ed. Konstantin Mitgutsch, Christoph Klimmt and Herbert Rosenstingl (Vienna: Braumüller, 2010), pp. 147-56.

2 | Henri Lefebvre, *The Production of Space* [1974] (Oxford/Cambridge MA: Blackwell, 1991).

3 | Edward W. Soja, *Thirdspace: Journeys to Los Angeles and Other Real-and-Imagined Places* (Oxford/Cambridge MA: Blackwell, 1996), pp. 53-82.

tion *Postmodern Geographies*, in which the term "spatial turn"[4] was coined for the first time (diagnosing the turn of Western Marxism towards spatial aspects of culture). As the title of this successive book, *Thirdspace*, suggests, with Lefebvre, Soja calls for an understanding of society as a synthesis of two spaces.

The reason why Lefebvre insisted on the existence of a third realm, or "space," is because he asserted that production can take place at any of three possible stages. Physical space, the first realm, is as produced as the second realm of imaginations: landscapes are a reworked form of "second nature," and social or architectural utopias are manmade ideas. Both stand in a dialectical relation to one another, and the outcome of their concurrence is social space. Therefore, Soja subsequently referred to cultures as "thirdspaces"—a term originally coined in postcolonial studies[5]—to denote spaces that are "real-and-imagined places" alike.

Fig. 71: Triad of Space according to Lefebvre and Soja

Spaces	Forms	Modalities	Equivalents
1st	**Spatial practice** [*pratique spatiale*]	**perceived** [*espace perçu*]	subjective | real everyday live/nature
2nd	**Representations of space** [*représentations de l'espace*]	**conceived** [*espace conçu*]	objective □ imaginary urbanism/cartography
3rd	**Representational spaces** [*espaces de représentation*]	**lived** [*espace vécu*]	collective □ symbolic lifeworld/culture

Extending Lefebvre's idea of a dialectical production of space, Soja speaks of a "trialectics of spatiality," and this is for at least two reasons. The first is that the results of the imaginary (re)production of physical space as culture feeds back into the first (as well as the second) kind of space. In this, the first space is affected by the third (and the second). The other reason is

4 | Edward W. Soja, *Postmodern Geographies: The Reassertion of Space in Critical Social Theory* (London/New York NY: Verso, 1989), p. 39.

5 | Homi Bhabha, "The Third Space: Interview," *Identity: Community, Culture, Difference*, ed. Jonathan Rutherford (London: Lawrence&Wishart, 1990), pp. 207-221, here p. 211.

that Lefebvre describes each of the spaces as "two-fold," hence as dialecti-cal in and of themselves.[6]

Production of space on the first level takes place as an everyday spatial practice, in which space is not only acted out or performed, but simulta-neously, it is individually perceived: this describes the *phenomenology* of space. Production of space on the second level takes place due to the rep-resentation of (perceived) space in architecture, geography, urbanism, and so forth, but is also objectively conceived: this describes the *epistemology* of space. Production on the third level takes place as the constitution of "rep-resentational spaces" (as Lefebvre calls them) or "spaces of representation" (as Soja calls them), i.e. *culturally significant places*. These places are signif-icant due to their collective production as an interpretation, or a collective reproduction as preservation of certain traditions; Lefebvre refers to both of these as "lived space."

Lefebvre's (and Soja's) triad of space has become very popular in recent discussions and has been used to describe the various modes of cultural production. However, there is significant confusion about the model. This is not only due to the third term, the "lived space," which is hard to sep-arate from the "spatial practices" of the first level (indeed, this confusion was Lefebvre's intention, as he did not want space to be conceptualized as static, but rather, as a process). Confusion also resulted from the fact that the second and the third space are both denoted as "representations." This duplication, or bifurcation, is particularly useful in re-examining the medium in question: computer games.

LEFEBVRE AND SPACE IN GAME STUDIES

In computer games studies, Lefebvre's approach was used shortly af-ter Soja's reading in 1996. In a paper entitled *Allegories of Space*, which was initially published online in 1998, the Norwegian hypertext-theorist Espen Aarseth (*1965) referred to Henri Lefebvre, making him first to mention the theory of spatial production in regard to games. In his text,

---

6 | *Dialectics*—based on the Greek word *logos* for spirit, speech, or meaning—does not literally designate a movement between only "two," since the prefix is derived from *dia*- meaning "through" and not from *di*-; "tri-alectics," as Soja names the process, is therefore almost a nonsensical term.

Espen Aarseth utilizes the popular reading of the three forms of space as the physical, the abstract, and the social.[7] In doing so, Aarseth claims that the spatial practice of games—i.e. the first space as (simulated) *physical space*—is derived from a relational space of navigation—i.e. the second space as (imaginary) *abstract space*—as well as from what Aarseth calls an "aesthetic space"—i.e. the third space as (conventional) *symbolic space*. Thus, according to Aarseth, games are allegorical representations of space. In other words, they are metaphors of space, and not space itself. "Representation," again, refers to an incomplete copy or an ontologically deviant "image" of the real world. It is "only" a representation; games can never depict space as it is perceived, completely, as it exists "in real life."

Since Aarseth's article on game space, Lefebvre's triad of space has been used frequently in game studies—notably, without following Aarseth's interpretation. The first further instance is a paper on *Virtual Real(i)ties* by Shawn Miklaucic, who discusses *SimCity* (1989) as a quite negative example of second space, i.e. as an abstract space, or the representation of space. In his perspective, the representation dominates the first as well as the third space alike: there is no "lived" (or perceived) space in *SimCity*, only its (cartographic) representation.[8] Miklaucic uses the term "representation" in an ambiguous way, since he addresses both in-game representations and the game itself as an image. Furthermore, Miklaucic does not seem to be aware of the fact that, in *SimCity*, the first space is not a map at all, even though the game world is visible from a birds-eye view. A map exists in the game, too, but only as a miniature that represents the frame or cover of the first space; that is, the border between on-screen and off-screen space. On the contrary, the primary view is the first space of the game—the lived space of *SimCity*.

A second example is Axel Stockburger's dissertation, *The Rendered Arena*, in which the three modalities of space are used to differentiate

---

7 | Espen Aarseth, "Allegories of Space: The Question of Spatiality in Computer Games," *Cybertext Yearbook 2000*, ed. Markku Eskelinen and Raine Koskimaa (Jyväskylä: Research Centre for Contemporary Culture, 2001), pp. 152-171.

8 | Shawn Miklaucic, "Virtual Real(i)ty: SimCity and the Production of Urban Cyberspace (2001)," *Game Research: The Art, Business and Science of Computer Games* (2006), http://www.game-research.com/index.php/articles/virtual-reality-simcity-and-the-production-of-urban-cyberspace (accessed June 17, 2019).

between the physical medium of the game device(s)—the first space—the narrative as well as rule-based representations of space on the computer-screen—the second space—the realm, constituted by the players' kinesthetic actions—the third space.[9] Another author using Lefebvre's schema in a similar way is Michael Nitsche, in his 2008 book *Video Game Spaces*: Just like Stockburger two years before him, the representation of space is the visible space on screen, as a form of second space. However, Nitsche separates the rule-based space—which Stockburger includes in second space—and identifies it with the first space, as the set of rules underlying secondary visual space. "Representation" is thus understood as the visualization of otherwise invisible space. Like Aarseth, Nitsche takes into consideration the dialectic of aesthetics and knowledge (symbolic space and relational space in Aarseth), or fiction and rules, from which the spatial constitution of a particular game arises. And like Stockburger, Nitsche also incorporates the aspect of the social as a third space, claiming that the "thirdspace" is the "combination of fictional, play, and social spaces".[10]

As evident in these examples, Lefebvre's triad of space is a stimulating heuristic model for a rich description of computer games. And this is not to speak of the simple possibility of applying Lefebvre to his original subject-matter—urban space—which now is pervaded by virtual game space. Nevertheless, the next section provides another reading of Lefebvre in regard to computer game spaces, which is quite different from the ones mentioned above: games themselves as spatial concepts.

REPRESENTATION AS DENOTATION AND REPRESENTATION AS EXEMPLIFICATION

Understanding games as spatial concepts requires a closer look at what a "representation" is (or could) be. Representation has a *semiotic* dimension,

9 | Axel Stockburger, *The Rendered Arena: Modalities of Space in Video and Computer Games*, unpublished PhD dissertation (London: University of the Arts, 2006), http://www.stockburger.at/files/2010/04/Stockburger_Phd.pdf (accessed June 17, 2019).

10 | Michael Nitsche, *Video Game Spaces: Image, Play, and Structure in 3D Games Worlds* (Cambridge MA/London: The MIT Press, 2008), p. 16.

beyond its *ideological* meaning, in which a representation is always suppressive and dogmatic, and besides an *ontological* understanding of representation as something that lacks reality or materiality. Indeed, Lefebvre himself, as previously indicated, seems to have had all three dimensions in mind: he refers to *phenomenological dialectics* (in respect to the ontologies of space: perceived, conceived, and lived) and *ideological dialectics* (in respect to the means of social reproduction: biology, knowledge, and culture), but also to *semiotic dialectics*: referencing the first space, in which the lived, cultural space feeds back into the individual perceived space. Lefebvre refers to this as the realm of "performance," or the sphere in which meaning is acted out. This idea was originally invented by John L. Austin (1911-1960), who insisted on differentiating between "performatives" and "constatives,"—both *how* something is said and *what* is being said (as the content of an utterance).[11]

Thus, the relationship between the first and second kind of space, in respect to semiotics, could be understood in the sense of Nitsche: as the dialectics between (rule-based) performance and (on-screen) representation. Still, the question remains: what is the difference between a representation in the second space and a representation in the third space, if not understood ideologically or ontologically? Semiotically, one could argue for two means of representation. An entire book by Nelson Goodman (1906-1998) was devoted to the problem of representation; in his lectures on *Languages of Art* from 1968, Goodman tried to outline a semiotic approach that avoids any ontological understanding of signs. In this, images as "mere representations" are no longer considered to "lack reality."

Goodman distinguishes between representation as "denotation" and representation as "exemplification," which are the two ways of using a sign in specific contexts. When *denotating* something, a term used to refer to an object or the "content" of the sign, it cannot be like what is referred to in respect to its appearance.[12] For example, most words humans use to designate objects have nothing in common with the object itself. Some onomatopoetic words may resemble an object, or an aspect of it: for example, sounds of animals used as common nouns for the species in question. But

---

11 | John L. Austin, *How to Do Things with Words* [1962] (Cambridge MA: Harvard University Press, 1975).

12 | Nelson Goodman, *Languages of Art: An Approach to a Theory of Symbols* [1968] (Indianapolis IN: Hackett, 1976), pp. 52-57.

such examples are rare; most words are symbolic, in the sense that they have nothing in common with the object.

Another means of representation, or representing something, is *exemplification*. In the act of exemplification, something is used to refer to another thing that possesses similar properties; or at least those characteristics relevant for the context in which referencing occurs. For example, when one goes to a hardware store to buy nails, one could ask for a certain type or nail by utilizing a proper noun—which would be an act of denotation. However, if one has forgotten the name or type of nail, one could just show a remaining nail in the package and ask the salesperson to hand out a(nother) one "of those."

Speaking in terms of diagrammatic topology, the nail presented as a sign for other nails belongs to a set of objects that share common properties, such as size or hardness. However, they might vary from one another in regard to color or brand. Thus, a denotation is an *asymmetrical* representation (the signifier does not share the properties of the signified), and an exemplification is a *symmetrical* representation (the signifier shares the properties of the signified).

ICONOLOGY OF SPACE

With Goodman, it is possible to conceive computer games as more than just an allegory for physical space (or only as "metaphors"). As asymmetrical representations, in the sense of denotations, games do lack the "real-being" of space. Nevertheless, they are symmetrical representations of theories of space, i.e. *the game exemplifies a spatial concept*. With Lefebvre, this means taking into consideration representations of space not just as perceived representations of physical space, but also as conceived representations in relation to thirdspaces: culturally produced space, in which symmetrical and asymmetrical representations, together, constitute "symbolic" space, which is lived.

Thus, philosophies of space are—in Lefebvre's schema—not only located on the conceptual level, in the way that geography and physics are spatial sciences. Instead, they mark the transition from second to third space, or define the dialectics in between representations of space and spaces of representation. With Goodman, a philosophy of space may exemplify a contemporary conceptualization of space, which the same time denotates (and thus produces) physical space. Philosophical concepts of space, then, are not about a "true" or "false" *representation of nature*, but rather, they are the *expression of culture*.

This approach has also been claimed by iconology, namely by Erwin Panofsky (1892-1968), in the early twentieth century. This school of thought simply called the difference between denotation and exemplification that of *iconography* (what is shown in a picture) and *iconology* (how it is shown in a picture).[13] If philosophies are understood in this way, as a structural resemblance of scientific conceptualizations, they provide much deeper insight into cultural processes than they do on the level of their own argumentation.

GAMES AS SPATIAL CONCEPTS

Building on this, we can now look at computer games as more than just a critique of our epoch and its understanding of space, which can indeed be done. Certain readings of *Tetris* (1984), for example in Janet Murray's work, conceive of it as a (critical) resemblance of contemporary capitalism.[14] But we could also attempt to understand computer games as exemplifications of spatial concepts: symmetrical representations of asymmetrical denotations or, in short, as thirdspaces of representational spaces. Computer games, then, are not conceived of as designating a certain space or place, but as demonstrating what a certain (historically contingent) truth of space can look like. So it is not the *what?* of space or the *where?* of place, but the *how?* of space—or its likeness.

The task of interpreting games as representational spaces, therefore, must be to use spatial theory to analyze games, to the extent that they express or enact spatial concepts—or possibly contradict them. Jon Cogburn and Mark Silcox, in their book on *Philosophy through Video Games* (2009), included a chapter discussing the success of Nintendo's *Wii* console from

---

13 | Erwin Panofsky, "Iconography and Iconology: An Introduction to the Study of Renaissance Art," *Meaning in the Visual Arts: Papers in and on Art History* [1939] (Garden City NY: Doubleday, 1955), pp 26-54.
14 | Janet H. Murray, *Hamlet on the Holodeck: The Future of Narrative in Cyberspace* (New York NY: Free Press, 1997), p. 144.

2006 in contrast to Microsoft's *Xbox 360* and Sony's *PlayStation 3* systems. They apply a similar idea to the one presented here, when they argue that:

[...] very few people predicted the success of the Wii because nearly everybody's view of the human-computer interface presupposed the truth of phenomenalism. According to this philosophical theory, people do not directly perceive the actual world, but instead experience a realm that is a function of their own private sensory manifolds. [...] By contrast, enactivist theories of perception hold that human beings do directly perceive the world. According to enactivism, this direct perception is a function of the way we physically manipulate ourselves and our environments. Unlike phenomenalism, enactivism provides a compelling explanation of why Wii gameplay is more realistic.[15]

Even though the final claim of "realism" should be viewed critically in the long term, Cogburn and Silcox propose the possibility that, on the level of hardware, different exemplifications of philosophical world-views can already be found: rationalistic dualism (in the style of Descartes) and embodiment (as presented in the concept of phenomenology in the early twentieth century).

"TETRIS" AS TOPIC SPACE

From the classical period of ancient Greece through the Middle Ages, a negative concept of space (in the modern sense) prevailed. Such conceptualizations have since been characterized as related to the phenomenon of *horror vacui*: the experimental demonstrations of empty space as a "vacuum" carried out in the seventeenth century by Blaise Pascal (1623-1662) and Otto von Guericke (1602-1686). The dominant spatial concept of antiquity was based on the idea that the divinity of the cosmos does not allow for space to be empty ("without God"). Even though concepts such as the Platonic *chora* (which originally referred to one acre outside the city-walls) could be understood as "open space" or "absolute space," this was basically a modern projection of Isaac Newton's (ca. 1642-1726) physics onto an-

---

15 | Jon Cogburn and Mark Silcox, *Philosophy through Video Games* (New York NY/London: Routledge, 2009), pp. 20-21.

cient concepts.[16] The dominant interpretation of physics can be found in Aristotle's *Physics*, in which he assumes that every object has its own place (*topos*), i.e. the object occupies "a space," from which derives the belief that—as there is no empty space—even air and other natural phenomena are objects or elements.

Fig. 72: Aristotelian space in Tetris

However, those *topoi* are not part of a greater space, as an encompassing *topos* that exists prior to objects—as Plato suggested—but rather, all places are "attached" to things. From this perspective, one could conceive of the game *Tetris* as an exemplification of *topic* space also related to the *horror*

---

16 | Jacques Derrida, "Chora," *Chora L Works. Jacques Derrida and Peter Eisenman* [1987], ed. Jeffrey Kipnis and Thomas Leeser (New York NY: Monacelli Press, 1997), pp. 15-32.

vacui: even though there is something like an "empty" space, in which things seem to move freely, that space is defined only by the shape of the objects themselves, which block out space occupied by "air." Each possible location is already defined and there is no way to "place" the tetraminos other than in these *topoi*.

Even though it looks like they would fall due to the force of gravitation, once they are placed, the tetraminos do not move anymore, even if they would naturally fall over. As an exemplification of a spatial concept, the variation *Not Tetris* (2010) then demonstrates how *Tetris* would perform if it were representing Newtonian space: blocks have no predefined places, but fall over due to gravitation. Thus, the possible variations of gameplay in *Tetris* serve to enforce the modern understanding of space compared to the ancient one.

Fig. 73: Newtonian space in Not Tetris, "Advent" as Relational Space

Compared to the *topic* space of antique physics, *relational* space is a topological concept that stems from graph theory. This dates from the early eighteenth century, namely from the Swiss-Russian mathematician Leonhard Euler (1707-1783), who used games like chess to pose mathematical problems. For example, with chess: how could one calculate the possible moves with the knight and touch every square on the board, but all of them only once? Another game Euler discussed is *Seven Bridges of Königsberg*, in which the quest involved crossing all seven bridges of the capital city of Eastern Prussia over the river Pregel and returning to the starting point without using one of them twice, but using *all* of them once.[17] As Euler demonstrated, this is impossible due to the position of the bridges. He provided a proof of this impossibility by reducing the topography of the city's inner island, canals, and shores to a pure space or relations of points, i.e. a topological net, system, or labyrinth. For such a labyrinth to be "unicursal," two connections (or edges) are always necessary between every knot (or vertex) of the graph, in order to constitute a walk, in which a return to the starting point is possible.

Fig. 74: Euler's topological drawing of the seven bridges of Königsberg across the river Pregel

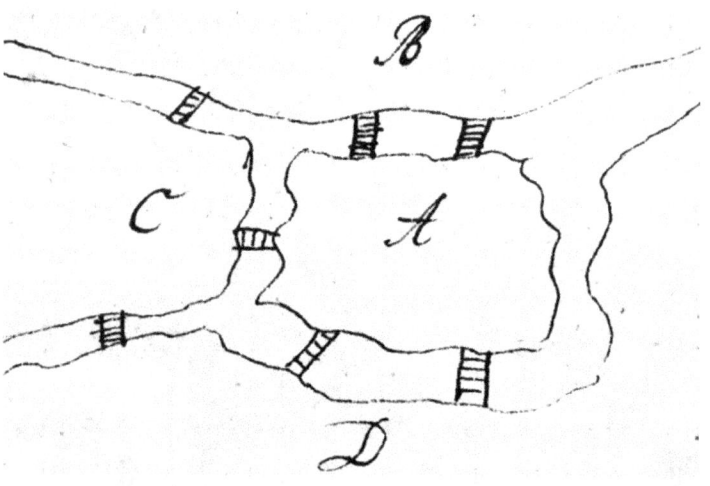

Even though there is a digital game entitled *The Seven Bridges of Königsberg* (2015), which reenacts as well as provides variations of the mathe-

---

17 | Leonhard Euler, "From the Problem of the Seven Bridges of Königsberg," *Classics of Mathematics* [1736], ed. Ronald Calinger (Englewood Cliffs NJ: Prentice Hall, 1995), pp. 503–506.

matical problem, there were also earlier works that exemplified its specific spatial task. *Adventure* (1976) and its successor *Zork* (1980), as well as other "text only" adventure games, exemplify a relational space in which the task is not only to find the way to the final knot, but also to find the most efficient walk between the starting point and the end point (as this is what the game counts in order for users to play). In fact, Newtonian space is present in *Zork* as an illusion of a world, too, but primarily as predetermined descriptions rather than related to players' actions, who were mostly limited to giving topological orders such as typing "n" for the action "going north."

Fig. 75: A fan's drawing of Zork's topological space

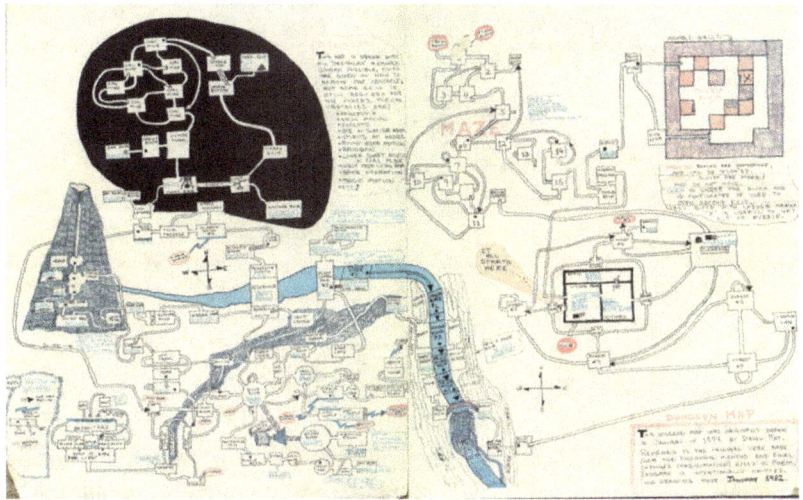

"Portal" as Curved Space

Closely linked to the concept of relational space in mathematics is the physical idea of curvature, which was initiated by nineteenth-century non-Euclidian geometry and further considered by theories of relativity in the twentieth century. As the assumption of parallels in Euclidean space could not be proven, a need for an alternative geometry gave rise to new concepts of space. Whereas, for Euclid, a plane was defined as the (non-spatial) surface of an object, Carl Friedrich Gauss (1777-1855) defined a plane as a spatial object that could be curved. Thus, it could be three dimensional in and of itself (with a "flat plane" being a special case).[18] Applied to three-dimensional object-space, this means that it could be conceived of as curved in the fourth dimension.

Fig. 76: Curved (outer) space with portal or "wormhole"

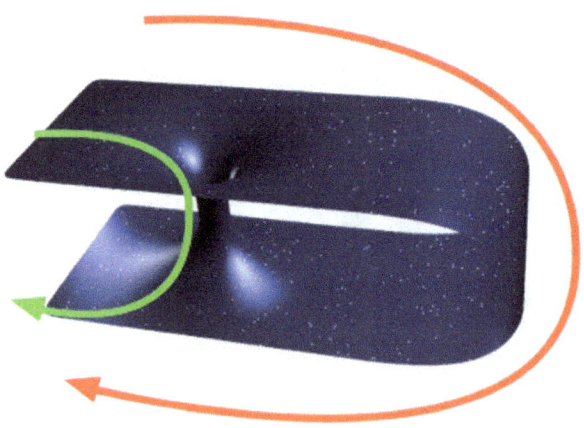

But, as opposed to the curvature of the plane in three dimensions, the curving of space itself cannot be perceived by humans; rather, it becomes an object of speculation.[19] Since Edwin A. Abbotts novel *Flatland* (1882), artists as well as scientists have been looking for an example of four-dimensional space—not to be confused with the problem of time being an additional dimension of space, hence "space-time." One way to demonstrate this is to show the consequences of the folding or bending of space, and not the curvature as such. This is precisely the situation in *Portal*

18 | Karl Friedrich Gauss, *General Investigations of Curved Surfaces* [1827] (Mineola NY: Dover Publications, 2005).

19 | Linda Dalrymple Henderson, *The Fourth Dimension and Non-Euclidian Geometry in Modern Art* [1983] (Cambridge MA/London: The MIT Press, 2013).

(2007), in which three-dimensional space is (hypothetically) folded back onto itself, without giving the visual impression of a curvature.

Fig. 77: Portals in Portal

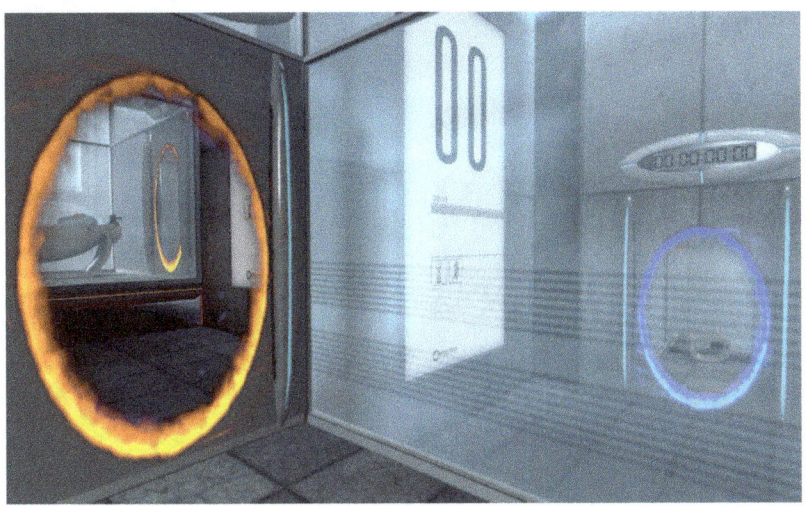

Again, this is not a claim that the four-dimensional concept of space is "true," it only states that computer games can exemplify philosophical concepts—perhaps more accurately than any other medium.

The Architectural Continuum

Choropoietic Media and Post-Physical-World Environments

Constantinos Miltiadis

> "Space is, of course, one of those words that frequently elicits modification. The complications perhaps arise more out of the modifications [...] rather than out of any inherent complexity of the notion of space itself. When, for example, we write of "material," "metaphorical," "liminal," "personal," "social," or "psychic" space [...] we thereby indicate a considerable diversity of contexts which so inflect matters as to seem to render the meaning of space itself entirely contingent upon the context."
> David Harvey, 2004[1]

INTRODUCTION

There is something about the notion of space, Harvey writes, that defies any universal definition. But it's not only the very notion of space that is contingent upon its context, he continues; it's also the methodology with which to approach space. The range of approaches to the architectonic rhetoric of the videogame that this volume presents cannot but prove the same claim.

What I want to discuss in this chapter is architectonics—not as phenotypical relationship between videogames and architecture, through stylistic, urban design or visual analyses.

---

1 | David Harvey, „Space as a Keyword," *Inaugural Marx and Philosophy Conference*, Institute of Education (London: University of London, 2004).

Fig. 78: Entrance to the Rotunda Room, Werner Oechslin Library, Einsiedeln, 2018

Instead, I want to focus on the concept of western design-space, its evolution and tradition, which has been inherited by videogame and architectural design. As such, I want to suggest that through technology, we can achieve media-specific architectures, which, whether tangible or not, could lead to an expansion of architectural aesthetics.

SPACE AS EMBODIED CULTURE

"Ουδείς αγεωμέτρητος εισίτω" read an epigraph on the door of Plato's Academy, according to legend. Often loosely interpreted, a literal translation would be "let no *ungeometered* people enter." For geometry was seen not as mere knowledge, but an embodied modality of being and a form of reasoning. To be *geometered* was to be cultured, cultivated, as geometry was a noble practice. Besides, proportionality—embedded in the Greek *λόγος* and its Latin synonym *ratio*—betrays the mathematics as the root of the western notion of reason.

A few centuries before that, Pythagoras had been studying mathematics as well as music to understand the world, and discover the divine proportions with which God, the Great Geometer, designed it.[2] So deep was this belief that when Hippasus proved that the square root of two is an irrational number—a number that cannot be expressed as a proportion of two others—the other pythagorians murdered him for his hubris, another legend has it.[3]

By the time of Plato, irrational numbers had become accepted. More importantly, geometry had been formalized when Euclid, his contemporary, published one of the most influential books in history in 300 BCE. Euclid's *Elements* provided a set of definitions and postulates, as well as propositions proven by using the standard instruments of unit-less Greek geometry: a straight edge and a compass. To fathom his contribution, we have to consider that *Elements*, through geometry, not only inaugurated Western mathematics but that it also produced for the first time, a rigorous system of axioms and proofs: the first scientific method.[4]

---

2 | Brian Clegg, *A Brief History of Infinity: The Quest to Think the Unthinkable* (London: Robinson Publishing, 2003).

3 | Michel Serres, "The Origin of Geometry," *Hermes: Literature, Science, Philosophy* (Baltimore: The John Hopkins University Press, 1983), pp. 124-33.

4 | Clegg, 2003.

Fig. 79: God as Architect, the Frontispiece of Bible Moralisee, ca. 1220-1230

In light of this—of the association between geometry with logic and reasoning, and as a space of thought—we can better understand Plato's fixa-

tion with abstract geometry as meditation[5], which manifested both in his philosophy and in the curriculum of the Academy. What is important to consider is that Euclidean geometry, taught today in schools all around the world, is not only a common and shared form of knowledge. Practically a cultural universal, Euclidean space is also a shared instrument of reasoning: one of understanding the visual world[6]—and by the time of René Descartes (1596-1650)—also one of modeling, or transposition of the perceivable to the sensible.

THE PERSPECTIVE REVOLUTION OF THE RENAISSANCE

It wasn't until Medieval times that geometry became a standard course in university curricula. Instrumental to the shift from the *Trivium* to the *Quadrivium* model of education was the philosopher Roger Bacon (1220-1292), who in his *Opus Majus* (1267) urged artists to study optics and geometry in order to produce more realistic religious iconography.[7] As Longo writes, it was through perspective that infinity—associated with the divine, and implied in what we now identify as the vanishing point— was first examined.[8] Fourteenth century artists like Giotto di Bondone (ca. 1267-1337) and Ambrogio Lorenzetti (ca. 1290-1348) among the first to attempt a realistic depiction of depth, reserved the use of perspective for annunciation scenes, when God enters the image in the form of an angel.

---

5 | Morris Kline, *Mathematics in Western Culture* (London: Oxford University Press, 2008), p. 41.

6 | Mark Wagner, *The Geometries of Visual Space* (Mahwah NJ: Routledge, 2006), pp. 12-29.

7 | Margaret Wertheim, "Lost in Space: The Spiritual Crisis of Newtonian Cosmology," *Seeing Further: 350 Years of the Royal Society and Scientific Endeavour* (London: Harper Colllins, 2010), pp. 42-59; Margaret Wertheim, "The Illusionistic Magic of Geometric Figuring," Cabinet Magazine, No. 26 (Summer 2007): 27–31.

8 | Giuseppe Longo, "Mathematical Infinity 'in Prospettiva' and the Spaces of Possibilities," *Visible, a Semiotic Journal* Vol. 9 (2011): pp. 1-10.

By 1425, architect Filippo Brunelleschi (1372-1446) had conducted his famous experiment on perspective.[9] Not far removed from modern day augmented reality, this experiment not only invented linear perspective, but it also demonstrated that mathematical rules can be used to faithfully represent the visual. To disseminate the technology of perspective, Brunelleschi's contemporary, architect and polymath Leon Battista Alberti (1404-1472), published two books on the subject in the subsequent years. The impact of the Renaissance invention of perspective is too extensive to summarize; however, the revolution that it brought about in visual culture had ramifications far beyond the field of architecture.

Fig. 80: Andrea Pozzo, Triumph of St. Ignatius of Loyola, Rome, 1685

Technical and perspective drawing were also adopted by the sciences.[10] Nicolaus Copernicus (1473-1543), Galileo Galilei (1564-1642) and Johannes Kepler (1571-1630), among the first generation to be educated in geometry and drawing, used their knowledge and belief in geometrical reasoning

---

9 | Samuel Y. Edgerton, "Brunelleschi's Mirror, Alberti's Window, and Galileo's 'Perspective Tube'," *História, Ciências, Saúde-Manguinhos* Vol. 13 (2006): pp. 151-179.

10 | Samuel Edgerton, "The Renaissance Development of the Scientific Illustration," in *Science and the Arts in the Renaissance*, ed. John William Shirley and F. David Hoeniger (Plainsboro NJ: Associated University Presses, 1985), pp. 168-197.

to painfully disprove established truths about the universe.[11] In the arts, by the seventeenth century, *trompe-l'oeil* managed to transcend the status of mere decoration, such that it was impossible to separate them from the—built—architecture they contributed to. More importantly, however, as Paul Feyerabend (1924-1994) states, perspective became the definitive technical knowledge of architecture, and the one which literally elevated the profession from artisanal craft to a technical one.[12] With the maturity of scientific drawing as a medium of communication, knowledge of geometry was enough to reproduce any drawing at any scale—or for that matter, a drawing to a building—rendering the straight edge and the compass inherited from Greek geometry "weapons for mass construction," as Mario Carpo (*1958) writes.[13]

ARCHITECTURE ACROSS CHOROPOIETIC MEDIA

A significant side effect brought about by this newfound ability to codify and instill a visual idea into a design language was the autonomy of drawing. Renaissance architects like Alberti considered drawing the medium of the unadulterated architectural idea, in which the architect-author had total control.[14] To him, the resulting building was a mere copy of the original architecture captured on paper, as Alberti, additionally, urged archi-

---

11 | More precisely that our solar system is heliocentric (Copernicus); that the moon is not a perfect celestial body (Galileo); and that the movement of celestial objects is not a perfect circle but rather, an ellipse (Kepler). Wertheim 2010; Edgerton 2006.

12 | Paul Feyerabend, "Brunelleschi and the Invention of Perspective," in *Conquest of Abundance: A Tale of Abstraction Versus the Richness of Being*, ed. Bert Terpstra (Chicago: University of Chicago Press, 1999), pp. 89-128.

13 | Mario Carpo, "Building with Geometry, Drawing with Numbers," in *When is the Digital in Architecture?* ed. Andrew Goodhouse (Montréal: Sternberg Press, 2017), pp. 33-44.

14 | Mario Carpo, "The Art of Drawing," *Architectural Design* Vol. 83, No. 5 (September 1, 2013) https://onlinelibrary.wiley.com/doi/abs/10.1002/ad.1646 (accessed June 28, 2019), pp. 128-33.

tects to leave the construction of their designs to somebody else.[15] Perhaps Étienne-Louis Boullée (1728-1799) put it best in the introduction of *Architecture, Essay on Art*:

What is architecture? Shall I join Vitruvius in defining it as the art of building? Indeed, no, for there is a flagrant error in this definition. Vitruvius mistakes the effect for the cause. In order to execute, it is first necessary to conceive. Our earliest ancestors built their huts only when they had a picture of them in their minds. It is this product of the mind, this process of creation that constitutes architecture and which can only consequently be defined as the art of designing and brining to perfection any building whatsoever. Thus the art of construction is merely an auxiliary art, which in our opinion, could appropriately be called the scientific side of architecture. Art in the true sense of the word, and science, these we believe have their place in architecture.[16]

Although material architecture would prevail as authorship, drawing, too, lived to occasionally be credited as a medium of architecture. Beyond buildings and plans, modern history books came to include architectures never intended to escape their medium of drawing. Besides Boullée and Giovanni Battista Piranesi (1720-1778) who are often acknowledged for their drawn architecture; Archigram, Archizoom, Lebbeus Woods (1940-2012), Zaha Hadid (1950-2016), and Bernard Tschumi (1944) are a few more recent Western examples.

With drawing as an established and valid medium of architecture, besides the one of building, we can consider architecture in other non-representational spatial substrates, or *choropoietic media*. According their own modalities of design-space, such media also allow for different aesthetic qualities by evoking different architectonics. In an analysis of the different readings and functions of space in Daniel Libeskind's (*1946) early drawing work, Robin Evans (1944-1993) showed that even drawing is not a unified medium.[17] On the contrary, for Evans "architecture without build-

---

15 | Mario Carpo, *The Alphabet and the Algorithm* (Cambridge MA: MIT Press, 2011), pp. 21-23.

16 | Etienne Louis Boullée, Architecture, *Essay on Art*, ed. Helen Rosenau, trans. Sheila de Vallée (London: Academy Editions, 1976), p. 82.

17 | Robin Evans, "In Front of Lines that Leave Nothing Behind. Chamber Works," *AA Files*, No. 6 (1984), pp. 89-96.

ing" is incorruptible, a potent rather than a latent, and a restoration of architectural practice beyond antiquated conceptions of space. Considering evocations of architecture across different and potential *choropoietic* media would not only liberate architecture from its grounded traditions, but also posit a new path forward. As Hans Hollein (1934-2014) wrote in his 1968 manifesto "Alles ist Architektur": "[a] true architecture of our time, then, is emerging, and is both redefining itself as a medium and expanding its field".[18] Unbounded by thinking in terms of building and "freed from the technological limitations of the past," Hollein's transdisciplinary architecture focused on both spatial and psychological qualities, for its redefinition and advancement. With *choropoietic* media as the different architectural substrates that can evoke their own, media-specific aesthetic qualities, we can consider architecture as a continuum—moreover, an expanding one, populated by the spectra of experience that different modalities of architecture can elicit.

THE 20ᵀᴴ CENTURY'S TROMPE-L'OEIL

New technologies will continue to fuel the fantasy of synthetic realism. As André Bazin (1918-1958) writes, the "myth of total cinema," marking the birth of the film medium, was nothing less than that of total realism.[19] Morton Heilig's (1926-1997) *Sensorama*—a later example published in 1958 that featured colored widescreen stereoscopic video, stereo audio, "aromas," wind, and vibrations—was admittedly a vision of a unification of the arts, a technological *Gesamtkunstwerk*. Ivan Sutherland (*1938), who would go on to invent the first head-mounted display, in 1968[20], wrote:

---

18 | Liane Lefaivre, "Everything is Architecture. Multiple Hans Hollein and the Art of Crossing Over," *Harvard Design Magazine*, No. 18 (2013): pp. 1-5.

19 | André Bazin, "The Myth of Total Cinema," *What is Cinema* No. 1 (1967): pp. 17-22.

20 | Ivan E. Sutherland, "A Head-Mounted Three Dimensional Display," *Proceeding of the December 9-11, 1968, Fall Joint Computer Conference*, Part I (ACM, 1968), pp. 757-64.

The ultimate display would, of course, be a room within which the computer can control the existence of matter. [...] With appropriate programming such a display could literally be the Wonderland into which Alice walked.[21]

Interestingly, Sutherland was also the inventor of *Sketch Pad*, the predecessor to modern CAD software, which begs the question as to whether experiencing digital space is the natural consequence of being able to draw digital geometry.[22]

By the mid 1980s, Jaron Lanier (*1960), who had previously been a game designer for *Atari*, created the first modern VR implementation, coining the term "virtual reality".[23] His vision for VR was not that of a consumer medium. On the contrary, he envisioned VR as an expressive design platform for "post-symbolic communication" between its users.[24] Architects were among the first to experiment with such technologies. Early pioneers such as Markos Novak[25], Daniela Bertol[26], Peter Anders[27], Monika Fleischmann and Wolfgang Strauss[28] and the lab of Gerhard

21 | Ivan E. Sutherland, "The Ultimate Display," *Proceedings of the IFIP Congress* (New York 1965), pp. 506-8.

22 | Ivan E. Sutherland, "Sketch Pad a Man-Machine Graphical Communication System," *Proceedings of the SHARE Design Automation Workshop* (ACM, 1964), pp. 6.329-46.

23 | The first recorded occurrence of the term "virtual reality" is in Artaud's essay "The Alchemical Theater." Antonin Artaud, *The Theater and Its Double*, trans. Mary C. Richard (New York: Grove Press, 1994), p. 49.

24 | Kevin Kelly, "Virtual Reality: An Interview with Jaron Lanier," *Whole Earth Review* No. 64 (Fall 1989), pp. 108-119

25 | Marcos Novak, "Liquid Architectures in Cyberspace," in *Cyberspace: First Steps*, ed. Michael Benedikt (Cambridge MA: MIT Press, 1992), pp. 225-54.

26 | Daniela Bertol, *Designing Digital Space: An Architect's Guide to Virtual Reality* (New York: Wiley, 1996).

27 | Peter Anders, Envisioning Cyberspace: Designing 3D Electronic Spaces (New York: McGraw-Hill Professional, 1998).

28 | Monika Fleischmann and Wolfgang Strauss, "The House of Illusion: Extending the Boundaries of Space," *AVOCAAD First International Conference Proceedings*, ed. K. Nys et al. (Brussels: Hogeschool vor Wetenschap en Kunst, 1997); Monika Fleischmann and Wolfgang Strauss, "Implosions of Numbers— Performative Mixed Reality," in *Disappearing Architecture: From Real to Virtual to*

Schmitt,[29] produced a significant amount of work exploring VR as an architectural medium.

By the 1990s, VR had become a buzzword, such that Simon Penny (*1955) declared it "the completion of the enlightenment project".[30] However, along with the aforementioned efforts, VR was abandoned for a few more decades, due to the untimeliness of technology.

CONTEMPORARY TECHNOLOGY AND TRADITION

Contemporary VR might have originated in gaming, but it has had applications in fields ranging from media art to experimental psychology. Architecture, too, was early to adopt this technology. Primarily, it has been used as a medium for visualization, simulation and design evaluation. Though subject to a historical bond with materiality and physical reality, architecture still appears reluctant to embrace VR as an architectural medium. Nevertheless, designating VR as a—new—tool to simulate architecture referencing the physical world has prevented architecture from recognizing or examining the degree of "architecturality" that media-specific VR environments can elicit.

Largely ignored by the field of architecture, videogames—facilitated by the popularization of personal computers and the advancement of computer graphics—have been doing so for decades. Since they first appeared, videogames have been recognized as a new form of literacy,[31] while game

Quantum, ed. Georg Flachbart and Peter Weibel (Basel: Birkhäuser Architecture, 2005), pp. 119-31.

29 | Gerhard Schmitt, Florian Wenz, David Kurmann and Eric van der Mark, "Toward Virtual Reality in Architecture: Concepts and Scenarios form the Architectural Space Laboratory," *Presence: Teleoper, Virtual Environ*, Vol. 4, No. 3 (January 1995): pp. 267-85; Gerard Schmitt, *Information Architecture: Basics of CAAD and its Future* (Basel: Birkhäuser, 1999).

30 | Simon Penny, "Virtual Reality as the Completion of the Enlightenment Project," in *Culture on the Brink: Ideologies of Technology*, eds. Gretchen Bender and Timothy Druckrey, Discussions in Contemporary Culture 9 (Seattle: BayPress 1994), pp. 231-48.

31 | Eric Zimmermann, "Gaming Literacy: Game Design as a Model for Literacy in the Twenty-First Century," *The Video Game Theory Reader 2*, ed. Bernard Perron and Mark J. P. Wolf (New York: Routledge, 2008), pp. 253-71.

studies, the academic field devoted to research of their phenomena, has noted the medium's preoccupation with space as instrumental to their form. Espen Aarseth (*1965) noted that "games celebrate their spatial representation as their central motif and raison d'être",[32] while Jenkins—comparing architecture and game design, citing both as preoccupied with design over a spatial substrate—suggested game design as "narrative architecture".[33] More recently, Stephan Günzel (*1971) proclaimed the "spatial turn" as a paradigm shift in computer game studies, reflecting both their design and practice.[34]

EUCLID'S FIFTH POSTULATE AGAINST THE SHAPE OF SPACE

While the importance and utility of Euclidian geometry is established and taken for granted in most fields of its application, it has troubled mathematicians since its early beginnings. In particular Euclid's 5th postulate—the infamous "parallel postulate," the last remaining proposition to prove the consistency of this ancient mathematical system—remained unsolved until it was deemed unsolvable in the early nineteenth century. Mathematician János Bolyai (1802-1860) and Nikolai Lobachevsky (1792-1856), independently inventing hyperbolic space, showed instead that conditions of parallelism are constitutive to space, or different forms of it.[35] In parallel, Friedrich Gauss (1777-1855), concerned with similar investigations, de-

32 | Espen J. Aarseth, "Allegories of Space. The Question of Spatiality in Computer Games," in *Cybertext Yearbook 2000*, eds. Raine Koskimaa and Markku Eskelinen (Jyyäskylä 2001), pp. 44-47.

33 | Henry Jenkins, "Game Design as Narrative Architecture," *Computer* Vol. 44 (2004): p. 53.

34 | Stephan Günzel, "The Spatial Turn in Computer Game Studies," in *Exploring the Edges of Gaming*, Vienna Games Conference 2008-9 (Vienna: Braumüller, 20190), pp. 147-56.

35 | Mich Wycoff, "Margaret Wertheim: Complexity, Evolution and Hyperbolic Space," *Evolution: Education and Outreach* Vol. 1m No. 4 (2008): pp. 531-35; Bertrand Russell, An Essay in the Foundations of Geometry (CreateSpace Independent Publishing Platform, 2018), pp. 7-15.

vised a means of studying two-dimensional surfaces intrinsically, instead of embedding them in a three-dimensional Cartesian box, published as *Theorema Egregium* in 1828. Continuing his work, Gauss's student Bernhard Riemann (1826-1866) proposed a new generative geometry that could produce smooth and metric manifolds in his habitation, entitled *On the hypotheses which lie at the bases of geometry*[36], which essentially formalized non-Euclidean geometry.

This information might seem redundant until we recognize that Albert Einstein's (1879-1955) theory of *Special Relativity* in 1905, which collapsed space and time into space-time, did so by implementing a four-dimensional Minkowskian manifold.[37] In other words, besides cancelling the autonomy of space as a unique entity, the current and corroborated scientific theory of space answers to a completely different geometry than the one described by Euclid. It is crucial to mention that, unlike Cartesian space, such geometries do not afford or privilege an origin point—as a reference of absolute difference. Instead, manifolds only allow for subjective difference, or—as described in philosophy—pure difference.[38] As is also manifested in the paradigm shift of relativity physics, reality, in the form of space-time, is not external. Rather, it is intrinsic to the observer and their frame of reference.

Western culture's insistence on visual interpretations of space is not a new phenomenon.[39] However, it's not only our culture and design thinking that are rooted in Euclidean space, but also our design tools. It wouldn't be an exaggeration to say that contemporary spatial design software packages, both in architecture and in game design are flat-earth-

36 | Bernard Riemann, *On the Hypotheses Which Lie at the Bases of Geometry* (University of Göttingen, 1854).

37 | Linda Dalrymple Henderson, "Einstein and 20th-Century Art: A Romance of Many Dimensions," in *Einstein for the 21st Century: His Legacy in Science, Art and Modern Culture*, eds. Peter Galison, Gerarld Holton and Silvan Schweber (Princeton University Press, 2018), pp. 101-29.

38 | See Gilles Deleuze, *Difference and Repetition* (Bloomsbury Academic, 2014), pp. 28-69.

39 | Martin Jay, "Scopic Regimes of Modernity," in *Vision and Visuality*, ed. Hal Foster (Seattle: The New Press, 1999), pp. 3-28; Erik Davis, "Acoustic Cyberspace," *Xchange On-Air Session* (November 11, 1997), https://techgnosis.com/acoustic-cyberspace/ (accessed June 27, 2019).

Fig. 81: Patterson Hume and Donald Ivey, Frames of Reference, Directed by Richard Leacock. Physical Science Study Committee, University of Toronto, Canada, 1960, Film Still

simulators: they rely on obsolete spatial concepts, disregarding the actual science of what they are supposed to model. The problem with enforced Euclidean design-space is not that design software ignores phenomena as fundamental as earth's curvature. It's that they make it almost impossible to take them into consideration, or to employ them creatively. And while such phenomena might be negligible, or even irrelevant to building, are they irrelevant to design and architecture? Few are the analyses of the lack of spatial sophistication in videogames,[40] as well as the ones that speculate on the extended spatial constitutions that the digital medium can afford design.[41] Margaret Wertheim (*1958) blames a deeper existential cause for this dissonance:

---

40 | Benjamin Fraser," Why the Spatial Epistemology of the Video Game Matters: Metis, Video Game Space and Interdisciplinary Theory," *Journal of Gaming & Virtual Worlds* Vol 3, No. 2 (2001): pp. 93.-106; Natalija Majsova, "Outer Space and Cyberspace: An Outline of Where and How to Think of Outer Space in Video Games," *Teorija in Praksa* Vol 51, No 1 (2014): p. 106.
41 | Edvin Babic, "On the Liberation of Space in Computer Games," *Eludamos, Journal for Computer Game Culture* Vol. 1, No. 1 (2007).

In essence, concepts of space and concepts of self are inextricably entwined so that when a culture adopts a new conception of space, as Western culture did in the seventeenth century, it impacts our sense of not merely where we are but of what we are.[42]

However, the few examples from the tradition of videogames, such as *Portal* (2007) or *Antichamber* (2013), are promising for their investigations of experience in spatial constitutions of post-physical-world environments.

Fig. 82: Digital Design Software for both Architecture and Videogames simulate a Flat-Earth Space

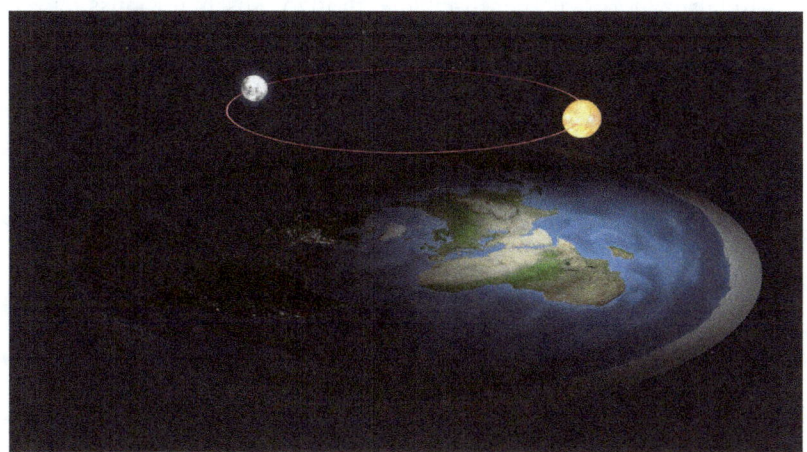

---

42 | Wertheim 2010, pp. 61-2.

Towards Virtual Architectures

This chapter attempted to demonstrate that space and design-space are not neutral entities. Examining and embracing new notions of space through digital media can provide new grounds for architectural experimentation and contribute new spectra of its experience. Videogames, as theoretically suggested[43] and experimentally proven, engage with and improve actual, concrete skills.[44] Additionally, not unlike flight simulators for pilots, the practice of videogames can cultivate and further develop spatial-cognitive capacities,[45] while VR is already serving as an ideal framework for testing extended notions of spatial presence and experience.[46]

To borrow form another discipline, in 1979, Rosalind Krauss (*1941) identified the fact that contemporary sculpture could no longer be described by historicizing narratives, which normalize the new by making the category of sculpture "almost infinitely malleable".[47] Less permissive

---

43 | Espen J. Aarseth, "Virtual Worlds, Real Knowledge: towards a Hermeneutics of Virtuality," *European Review* Vol. 9, No. 2 (2001): pp. 227-232.

44 | Isabela Granic, Adam Lobek and Rutger C. M. E. Engels, "The Benefits of Playing Video Games," *American Psychologist* Vol. 69, No. 1(January 2014), https://psycnet.apa.org/record/2013-42122-001?doi=1 (accessed June 28, 2019), pp. 66-78.

45 | Kaveri Subrahmanyam and Patricia M. Greenfield, "Effect of Video Game Practice on Spatial Skills in Girls and Boys," *Journal of Applied Developmental Psychology* Vol. 15, No. 1 (1994): pp. 13-32; Diana Gagnon, "Videogames and Spatial Skills: an Explanatory Study," *Educational Communication and Technology* Vol 33, No. 4 (1985): pp. 263-75.

46 | Khrystyna Vasylevska, Jana Podkosova and Hannes Kaufmannm, "Walking in Virtual Reality: Flexible Spaces and Other Techniques," in *The Visual Language of Technique* (London: Springer, 2015), pp. 81-97; William H. Warren et al., "Wormholes in Virtual Space: From Cognitive maps to Cognitive Graphs," *Cognition* 166 (September 1, 2017): pp. 152-63 https://doi.org/10.1016/j.cognition.2017.05.020 (accessed June 27, 2019); William H. Warren, Daniel B. Rothmann, Benjamin H. Schnapp and Jonathan D. Ericson, "Non-Euclidean Navigation," *Journal of Experimental Biology* Vol. 222 (2019), https://jeb.biologists.org/content/222/Suppl_1/jeb187971 (accessed June 27, 2019).

47 | Rosalind Krauss, "Sculpture in the Expanded Field," *October* 8 (1979): pp. 31-44.

than Hollein, Krauss's "expanded field" argues for an art form that is negatively defined by what it is not rather than by what it is. Similarly, utilizing this articulation for architecture would generate a more generous and plural field for itself and its aesthetics, rather than of a singular point.

In other words, can we consider a continuum of architecture in the model of the continuum of real numbers? Could we envision imaginary architectures—not imaginary as fictional, but rather as the imaginary in complex numbers? What could $\sqrt{-1}$ architectures be, that are to concrete architectures as paramount and tangible as imaginary numbers are to the real number set? Embracing transdisciplinary articulations—and given their knowledge and available tools—today's architects can play a decisive role in exploring the future of architecture across *choropoietic media*, uncovering the latent aesthetic domain of it's "expanded field."

From Asteroids to Architectoids

Close Encounters between Architecture and Game Design

Ulrich Götz

FUNDAMENTALS OF A MISUNDERSTANDING

The frequently assumed proximity between architectural spaces in reality and their virtual counterparts in video games is based on a misunderstanding. The architectural discourse, when it occasionally comes into contact with disciplines related to the development of virtual realities, notes that today's video games provide entire cities as fields of play! But how would these vast spatial entities have been designed if experts in architecture and urban planning were not involved?

The gaming industry, on the other hand, dedicates entire research departments to the development of its scenarios, which are based on examples from architecture and urban planning. These teams investigate the formal typologies of natural or culturally shaped landscapes, whether these environments would be suitable as scenarios for game actions, and how they could be authentically staged. The bounty of these expeditions into real space not only flows into internal production processes, but is even used as advertising for new game titles.[1] Such references prove how hyper-realistic visualizations with "exceptional graphical quality"[2] can be achieved with intensive technological effort. At the same time, the con-

---

1 | The game engine *CryEngine* by Crytech GmbH is known for its high degree of realism in visual presentations. For the introduction of the game *Crysis* (2007), juxtapositions were published comparing the visualizations of the game engine with original photographic models.
2 | Manuel Lacoste, "Why developers choose CRYENGINE – Part 5" (March 5, 2019).

fessions of an internationally renowned game corporation reveal that it "sends teams out to capture the essence of a place"[3]: what matters is a perfect copy of real scenarios, including correctly depicted fauna and flora, credible reactions of NPCs[4], and even convincing social customs and actions. The "shot on location" seal of quality from the film industry's location scouting practices seems to be reflected in a similar search for legitimacy by some game productions, apparently looking for a similar label "based on real locations".

However, these developments in both disciplines are based on fundamentally false assumptions. They are grounded on a selective and superficial discussion, which simply overlooks the thematic core of the other discipline. The architectural perspective neglects to even perceive the sets of rules that exist in games, and the strategic actions derived from them. This, however, would be the prerequisite for understanding the effect of typical design laws in game spaces. Only then would it be possible to reveal the relationship between functional conditions and spatial order in game spaces—a relationship that, by the way, is certainly architectural. Just as in urban planning or architectural design, general conditions shape the artificial spaces of game design: "game spaces represent a spatial expression of the set of rules".[5]

The game industry's unshakeable conviction that it can transpose the highly complex structures of real environments into virtual space is based on a comparably robust ignorance. Mutually constitutive conditions of physical, geographical, ecological, functional, historical, and cultural processes—which led to the current state of an artificially-shaped "real" environment—are necessarily skipped in games that appear realistic. The image of such games, therefore, results from a montage of selected, for-

https://www.cryengine.com/news/why-developers-choose-cryengine-part-5 (accessed July 7, 2019).

3 | Dean Takahashi, "How Ubisoft visits real places to make its open-world games like The Division" (February 17, 2019) https://venturebeat.com/2016/02/17/how-ubisoft-creates-open-worlds-in-games-like-the-division/ (accessed July 7, 2019).

4 | NPC: non-player-character, or non-playable character.

5 | Ulrich Götz, "Rules shape spaces – Spaces shape rules," *Games and Rules. Game Mechanics for the "Magic Circle,"* eds. Beat Suter, Mela Kocher and René Bauer (Bielefeld: transcript, 2018), pp. 259–65.

mal fragments, which may be indebted to a composition of the real, but which cannot comprehend its inner effects and are only able to reproduce its exterior appearance. The disciplinary exchange between architecture and games currently remains purely superficial. The two fields only recognize and copy the outer shell of the other discipline, but do not understand the core.

INTERACT WITH UTOPIA

In the history of computer games, magical moments have marked the decisive steps in which machines for calculation became stages of fantasy. Such a transformation happened, for example, when William Crowther created a narrative space for fantastic actions in *Colossal Cave Adventure* (1976), uniting the most contradictory worlds imaginable: namely, the worlds of mathematical machines and those of fictional storytelling. As the gaming industry developed over the following decades, this unexpected connection between advanced technology and the elemental human need for play and narration became one of the most powerful tools of utopian design.

In their attempts to penetrate the representation of utopias, Surrealist painting was well aware that depictions were not synonymous with what was depicted.[6] These remarks came from a time when the recipients of a work were still mostly in a passive position, while authors actively determined the process of creating an artifact. The development of virtual worlds reverses this clear allocation of roles; probably very few developers involved in the lengthy creation process of large game productions, with hundreds of other collaborators, have an overview of both the totality of creative and technical contexts of the final result as well as the internal laws of the original model in reality. The recipients, on the other hand, are called upon to engage with seemingly realistic virtual environments through the profound possibilities of intervention in design and use, as if this artificial environment actually had to trigger realistic actions. In games that depict architectural environments, players internalize virtual

6 | See René Magritte, *La Trahison des images* (Oil on canvas, 60.33 cm x 81.12 cm, 1929) The subtitle of the painting entitled *The Trechery of Images* reads: "Ceci n'est pas une pipe" (this is not a pipe).

spatial orders and their utility patterns without the need for deeper understanding. A direct return of such game principles to real space is therefore
impossible, since the player learns behaviors for virtual space that have no
validity in reality.

*Fig. 83: Exhibition "Cités Millénaires" at the Institut du Monde Arabe
(Paris)[7], Oct 10 2018 – Feb 10, 2019*

However, the visual perfection of the realistic representations in some
game worlds often makes it difficult to ascertain whether their fictionality
originated in fantastic creations, or whether their source material is tak-
en directly from reality. In order to adapt the animation of avatars to the
motion sequences of their two-legged human role models, *motion capturing* transfers the complexity of human body movements to the computer.
Parallel *facial capturing* complements these natural-looking movements
with the transformation of faces. It seems to be only a matter of time—
and comparatively simple technological developments—until the survey-

---

7 | See Arts in the City, "Voyage virtuel au coeur des cités millénaires .
l'Institut du Monde Arabe" (October 16, 2018), https://www.youtube.com/
watch?v=0xPp9XoyuBM (accessed July 7, 2019).

ing technologies used in architecture and urban development can deliver spatial data through three-dimensionally scanning drone flights, which can immediately become virtual scenes in games. The virtual realities of digital games offer unique opportunities to give visual expression to the creation and use of utopian designs. Therefore, the ever-more established design approach of aiming for the most correct possible representation of real space in the virtual, can only result in one judgment: in several respects, this approach is extremely annoying.

VIRTUAL ARCHITECTOIDS

The aforementioned examples illustrate how strong the mutual attraction is between the design methods of real and virtual space. But the "flirtation" of these disciplines is not without consequences—for after mutual exchange, it creates chimeras. The interdisciplinary debate, which only takes place on the surface, imports the appearance, but not the essence, of the two neighboring subject areas. Architecture and urban development do not become more utopian or more playful through the contact with games, but prefer to use the possibilities of virtual reality technologies to impress potential investors. Concepts for games do not become more spatially well-devised or more architecturally sophisticated, but rather, content themselves with conceiving game actions that match the imitation of traffic infrastructure buildings—such that, for example, car chases can be played. The results of the exchange follow fixed, primarily visual platitudes; their objectives bind and waste creative resources. Admittedly, however, the results of photorealistic representations are so powerful and impressive that they become guiding images in the discussion of how space can even be depicted in the virtual at all. In both disciplines, a "third" thing arises from the use of functionless bits and pieces of the respective other discipline: if real constructions are called "architecture," these results could instead be described as "architectoids".[8]

---

8 | The term "architectoid" is used to describe an architect-in-training in the English language. There is no corresponding name for a spatial structure that is in the intermediate stage described.

Fig. 84: Grand Theft Auto V: Particularly realistic Appearance with NaturalVision Mod

The games industry spends billions on exploring the qualities of the virtual. But especially with the most elaborate productions, these efforts often lead to mere functionally-depleted images of reality. However, if the design of the real space corresponds to its functional conditions, the design of a game environment is linked to the concept of game mechanics and motivation[9] and artistic staging.[10] Therefore, the image of real spaces is not functionally useful for game design—at least at first. Instead, the benefit of realistic visualization for games has to be constructed at great expense. Paradoxically, for this reason, the architectural idea is never reduced more to a mere background than in realistically visualized game productions, which are not able to emulate architectural logics, *per se*: they only use their empty shells.

Game studios have long been aware of the hunger for realism their representations generate. On one hand, they know the criticism they will face with the smallest deviations from the real detail; on the other hand, they realize that the goal of creating perfect images within the framework of available budgets can only be achieved to a certain degree. As such, they have come up with a workaround: almost akin to the architectural concept of "participation," large game productions set up interfaces through which fan projects, after the first release, work on how the visual impression can

---

9 | René Bauer, "Games as a special zone," in Suter, Kocher, Bauer 2018, pp. 259–265.
10 | Stephan Schwingeler, *Die Raummaschine* (Boizenburg: Verlag Werner Hülsbusch, 2008), p. 103.

be further improved in order to become "as photorealistic as possible"[11]. Extensive community contributions expand and refine the visual appearance of games in what are called "mods"—modifications—and thus represent a thought-provoking attitude toward central questions of artistic and creative authorship.

These game productions organize their work for the visual plausibility of the supposedly real, and not for the qualities of the fictional in the virtual. The trend towards visual realism in games is not new, but it persists: "Games are no longer about using the freedom of virtual creative space to make the impossible possible, but are instead about making what is in reality improbable possible to experience".[12] When such games are used, the "wear and tear effect" is already noticeable after a short time; this describes how a game action presents as very thin in comparison to graphic representation, and one becomes indifferent to the visual effects. This could hardly contradict the effort of the research more—all of which was necessary to create realistically coherent scenarios in the first place. It is precisely this contradiction that game critics find problematic when they point out a lack of contextualization in what is depicted".[13]

Amazingly few game productions dedicate themselves to their own research on spatial qualities in the virtual. This statement even applies to productions that pursue visual abstraction and stylization, such as comic or fantasy styles. A remarkably small number of games play with the actual material of the virtual by, for example, questioning readability and patterns of use, presenting graphics with previously unseen imaging techniques, or designing spatial logics that make progress in a game space a challenge. However, when these rare experiments are made public, they often receive above-average recognition for their courage, such as *Memory*

---

11 | John Papadopoulos, "NaturalVision mod aims to make Grand Theft Auto V as photorealistic as possible," (July 26, 2016), https://www.dsogaming.com/news/naturalvision-mod-aims-to-make-grand-theft-auto-v-as-photorealistic-as-possible/ (accessed July 7, 2019).

12 | Ulrich Götz, "Load and Support," in *Space Time Play. Synergies Between Computer Games, Architecture and Urbanism*, eds. Matthias Böttger, Friedrich von Borries, Steffen P. Walz (Basel/Boston/Berlin: Birkhäuser, 2007), p.134–137.

13 | Matthias Kreienbrink, "Viel Kulisse, nichts dahinter" (April 27, 2019), https://www.zeit.de/digital/games/2019-04/the-division-2-videospiel-realitaet erzaehlung/komplettansicht?print (accessed July 7, 2019).

of a *Broken Dimension* (2017), *Portal* (2007), or *Portal 2* (2011). Usually, it is only particularly small groups of developers who tackle such projects (and who, after initial success, then merge into larger studios). It would be hard to imagine what visionary results could be achieved if large-scale productions opened themselves to such experiments, and the effort of their developments were to flow into the creation of truly fantastic worlds.

Fig. 85: Memory of a Broken Dimension (2017): Researching an Independent Quality of the Virtual

THE SHELL OF A GHOST

The architecture of the twentieth century saw itself as a driving force for the renewal of society. Individual architects or groups of architects, as well as entire architectural trends, worked with this self-image to shift the boundaries of what could be possible. Frank Lloyd Wright's utopian contributions to this are legendary. In the *Gläserne Kette*,[14] Hans Scharoun anticipated iconic architectural visions that later culminated in the buildings of the Philharmonie (1963) and the Staatsbibliothek (1978) in Berlin. The Munich Olympic Stadium (1972)[15], the Centre Pompidou in Paris (1977)[16],

---

14 | Die Gläserne Kette (1919-1920) was a group of architects and artists in Berlin, surrounding Bruno Taut, that discussed visionary forms of architecture.
15 | Architects: Behnisch & Partner.
16 | Architects: Renzo Piano and Richard Rogers.

or the projects of the architectural group Archigram[17] are representative of the established belief in progress that was inherent to twentieth-century architecture. Some architectural trends were devoted to social renewal through new forms of urban coexistence, others attempted to break the formal canon of the existing (for example, in deconstructivism). Where innovations were not pushed forward within their own discipline, excursions and contacts with other disciplines and media provided inspiration. Some positioned themselves at the intersection with art, such as Constant (1920-2005)[18], who conceived previously unknown urban plans as part of the Situationists. The architectural discourse discussed philosophical views or even turned to comic film adaptations such as *Ghost in the Shell* (1989/1995), which provided material for architectural discussions about the effects of the digital revolution on society.[19]

As future-oriented as these approaches were in comparison to previous epochs, it is remarkable that they were created using highly traditional tools and methods of production. Visions were created with paper, ink, watercolor, and architectural models; their complexity made new tools— this time digital— possible and necessary. Such software tools for spatial planning in architecture and urban planning are available today, and they are closely related to the design methods used in virtual-world construction. In these reformed architectural design processes, a realistic portrayal of ideas appears to be the ultimate goal. The preliminary culmination of this architectural design approach is an alliance with game technologies, which allows virtual access to designs that have not yet been implemented by using virtual reality devices. In the resulting struggle for the coherence of a realistic aesthetic, what can be formally depicted becomes the focus of attention in an inflationary way, while the only vague narrative hint at the possibilities of action and use receives hardly any recognition. But it was precisely such methods that architectural visualization used only a few decades ago, when atmospheric sketches or model photographs intentionally generated ambiguous images to open up bold, epochal visions.

The use of new methods does not necessarily lead to reforms of their content. In an unholy analogy to video games, an open contradiction in

---

17 | British group of architects (1960-1974).

18 | Constant Nieuwenhuys, a Dutch Artist better known as Constant.

19 | See Masamune Shirow, *Ghost in the Shell* (Kodansha: Tokyo, 1989); Mamor Oshii, *Ghost in the Shell* (Production I.G., 1995).

the construction industry can be seen between the readily available design possibilities of new software tools and the results that are actually achieved. In the breadth of their application, these tools often seem to be more regressive than their predecessors—as if less imagination were used not only to read, but also to develop these designs. What remains are architectural platitudes, ghostly shells.

Fig. 86: Constant Nieuwenhuys, New Babylon, 1964

FICTITIOUS NARRATION – DOGMATIC REALITY

Despite all displeasure with decorating virtual worlds with objects whose meaning lies in reality, there are also legitimate reasons for realistic design approaches. Why should a crime story, for example, not become the subject of a game—and is it not important, then, to choose a setting from reality? How should a horror game be told if tension is not constructed through references to reality?

Assessing the suitability of a visualization style must be evaluated on a differentiated basis. Some games lean closely on the traditions of cinema and film, and therefore continue the aesthetics of the camera. In their extension of the cinematic experience, these games openly commit themselves to the themes and perspectives of film production: the broken, small-town idyll of the horror game *The Last of Us* (2013) is told in cinematic form all the way through; the clear reference to classics from Western films is the central argument of *Red Dead Redemption* (2010). Using historical references, the multilayered *Fallout* series shows, in a post-apocalyptic setting, how the framing of the plot before and after the nuclear catastrophe demand a realistic visual description. *Fallout 4* (2017) only permits a step-by-step exploration of the "open world," in which players must set up their own bases in expeditions, in order to slowly occupy the virtual space and literally install themselves there.

These examples put narration at the center of the game, and plausibly explain why such stories must be sensibly located in realism. The consideration of the theme of the game, therefore, is a key with which the choice of visual presentation can be discussed. However, it also reveals the superficiality of games in which the plot is primarily governed by rules without any notable narrative depth—and which nevertheless make use of realistic modes of representation. The short, conflict-oriented rounds of *PlayerUnknown's Battlegrounds* (2017) are based exclusively on the principle of "last man standing," in which the first rank in the competition is determined by eliminating all other opponents. But why should the resulting hide-and-seek game require a visualization in which the player hides a human-like avatar with a camouflage suit in virtual grass? Wouldn't an abstract, monochrome figure in front of a background of the same color result in the same gameplay according to this simple set of rules?

But not all decisive arguments for the development of games are derived exclusively from the actual game concept. This desirable approach is contradicted by the laws of a global gaming market worth billions. It is not only oriented toward the goals of innovative conception and design, but it also creates dependencies on investments, target groups, branding, profit maximization, and so forth. Looking for similarities in the most successful games, one notices what seems to be a mere formality: games with high sales numbers in the global mainstream market quite often use visualizations that show realistic (urban) environments, or convert such representations into easily recognizable comic styles (such as *Fortnite*, 2017).[20] Especially in the case of interactive objects, selected designs are found in very similar form both in titles with a high demand for realism as well as in comic-strip stylizations (this applies, for example, to buildings, furnishings, vehicles, and weapons, but also to movement behavior and

---

20 | See Technobezz, "20 Meistverkaufte Videospiele aller Zeiten" (May 27, 2019) https://www.technobezz.de/best/20-best-selling-video-games-of-all-time/ (accessed July 7, 2019).

animation patterns[21]). These common design paradigms can be found in action, adventure, sports, fantasy, and role-playing games—and they extend far into the party and family games sector. The often opulently decorated worlds of these games can only be achieved with high production costs.

On the other hand, there are strategy, logic, and puzzle games, which rely on the persuasiveness of their game mechanics with abstract visual representations. The effects of their "game motivation" do not lag behind games with a high degree of realism, which is why they also successfully position themselves on the market. Since the production effort of such games is relatively low in comparison to extensive fantasy worlds, and they can be kept on the market for a long time through constant updates, their operators like to refer to them as "cash cows."

This competition pushes productions with smaller budgets into niche positions, where they explore design possibilities that are unoccupied by the mainstream. Typically, they also switch to stylized forms of representation, because they cannot afford to spend a lot of money creating realistic worlds. However, they are much more experimental in their approach in order to come up with unique creative features.

Although the rankings of the most successful games are based on very inconsistent criteria, a rough equation can be made: high financial production costs tend to result in realistic visualization quality, while cheaper productions tend to be more experimental. Conversely, the realistic quality of the appearance is based on high financial production costs, while the experiment tends to emerge in a niche. In this way, a calibration of contents and their visualizations occur, which generates a powerful feedback loop. In this cycle, mainstream game users seem to be conditioned in such a way that the "return on investment" for particularly expensive productions can only be achieved with games that have typical content, and an appearance that is realistic or close to reality. The aforementioned formality actually becomes an internal characteristic that says a lot about the nature of such productions. Ultimately, there is a direct connection between mediated aesthetics and the laws of the globalized market.

---

21 | For example, compare the competing products *PlayerUnknown's Battlegrounds* (2017) and *Fortnite* (2017), which use very similar interaction objects for quite different visual styles.

The Danish film directors Lars von Trier and Thomas Vinterberg initiated a catalogue of regulations in *Dogma 95* (1995), which was intended to lead film art from formal restrictions back to cinematic authenticity.[22] This set of restraints were intended to guarantee the plausibility and authenticity of film material once again, as well as to fight against false themes and means of presentation. Games, as freefloating narration machines and utopia producers in the virtual world, are—in principle—among the most visionary media of all, and they limit themselves with the conventions of their visual presentation. A special "dogma" for this medium would therefore also have to demand a new authenticity, one that isolates the patterns in which trivial content arises. This includes the understanding that games should not automatically take culturally-shaped space that we know from architecture and urban planning as the setting for their events. Instead, they should rather turn their attention to researching the principles of game space.

NEIGHBORS AT A FENCE

Hidden dependencies, misinterpretations and misunderstandings, but also creative lethargies define the image that the developers of real and virtual space—game designers and architects—have of one another. These two parties behave like neighbors at a fence, respecting each other and possessing established opinions about one another—but not exchanging their views. Sometimes, they secretly pick a fruit from a branch that grows over the fence—but of course, only when the other is not looking. Shouldn't there be a means for a more constructive dialogue? How could these two areas of expertise be better combined, and which of their counterparts' skills could the neighbors use more effectively?

The essence of architecture results from its innermost, functional demands. Architectural typologies are defined as frames, in order to integrate them into culturally-shaped space. Façades are shells that cover architectural content. Trained in analytical design, architects should be highly opposed to reducing games to constructs of the virtual on the

---

22 | With a commitment to the "Dogme 95 Manifesto," film directors vowed to act according to the guidelines of the Dogme 95 collective, which came to an end in 2005.

surface, and failing to deal with their functionalities inside and outside the game. The architectural design must open itself to the narrative and utopian qualities of the virtual, instead of using its possibilities only for illustration with glossy renderings. Isn't it the highest honor for architectural design if it survives the times, and proves its independent qualities through ever-new stories that unfold inside it?

How could games approach architecture? The competition in their graphic output obscures the potential of a fantastic medium—to use the freedom of the virtual for games as a central cultural need. With regard to architecture: it is not the copying of buildings that takes game design further, but the analysis of architectural concepts. How does the small fit into the big picture, what structural principles are underlying, how can a construct be adapted and expanded, and what gesture is communicated to the outside world?

From the point of view of architecture, the call for game design must be: Have the courage to show the unfinished, turn games into islands in the virtual, which dissolve at their edges like drawings in a sketchbook! Put your work into the mechanical and functional nature of the game space, and not into the copy of real space! And game designers answer architects: Play games! But be selective and play them architecturally! For only a few games stand out from the crowd, truly facing the challenging, inspiring questions of game space.

Piercing all Layers of the Anthroposphere

On Spatialization and Architectural Possibilism in *Hitman*

Marc Bonner

ARCHITECTURE AS A MEDIAL HINGE

Defining architecture as a "medial hinge"[1] loosely refers to German architect Hans Hollein's (1934-2014) postulation in 1968 that everything is architecture.[2] Architecture has to be understood anew in its *medial* potential, or how it can mediate the environment to the observer by enabling new spheres of action.[3] Hence, the concept of architecture as a medial hinge focuses on the role and importance of architecture, in all its possible forms, as a total work of art.[4] It is a predominant means (in the sense of the

---

1 | Marc Bonner, "Architektur als mediales Scharnier—Medialität und Bildlichkeit der raumzeitlichen Erfahrungswelten Architektur, Film und Computerspiel," *Image. Zeitschrift für interdisziplinäre Bildwissenschaft* Vol. 21, No. 1, (January 2015), pp. 5–22.

2 | Hans Hollein, "Alles ist Architektur," *Bau. Schrift für Architektur und Städtebau*, No. 1/2 1 (1968): pp. 1–28.

3 | Hollein's primary example is the head-up display (a transparent display that presents data without requiring the user to change their line of sight) inside of a fighter pilot's helmet. This architecture enhances sensual perception and synesthetic experiences of the environment, whether it is at hand or far in the distance.

4 | Architecture is constituted by arrays of different materials, medias, and entities: these range from concepts, theories, ideologies, or abstract atmospheres to drawings, analogue and digital graphics, analogue and digital models; as well as from algorithms and level structures to actual buildings, groups of buildings, built environments, urban complexes, landscape architecture, or film sets.

German term "Agent") of understanding and perceiving reality, as well as the fictional worlds of mass media. Architecture as a medial hinge merges different disciplines of media and art with the realm of the everyday, folding them onto each other and encapsulating one another. Thus, architecture is a medium within a medium: it rhythmizes and regulates our experiences of the world. In its current digital, pictorial, viral ubiquity, architecture no longer has to be bodily present, but "it always has a mediating role instead of being the end itself".[5]

In particular, the enactment of architecture and the perception of 3D game spaces are tightly interwoven, as performative interaction within nonlinear environments and spatial involvement, in the sense of Gordon Calleja[6], is crucial. Speaking of architecture as a medial hinge thus refers to the corresponding architectonics of built reality and digital game worlds.

On Movement, Interaction and Inhabitation

To a certain degree, the observation above is not new to some fields within game studies. Michael Nitsche defines game-intrinsic space as nonlinear exploration, while filmic space is a linear description: "The necessary eye of the virtual camera makes these spaces cinematic and the interaction makes them accessible much like architectural structures".[7] Ernest W. Adams stresses that architecture is used in order to define what a place is supposed to feel like, as well as "what might happen to you there, and even sometimes what you ought to be doing".[8] Ulrich Götz highlights 3D nar-

---

5 | Juhani Pallasmaa, *The Embodied Image. Imagination and Imagery in Architecture* (Chichester: John Wiley & Sons Ltd., 2011), p. 100.

6 | Calleja's concept of involvement in game worlds will be elucidated later. Gordon Calleja, *In-Game, From immersion to incorporation* (Cambridge, MA/ London: MIT Press, 2011).

7 | Michael Nitsche, *Video Game Spaces. Image, Play, and Structure in 3D Worlds* (Cambridge MA/London: MIT Press, 2008), p. 82.

8 | Ernest W. Adams, "Designer's Notebook: The Role of Architecture in Video Games," *Gamasutra* (October 9, 2002) https://www.gamasutra.com/view/ feature/131352/designers_notebook_the_role_of_.php. (accessed March 15, 2019).

rative spaces as points of convergence with physically real architecture,[9] which is only fully revealed to explorers who appropriate all of its places and paths.[10] Gordon Calleja also highlights the quality and freedom of player-induced movement, which "is the key ingredient that allows players to act upon the environment and is thus a necessary condition for the sense of agency that is a crucial factor in the game experience".[11]

The convergence between game-intrinsic architecture, built reality, and the spatial perception thereof differs from linear, restrictive, and enclosed level structures seen in *Quake* (1996) to the labyrinthine, multicursal stacks of *System Shock* (1994); from open cityscapes such as Paris during the French Revolution in *Assassin's Creed Unity* (2014) to the coherent building types of *Dishonored 2* (2016). Except for the latter, few game worlds enable the creation of individual narratives through an intricate architectural experience like the current editions of the *Hitman* series. Therefore, the distinct architecture and groups of buildings from *Hitman* (2016) will serve as a case study in this work, as they interweave

---

9 | In addition, according to Götz, game designers as well as architects are confronted with overlapping design aspects like visual presentation und spatial experience. Both occupational fields must cope with similar problem-solving and construction methods. Ulrich Götz, "Load and Support. Architectural Realism in Video Games," in *Space Time Play. Computer Games, Architecture and Urbanism: the Next Level*, ed. Friedrich von Borries, Steffen P. Walz, and Matthias Böttger (Basel: Birkhäuser, 2007), pp. 134–37, here p. 134. This has resulted in several architects or product designers working in the game industry, see: Marc Bonner, "Analyzing the Correlation of Game Worlds and Built Reality: Depiction, Function and Mediality of Architecture and Urban Landscapes," *DiGRA Conference 2014*, Utah (August 3-6, 2014), conference proceedings (2014), pp 1-14.

10 | Götz, 2007, p. 134. In terms of the role of exploration in open world games, see: Marc Bonner, "On Striated Wilderness and Prospect Pacing: Rural Open World Games as Liminal Spaces of the Man-Nature Dichotomy," *DiGRA 2018. The Game is the Message*, University of Turin (July 25-28, 2018), conference proceedings (2018), pp. 1–18; Marc Bonner, "Erkundung als virtuell-fiktionale Immersionsstrategie—Das prospect pacing der Open-World-Computerspiele als Spiegel nicht linearer Spieler-Einbindung," *Jahrbuch Immersiver Medien 2016*, Interfaces—Netze—Virtuelle Welten, ed. Institut für Immersive Medien Kiel (Marburg: Schüren, 2017), pp. 38–57.

11 | Calleja, 2011, p. 27.

Le Corbusier's (1887-1965) concept of the *promenade architecturale* with the French urban palace layout of the *hôtel particulier* into ludic analogies of built reality.[12]

The corporeal potential of this is characterized by the open-endedness of the game-intrinsic buildings. As Calleja concludes, it is all about spatial and kinesthetic involvement. He defines the "incorporation" of the player as "immersion as transportation," which is characterized "not just [by] an engaging activity, but also [by] a world to be navigated".[13] Thus, spatial qualities such as navigation, interaction, and exploration must play with multiple sizes of space, interior-exterior dynamics, while remaining effectually complex at the same time:

> When a player plots a route through a geographical expanse and then navigates it, it is more likely that she will feel a sense of habitation within the game environment. There is the added satisfaction of having expended effort to reach a particular destination, especially when reaching this goal is challenging.[14]

Therefore, architecture as a medial hinge, and its role in different modes of perception among contiguous media, relies heavily on phenomenology. Both the spatiotemporal experience of space in physically real architecture and the spatiotemporal experience of game-intrinsic buildings have a close relationship. In contrast to film or literature, "[g]ame environments afford experiences that are not available through non-ergodic media".[15]

---

12 | For more information on the building type entitled *hôtel particulier*, see: Frédérique Lemerle, "L'émergence de l'hôtel particulier à Paris," *Marquer la ville, Signes, traces, empreintes du pouvoir (xiiie-xvie siècle)*, ed. Patrick Boucheron and Jean-Philippe Genet (Paris/Rome: Publications de la Sorbonne, 2013), pp. 109–123. https://books.openedition.org/psorbonne/3275?lang=de (accessed June 17, 2019).

13 | Calleja, 2011, p. 27.

14 | Ibid., p. 75.

15 | Referring to Aarseth's concept of ergodicity, Calleja states that players must provide active input into a gameplay session. The term "expresses the active participation of the player within" the man-machine feedback loop "that is formed by the game's hardware, the representational layer, and the underlying rules and environmental properties." Ibid., pp. 41, 167–172.

THREE CATEGORIES OF ARCHITECTURAL EXPERIENCE

Eventually, this leads to Carney Strange and James Banning's categories of design for human behavior in real-world college and university campuses, namely those of "architectural determinism," "architectural probabilism," and "architectural possibilism".[16] According to John McArthur, these categories also apply to digital technologies. Thus, they can become new kinds of spaces, which we then have to appropriate.[17] Architectural determinism "suggests that there is a rather direct link between the built environment and behavior within it".[18] McArthur clarifies that choices "are dictated by the physical structure".[19] Not only is this evocative of the promenade architecturale, but also of the kind of single-path architecture that exists in games like Half-Life (1998) or The Last Guardian (2016).

Architectural probabilism enables multiple behavior patterns and courses of action. Such "probabilistic links" channel certain ambiances and affordances, and can exhibit multicursal configurations. This evokes preferences, but also suggests a kind of freedom in the architectural experience.[20] Here, "the design of a built environment can increase the likelihood of some actions over others".[21] This is the case with games of the immersive sim[22] subgenre, such as Dishonored 2 (2016) or Deus Ex: Human Revolution (2011), as well as with nonlinear stealth games like Hitman: Absolution (2012). Architectural possibilism "views the physical environment as a source of opportunities that may set limits on, but not restrict, behav-

---

16 | C. Carney Strange and James H. Banning, *Educating by Design, Creating Campus Learning, Environments That Work* (San Francisco: Jossey-Bass/Wiley & Sons, 2001), p. 13.

17 | John A. McArthur, *Digital Proxemics, How Technology Shapes the Ways We Move* (New York, NY: Peter Lang Publishing, 2016), p. 8.

18 | Strange and Banning, 2001, p. 13.

19 | McArthur, 2016, p. 6.

20 | Strange and Banning, 2001, p. 14.

21 | McArthur, 2016, p. 7.

22 | For better insight into the characteristics of the immersive sim games and its roots in certain developer studios, see: Hans-Joachim Backe, "Metareferentiality through in-game images in immersive simulation games," *Proceedings of Foundations of Digital Games (FDG 2018)*, (August 07-10 2018), Malmö, Sweden (2018), pp. 1-10.

ior".[23] These buildings have an open-ended modular and nonlinear character, and enable context-sensitive interaction for each visitor or player:

[A] built space sets limits on the actions a user might take, but that the user is free to use the space in any number of unrestricted ways. [...] [T]he environment is passive and the user is active [...]. The environment remains malleable based on the whims of actors; the environment accepts multiple viewpoints without restriction; actors control their own behaviors.[24]

What McArthur states here seems to apply to most open-world games, such as *Far Cry 3* (2012) or *Assassin's Creed Origins* (2017), in which networked places and points of interest like hostile outposts are "quest places" that can be appropriated through multiple play styles and from multiple directions, due to the open topography and architectural configurations. In addition, this applies to the current *Hitman* series as well as to certain *immersive sim* games, once again including *Dishonored 2*.[25]

As the chart illustrates, Strange and Banning's categories are congruent with later models of architectural experience, including the filmic ap-

---

23 | Strange and Banning, 2001, p. 13.

24 | McArthur, 2016, p. 6.

25 | For example, in *Dishonored 2*'s eighth level, "The Grand Palace," players can explore a nested, multi-story building that merges the minimalist geometry of Walter Gropius's Bauhaus homes with elements of Northern Italian fortification architecture, such as the ravelin and bastion systems, whose slanted polygonal geometries are best known from forts by Domenico dell'Allio (1515-1563) or Sébastien Le Prestre de Vauban (1633-1707). That said, with the ability to teleport or making long jumps on all the nooks and crannies of these eclectic façades, players can traverse and explore the architecture at places and on paths unreachable for NPC (non playable character) pedestrians.

proach of Doris Agotai[26] and the sociological approach of Theresia Leuenberger.[27]

Fig. 87: Congruent categories of architectural experience of different disciplines

Architectural implication	Strange/Banning (2001)	Agotai (2007)	McArthur (2016)	Leuenberger (2018)	Examples
linear, restricted, enclosed	architectural determinsim	directed gaze	passive actors and active environment	differential in power in favor of the architecture	Half-Life, Quake, The Last Guardian
nonlinear, multi-cursal, branched	architectural probabilism	controlled movement	actor and environment are active	balance	Deus Ex: Human Revolution, Dishonored 2, Hitman: Absolution
nonlinear open-ended, networked	architectural possibilism	free wayfinding	passive environmant	differential in power in favor of the perceiver	Assassin's Creed Origins, Dishonored 2, Hitman

26 | Agotai stresses that openings like doors, windows, galleries, and stairs channel gazes and movements into linear perceptions and behavioral patterns. This way, architects play with the presence of an observer, which leads to a heightened experience of reality: perceiving architecture as a spatiotemporal object and participating in it evokes spatialization. Agotai's three categories are inspired by filmic methods like framing and editing: directed gaze, controlled movement, and free multicursal pathfinding. Doris Agotai, *Architekturen in Zelluloid, der filmische Blick auf den Raum* (Bielefeld: transcript, 2007), pp. 59, 68, 133.

27 | Leuenberger emphasizes that experiences of architecture are situational. The arrangement or layout of objects and humans, and how they are experienced and contextualized, changes with each place and moment. Thus, every mode of experience of architecture is realized through one's intention towards it and usage of it. Her categories build upon architectural spheres of impact to the observer. Such differential in power can tilt in favor of the materiality of the building, in favor of the observer, or it can stage a balance between both. Theresia Leuenberger, *Architektur als Akteur? Zur Soziologie der Architekturerfahrung* (Bielefeld: transcript, 2018), p. 80.

ON PROMENADE ARCHITECTURALE AND HÔTEL PARTICULIER

The architectural realization of directed gazes on a linear path is best known from Le Corbusier's concept of the *promenade architecturale,* which enables a fluid movement riddled with *establishing shots* into several rooms within a building. *Villa Savoye* (1931) in Poissy is a prime example of this.[28]

Fig. 88: Le Corbusier's promenade architecturale at Villa Savoye, Poissy, 1931

Le Corbusier's intention is to provide a kind of total impression without having been in every single room. This might evoke an urge for further exploration, but can also enable a voyeuristic gaze. One starts in a long, narrow, and dark entrance; ascends on the winding ramp situated to the right, in the center of the building; performs the series of framed gazes into bright rooms; and finally, ends on a rooftop garden.[29]

---

28 | By 2010, Steffen P. Walz had already used the *promenade architecturale* in order to briefly describe the basic rhythmical way of game spaces. See: Steffen P. Walz, *Towards A Ludic Architecture* (Carnegie Mellon University/Pittsburgh: ETC Press, 2010), p. 30.

29 | In contrast, the *promenade architecturale* of Le Corbusier's *Villa La Roche* in Paris (1923) encloses the center of the interior with ramps, balconies, galleries, and openings instead of being the center itself. Here, the same

In contrast, until the nineteenth century, Parisian villas sported both representational halls and private cozy rooms according to the layout of the *hôtel particulier.* Besides monumental staircases, most rooms were connected via *enfilades* (a series of rooms connected by doors visible along one line of sight). Since every room is directly connected to the adjacent ones, and is thus accessible by at least two doors or more, the host can freely choose along which path the group of rooms will be presented to a guest. Which specific rooms one navigates to, and how far into a private area one reaches, depends on the room's status or role within the overall configuration of the architecture. Agotai highlights the symbolic power of this kind of architectural experience, as it requires crossing certain spheres of public and private usage.[30] This is epitomized in the *appartement double,* which means two parallel *enfilades* and an offset arrangement of rooms. Narrow intermediating corridors and several side stairs underlie the open layout. Thus, they embody an *architectural possibilism* that enables generating multiple paths, in order to circumvent occupied rooms. François Mansart's (1598-1666) *Hôtel du Jars* (1648) in Paris was the first example of such a nonlinear design solution.

THE ARCHITECTURAL IMPLICATIONS OF HITMAN

Promenade architecturale (determinism) and *hôtel particulier* (possibilism) embody two ends of the continuum of architectural experience. In the environments of IO Interactive's *Hitman* and *Hitman 2*, both ends build a characteristically interwoven and dynamic tandem, in order to stage a

---

space can be perceived from multiple places. The most iconic and sculptural example of the *promenade architecturale* can be experienced in Frank Lloyd Wright's (1867-1959) *Solomon R. Guggenheim Museum* in New York (1959), with its helical spiral ramp dominating the cylindrical atrium that is also the main exhibition space. Tom Tykwer's *The International* (USA/GER/GBR 2009) copies this structure for a massive film set, staging a dramatic shootout while using architectural determinism for a fluid and complex cinematography. See: Kristine Jaspers, "Alice im Wunderland, Die Gestaltungskunst des Szenenbildners Uli Hanisch," *film-dienst* No. 14 (2009), pp. 6-10.

30 | Agotai, 2007, p. 137.

Fig. 89: Jean Marot, Floor plan of François Mansart's hôtel principle of Hôtel du Jars

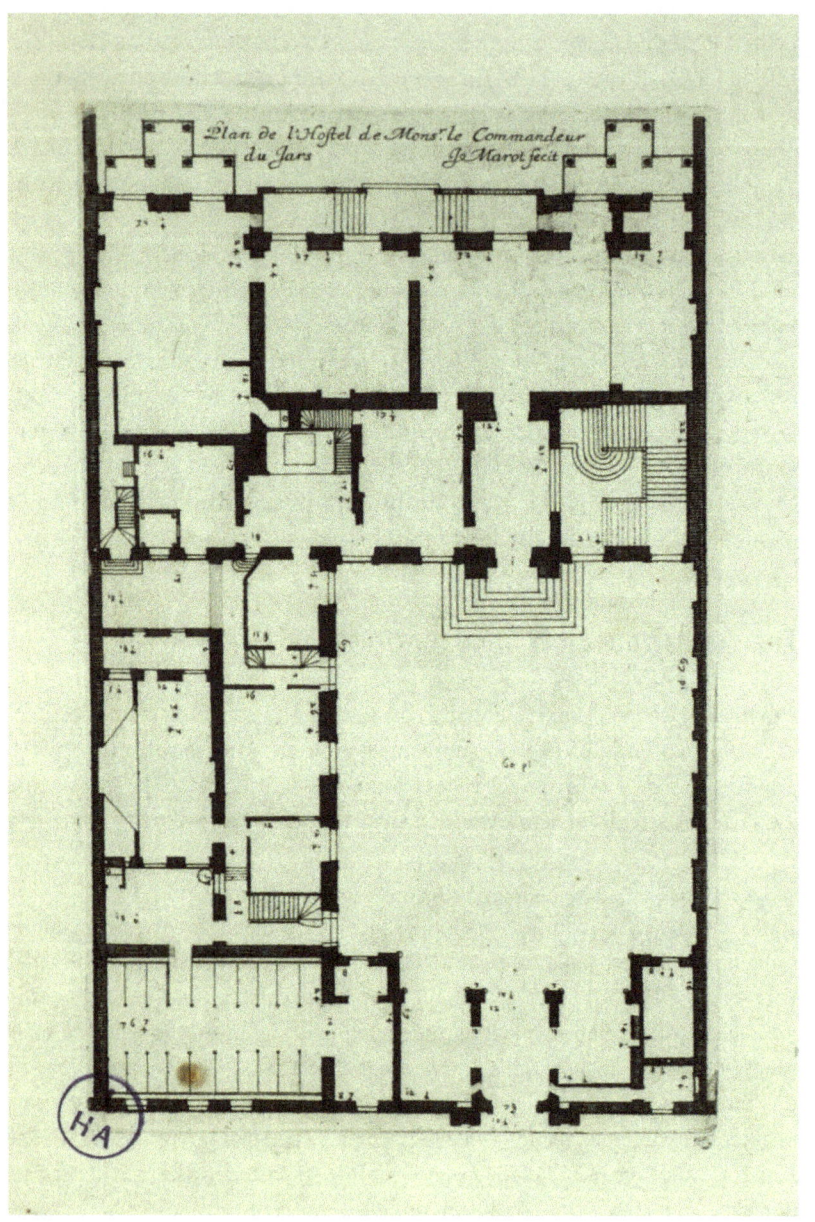

multilayered public urban space. Game directors Jakob Mikkelsen and Eskil Mohl even use the same categories in different terms, when speaking of the game intrinsic architecture as a combination of a "'snail house' with 'Swiss cheese'".[31] Mark Brown, of the Youtube channel *Game Maker's Toolkit*, compares this to a physically real IKEA store; he argues that, while IKEA packs the different functions of dwelling and multiple atmospheres into one enclosed hall, they want the customers to look at every interior and every single object. Therefore, "the store's layout provides an obvious and easy-to-follow path," meandering through all of the product groups and culminating at the checkout areas.[32] Yet, as a snail always winds up in narrower segments until it leads to a dead end, describing this mode of architectural experience through the metaphor of a snail shell is insufficient. The intended architectural functions and phenomenological effects are better described as a *promenade architecturale*.

A level in *Hitman* can have several *promenades architecturales*, providing the player with gazes onto spatiotemporal societal dynamics and hinting at different solutions. It is the starting point for delving deeper into crowded places, high security areas, or private rooms. Only by exploring the groups of buildings, interstitial spaces, and successive rooms—by combining several disguises, as someone with a certain type of job—do the possibilities of assassinating targets, which is the core premise of the game, unfold before the player's eyes.[33]

In this, the developers' metaphor of Swiss cheese describes the networked places and multicursal, modular layouts of the game world. In IKEA, it is "all the holes between the rooms that create shortcuts," so "seasoned IKEA veterans and staff members can bypass entire sections and get to where they're going more easily".[34] The Swiss cheese effect in *Hitman* not only refers to built-in shortcuts, such as obvious doorways, but

---

31 | Mikkelsen cited in Mark Brown, "The Making of Hitman 2's Miami Level, The Game Maker's Toolkit," youtube.com (February 18, 2019), https://www.youtube.com/watch?v=56iiP2xQn74 (accessed June 17, 2019). See 00:11:19.

32 | Ibid., 00:11:39.

33 | See Kevin Wong, "How 'Hitman' Uses Thoughtful Level Design to Tell Stories," *motherboard.vice.com*, (December 2, 2016), https://motherboard.vice.com/en_us/article/pgkvmn/how-hitman-uses-thoughtful-level-design-to-tell-stories (accessed March 15, 2019).

34 | Brown 2019, 00:11:58.

also to hidden or not easily evident paths, like a downspout to a rooftop or a maintenance duct. Traversing the explored game space with such short-cuts gives players "a feeling of mastery".[35] Combining this architectural experience with the fact that the designers try to avoid dead ends—and thus, design grouped rooms with multiple entrances and exits[36]—the Swiss cheese metaphor is congruent with the *hôtel particulier* layout.[37]

This is perfectly displayed in *Hitman*'s Paris mission "The Showstopper," in which players attend a fashion gala in fictional *Palais de Walewska*. While the exterior merges different French architecture styles, combining volumes and façades of three iconic buildings into a *Beaux-Arts* chimera,[38] the ground plan of the four-story *palais* resembles symmetrical concepts of the *hôtel* layout, complete with *enfilades* and the *appartement* principle.

Fig. 90: Levels of Hitman's Palais de Walewska maps

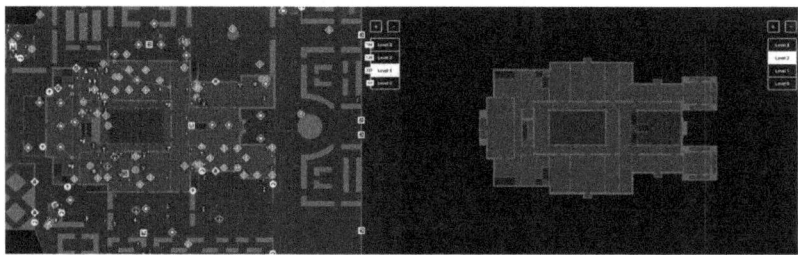

The environments in *Hitman* stage an alternation between "safety and opportunity," while enticing "participants with the promise of new information, tapping a natural yearning to know 'what's beyond the bend'" in a distinct, media-specific "person-environment dynamic".[39] This strategy of teasing items or points of interest from certain points of view is also a stat-

35 | Ibid., 00:12:45–00:12:57.

36 | Ibid., 00:13:14.

37 | This is especially true for the appartement double, with its hidden stairs, modular succession of rooms, and the possibility of multiple paths.

38 | To be more specific, this includes: Théodore Ballu's and Édouard Deperthes's *Hôtel de Ville* in Paris (1882), Hector Lefuel's *Pavillon de Flore* of the Musée du Louvre (1868), and Nicolas Fouquet's *Château Vaux-le-Vicomte* (1661).

39 | Strange and Banning, 2001, p. 28, 75.

ed objective of the game designers.[40] As such, the larger nonlinear levels of *Hitman* and *Hitman 2* can be described as semi-open world structures.

The game designers must construct a thorough disguise system that marks the core point of the person-environment dynamic, in order for players to delve deeper into *architectural possibilism*. Most levels have a layering of six public, security, and privacy spheres; these are convoluted within the spatial arrangements and buildings, and represent a distilled version of everyday society.[41] NPCs must be distracted, trapped, and knocked out in order to gain the desired disguise; behavioral patterns are deeply linked to certain areas within a building or compound.[42] Although there are traditional stealth passages—in the sense of circumventing enemies, or using shadowed areas in narrow labyrinthine layouts, as best known from *Tom Clancy's Splinter Cell* (2002-2013) or the *Metal Gear Solid* (1998-2015) series—*Hitman* and *Hitman 2* are all about "hiding in plain sight"[43] via the most heterogeneous jobs, characters, and thus, the horizon of agency within a built environment. Mikkelsen articulates the questions that initiate the structuring and layering of jobs and agencies during the design of a level: "what people would be working here," or "what gives

40 | Brown, 2019, 00:04:58.

41 | Level designer Mette Podenphant Andersen speaks of public open space, public purpose space, public rule space, private space, professional space, and personal space; she highlights the potential "involvement" of the players by public spaces. Andersen cited in Alissa McAloon: "Mapping out the subtle social cues throughout Hitman's level design," *www.gamasutra.com* (March 19, 2019), http://gamasutra.com/view/news/338996/Mapping_out_the_subtle_social_cues_throughout_Hitmans_level_design.php?fbclid=IwAR2RUrJzPfAoIBtQwgX WmcpiHzv1BYZHOdB-fU1tBISMRHI89_8EuuaUD54 (accessed March 19, 2019).

42 | A player has to assassinate different types of target NPCs that roam the area. Targets of the type "dweller" stick to one location, such as one building or a few rooms on a story, ever circling the same succession of waypoints contextualized with the character and the building's functions. The "roamer" type is more complex, and may have different phases of behavioral patterns and looped paths in more open areas of the semi-open world. Brown, 2019, 00:03:19, 00:03:49.

43 | Ibid., 00:14:03.

you access to when," and "how early do you meet them [the disguises or jobs]".[44]

This can also be experienced in and around *Palais de Walewska*: while switching context-sensitive disguises such as auction staff, a model, a chef, a stylist, palace staff, a member of the tech crew, or a security guard, players are able to roam the palace from the wine cellar to a kitchen, from representational rooms to a lounge bar, from a dressing area and backstage rooms to the catwalk, from the high security garden to a dusty attic.[45]

Fig. 91: Image series of Palais de Walewska in Hitman

44 | Mikkelsen cited in Brown, 2019, 00:15:09.

45 | That said, certain kinds of assassination are more likely than others, as they are either the easiest or most evident. For some players, this may lead to a performance of ludic probabilism, as an ideal combination of disguises enables them to directly achieve the goals. Thus, it is the most effective way in a linear manner. It is the dramaturgy of gaining ever-more powerful or empowering outfits. Therefore, the game system rewards players that plan and use the most creative or stealthiest means of assassination.

Through switching between jobs and varying agency, the player unfolds the game world into an *architectural possibilism,* becoming the host of a level and its distilled societal dynamics.[46] Staging such an intricate *hôtel* layout during an ephemeral modern day conversion, complete with authentic work routines, crowds, and infrastructures, it is no wonder that two of *Hitman's* game designers, Fredrik Gyllenhoff and Nils Damsgaard, are actually trained architects.[47] *Hitman's* Italy mission "World of Tomorrow" embodies the initial design that became the archetype and blueprint for the even more complex and sprawling areas of *Hitman 2.*[48]

---

46 | As Don Carson puts it: "As players learn to read a game space as a complex spatiotemporal setting, multiple roles position the player in different perspectives toward the game world and assist in a deeper exploration of it." Don Carson, "Environmental Storytelling: Creating Immersive 3D World Using Lessons from the Theme Park Industry," *Gamasutra* (March 1, 2000), https://www.gamasutra.com/view/feature/131594/environmental_storytelling_.php (accessed March 15, 2019).

47 | "[E]very object, placed or misplaced, had to tell a tale, or imply a prior action. It creates the illusion that this is a living breathing world. And it adds to a mood of invasiveness." See: Wong, 2016.

48 | Like the fictional racing track facing the high security research facility *Kronstadt*, complete with laboratories, paddocks, marina, racing team lounges, and numerous tunnels and gangways in Miami level "The Finish Line", or the vertically stacked eight-story high castle on the remote fictional Scottish *Isle of Sgàil* in the mission titled "The Ark Society", which is crowned with a glass cube as high-security area. In addition, especially the Columbia mission "Three-headed Serpent" mirrors core locations and topologies of the archetypal Italy mission. The level takes place in and around the fictional village *Santa Fortuna*. It is framed by a cocaine plantation, the dense jungle, a muddy river and a construction site. Like in *Sapienza* there exists a hidden cavernous facility underneath the spacious escapist villa that is situated on a higher altitude and besides the rural village full of stacked buildings and furrowed by narrow alleys. The locations differ in atmosphere and design, of course. For example, the villain's villa differs from the rustic-style *Villa Caruso* in it's architectural language and layout by merging aspects of Le Corbusier's *Villa Savoye* with Richard Meier's *Bodrum Houses* on Turkey's Bodrum peninsula (2012) as well as building materials or material aesthetics known from Frank Lloyd Wright's numerous prairie houses into a Modernism meets American Craftsman Style

It stages the fictional Italian coastal town of *Sapienza*, which is said to be nested on the Amalfi coast. *Sapienza* consists of a Medieval old town, complete with a piazza, beach, church, ruins, narrow alleys, several shops and flats, recreational places, the monumental *Villa Caruso*, and laboratories hidden in a cave underneath the villa. While this may sound like a James Bond film set, *Sapienza* is more than that. It is a fully explorable town, with a layout reminiscent of the real-world town of Vernazza, which clings to a picturesque cliffside in the Cinque Terre region of Liguria. With nearly forty-four sub-locations adjusted to the dynamics of a coastal tourist town, *Sapienza* is the first mission in the *Hitman* series that fully unlocks the potential of the game mechanics.[49] The newfound complexity of architectural and societal depiction can also be seen in the twenty-six disguises placed throughout the level.

Fig. 92: *Levels of Hitman's Sapienza map*

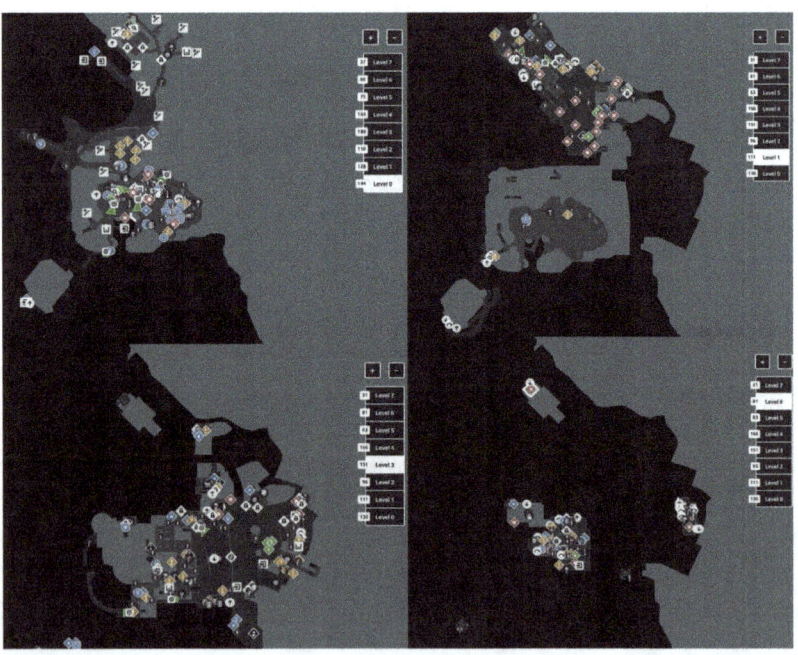

chimera. Having said this, *Santa Fortuna* sports more locations and may enable even more ways to fulfill the mission's goals.

49 | According to Andersen's analytic sheet of *Sapienza* in McAloon, 2019.

Torbjørn Christensen, who was the lead level designer of *Sapienza*, highlights the intention "to explore the verticality in coastal towns, and how streets and corridors connect everything".[50] Besides its vastness and complexity, it is also a characteristic of *Sapienza* that the targets are "dwellers" restricted to the villa compound on the rocky peninsula, while most of the level enables an "organic touristic exploring"[51] of public places. The means of roaming through the game world as a recreational place, and as a walkable picturesque diorama of an Italian coastal town society, full of altering atmospheres and congruous as an end in itself made for a path breaking level design within the game series.

Fig. 93: Image series of Sapienza level in Hitman

50 | Christensen cited in Phil Savage: "The making of Sapienza, Hitman's best level," *pcgamer* (January 1, 2017), https://www.pcgamer.com/the-making-of-sapienza-hitmans-best-level/2/ (accessed March 15, 2019).
51 | Savage, 2017.

CONCLUSION

In *Hitman* and *Hitman 2*, architecture as a medial hinge becomes a media-specific paradigm: it communicates a heightened comprehension of
complex building types, and the socio-urban dynamics of the real world by
fictionalizing "reality and culture through turning human settings into
images and metaphors of idealized order and life, into fictionalized architectural narratives".[52] Though *Hitman* stages real-world building types
like the *Palais de Walewska* in a coherently arranged manner, it is not only
about adapting the *promenade architecturale* or *hôtel particulier* principle
one-to-one in this, but rather, it is about staging media-specific architectonics for an analogous mode of architectural experience in the sense of
ludic logics. In other words: not every *promenade architecturale* must be
embodied as a ramp made of concrete; not every building volume has to
depict a palace in order to be rhythmized in the *hôtel particulier* manner
within the level structure. It is about its function within the person-
environment dynamic.

The game-intrinsic architecture of the *Hitman* series perfectly inter-
weaves the linear fluid *promenade architecturale* with the open, nonlinear,
networked concept of the *hôtel particulier*, and its multi-directional access-
es into coherent buildings and urban districts. Every level is a semi-open
world, where the player starts anew as a tourist or guest in a publicly unrestricted area; one proceeds by exploring and disguising, sneaking and
circumventing into ever smaller places of higher security clearance or
personal sphere. Appropriating the networked places enables a knowledge
of the architecture to arise. That said, the metamorphosis from tourist to
host, in terms of the horizon of agency, is only possible by exploring the
intricate interiors and spacious architectures, by piercing through all the
architectonical and societal layers of a staged but intricate everyday life.
Only then is one able to master *architectural possibilism*.

---

52 | Pallasmaa, 2011, p. 19.

Creating Fascinating Spaces

The Assignement for Designers of both Virtuality and Reality

Sinem Cukurlu

People playing games are able to immerse themselves in fascinating worlds that both involve them and allow them to make their own decisions. Game spaces invite players to keep revisiting them, to accomplish quests or (self-assigned) tasks, and to communicate and exchange with other players. Games permit interaction with their elements. While working in an architect's office as a student employee, and playing games during my leisure time, I felt like creating virtual worlds was better developed in regard to user interaction; this is why I chose to gain more insight into creating games. I promised myself that if I started working as an architect after my studies, I would create architecture that leaves a lasting impression. And if I were involved in urban planning, I would ensure that real spaces are as inviting and interactive as those of games.

WHY ARCHITECTS AND GAME DESIGNERS ARE RELATED

As I started researching the process game designers use to create their virtual worlds, I found several common challenges for the architects of each discipline: both must negotiate the constraints of their clients and contracts; they examine and analyze the correlation of space, as well as rooms and their functionality; and they draw details that are true to scale. Of course, there are important differences in planning real and virtual architecture: costs, rules, and limits exist in both worlds and must be observed. But, in the end, the true challenge for real-life and virtual architects is to create structures and spaces that people or players must enter, in order to experience them in the way that the architect has conceived. Both kinds of designers work on objects that live from their interactivity. "Good" games as well as architecture involve their users, and ensure that they write their own stories. In both worlds, architecture—the composition of space and positioning of elements within it—has more than just an aesthetic value. People remember how they moved through space and buildings, and how they experienced them. Regardless of whether the space is real or virtual, well-designed architecture in both worlds is narrative, arouses emotion, initiates and leaves an impact on the user—it creates "living" spaces that remain present in one's mind. Architecture is not only the exterior design of a building; it also forms space and leads its users through it. Jesse Schell, game developer and author, says that the primary function of architecture in both worlds is to control people's experiences and to "lead" them: "If all the experiences we wanted to have were to be found easily in nature, there would be no point to architecture. But those experiences aren't always there, so architects design things to help us have the experiences we desire".[1]

This is the reason why architects and game designers are more related than some might think. They need to create structures that invite users to interact, and which lead them to obtain the intended experience. Virtual spaces in 3D games can be seen as real spaces, because—just as in real spaces—virtual spaces are three-dimensional, modifiable, and provide the opportunity to explore them. Thomas Erickson, a social scientist and designer researching how people use technology for collaboration and communication, established that it is important to create spaces and rooms that not only lead the user, but that are used for more than just a single purpose in his studies "From Interface to Interplace: The Spacial Environment as a Medium for Interaction".[2] In order to be successful, or to create architecture that is successful, space must be open to a wide variety of activities. I personally experienced how the architecture of games can ascribe new meaning to space without the space suggesting it. Players

1 | Jesse Schell, *The Art of Game Design: A Book of Lenses* (Burlington MA: Morgan Kaufmann Publishers, 2008), p. 330.

2 | Thomas Erickson, "From interface to interplace: the spatial environment as a medium for interaction," in *Spatial Information Theory A Theoretical Basis for GIS.* COSIT 1993. Lecture Notes in Computer Science, eds. Andrew U. Frank and Irene Campari (Berlin/Heidelberg: Springer, 1993), pp. 391–405.

meet at a specific point in the game, such as on a bridge, to exchange items or leave their character when they are inactive. Differently than its original purpose—bridges are made for crossing—that place is imbued with a new function and meaning, due to the players' behavior. But what further functions can architecture have in games beyond the ones already mentioned?

FUNCTION OF ARCHITECTURE IN GAMES

In his essay "Designer's Notebook: The Role of Architecture in Videogames," game design consultant and lecturer Ernest W. Adams structures the function of architecture into primary and secondary functions.[3] He says that, firstly, architecture supports gameplay mechanics; secondly, it informs and entertains the player. For example, architecture in a game like *Mirror's Edge* (2008) determines which paths the player can use. The designer blocks specific paths and directions, or deliberately permits them. Players are subtly guided to look for new routes, while thinking the direction they are going is their own decision. But, in fact, they are being led and restricted: beams, pipes, railings, or crane masts that can be used, change the object's color to red. If they do not turn red, there is no new pathway or progress expected. In first-person shooter games, or "ego shooters," like *PlayerUnknown's Battlegrounds* (2017), architecture is used to take cover from enemies. In *World of Warcraft* (2004) a player seeks shelter from the hostile fraction in allied cities; here, architecture serves to protect players from a "boss's" abilities, and thus belongs to the gameplay. Architecture can also be a challenge and opponent. The player needs to proceed in a logical and skilful way to solve a puzzle and to progress in *The Legend of Zelda* (1986), where players interact with elements of the in-game architecture to gain access to the next room. Furthermore, there are games in which players have to explore the environment and surroundings to find out how the game space is structured, and which pathways

---

3 | Ernest W. Adams, "Designer's Notebook: The Role of Architecture in Videogames" *Gamasutra* (October 9, 2002), https://www.gamasutra.com/view/feature/131352/designers_notebook_the_role_of_.php (accessed June 17, 2019).

lead to which areas. In this case, it is useful for players to recognize the function of a building from afar, and can use it to orient themselves.

Often, maps are included for this purpose; but if no maps are given, the players must rely on their memories. Therefore, it is important that players are guided, or can orient themselves, with architecture in order to know which area or buildings they have already visited. Architecture requires its own clear color-language and use of forms, if it is to be a recognizable feature or symbol in games. Architecture also serves as a medium that can arouse emotions and create atmospheres by using specific materials, lighting, and space. In the words of architect James Sale: "As architects, our tools are the materials that the building is built of, but also light and space. We can contract and expand those as much as we want [...] It's what we use to give space different feelings. For example, a classic trick is to create a small threshold and then open out into a big space. You contract and then release".[4] That movement—from a small space to an exposed area—is used in many games. In *BioShock* (2007), the large, open world of *Rapture* is only revealed to the player after going through small doors and corridors. Just as in real-world architecture, such as cathedrals, the process of contracting and expanding is one way to give space a sense of narrative and feeling. Adventure games often use open and closed rooms or corridors as types of space. Virtual designers seem to consider the psychology of spaces, because every 3D game is composed of these spatial elements. How the components are dimensioned affects players' emotions or sensibility: narrow and small spaces appear threatening and oppressive, while wide spaces invite the player to explore and to journey through the environment.

Functions of architecture in games show some parallels to architecture in reality. Architecture provides shelter, protection, and orientation; it creates familiarity and atmosphere, and leaves an impression upon us. The tools that are used by real-life and virtual architects are the same: materiality, light, space, perspective, environment, shape, and form.

---

4 | James Sale, "From Dark Souls to Manifold Garden: How games tell stories through architecture," interview by Thomas McMullen, *Alphyr*, https://www.alphr.com/games/1002937/from-dark-souls-to-manifold-garden-how-games-tell-stories-through-architecture (accessed June 17, 2019).

DESIGNING GAME WORLDS—ASPECTS THAT CAN BE TRANSFERRED TO REAL-LIFE ARCHITECTURE

Designing virtual worlds is different than designing real-life architecture, and is obviously not limited by the same restrictions. In reality, architects must observe the constraints of construction, material, physics, safety, and land costs that are not relevant in every game. A virtual designer does not need to consider material thickness or material weight, nor construction detailing or fire safety regulations. Of course, game designers are limited, too: namely, by the costs and limits of the hardware being used. The game engine that renders frames can be very expensive. That engine illustrates a specific number of polygons, which comprise the objects, and this limits the element's precision. The more the hardware needs to "do," the more expensive it gets. Nevertheless, the virtual world does not serve real people inhabiting these constructions, but rather, it serves the playability of the game. But where to begin comparing how to design both worlds, if there are seemingly no limits (or let's say, another kind of limits)?

Designing a game or a level is not a standardized process for a specific person, nor is it the concern of video game developers. Generally, it is a process in which a game space is created that allows for interaction. The process includes not only the placement of objects or enemies, but determines their "behavior" when players interact with them. A virtual designer needs to analyze how players act in and with their surroundings, and—in the best case scenario—ensure that they explore the world and obtain the intended kind of experience. Designing both virtual and real architecture is a technical and artistic process, in pursuit of creating impressive worlds. Before creating an entire game, the gameplay—not the actual structures of the game, but how players should interact with it—is discussed and created. The game's plot, rules, and goal are therefore the main topics of this first step. Game designers and level designers draw diagrams that explain the gameplay.

Such illustrations only show the gameplay; they do not show an actual floor plan, but rather, the players' actions and possible strategies.[5] Accor-

---

5 | Michael Stuart Licht, "An Architect's Perspective On Level Design Pre-Production," *Gamasutra* (June 3, 2003), https://www.gamasutra.com/view/feature/131257/an_architects_perspective_on_.php (accessed June 17, 2019).

Fig. 94: Michael Stuart Licht, Gameplay diagram from Star Wars: Bounty Hunter, 2002

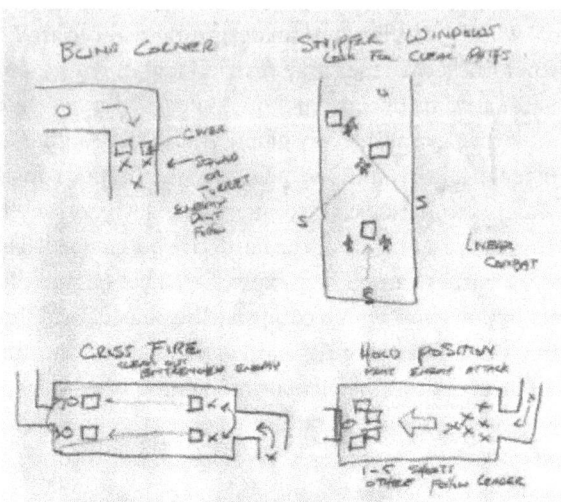

ding to my experience, this process does not happen when creating real worlds. Of course, architects examine spatial plans and consider the best configuration and dependencies of rooms—but the actual simulation of user behavior almost never occurs. Another point I find lacking in the creation of real worlds is that, in the process of game development, the specific aspects of the entire game and the concept of levels are reviewed at various stages. These aspects include the game's structure, the question of whether or not players are able to find their way, if they understand the purpose of elements, and of course, if elements fulfill their purpose. *Playtesting* helps to not only check a game's playability, but also to discover, fix, and remove errors. Does that happen in architectural offices? I don't believe so—even if it ought to occur. A construction could and should be tested for functionality, circulation, route guidance, and defects within the building's structure at an early phase. Visual and functional aspects can be adjusted through the real feedback of users, instead of relying solely on the experience of architects. When it comes to designing virtual worlds, the point is to create something that does not only delight yourself, but also the users; this is why it is so important to get real feedback at an early stage. One could even imagine that playtesting might be integrated in the building information modeling (BIM) system someday. This way, projects could be monitored and reviewed at any stage by all participants. This would facilitate communication between them when designing a new construction or renovating an existing building. The architect would not need to create a 2D floor plan, which the users might not be able to read and understand anyway.

The office of Mzo Tarr Architects in London uses "game theory" to involve users, planners, investors, and neighbors into their design process. They define this concept as follows: "Game theory is the mathematical study of decision-making between people in a situation of conflict or cooperation. [...] Any time a decision is going to be made between two or more people [...] you can use game theory to help identify which is the best decision or strategy to make".[6] By using this approach, they discover how and why a single user makes decisions, and then draw conclusions that flow into the building's design and function. Through this process, the user becomes a decision-maker in formulating the architecture without having to rely on floor plans that must be studied in order to be under- stood. After all, it is the users who must be satisfied with the realization of their new home, and feel comfortable in it. But, this London office does not take the process further than this. Game theory should be followed by 3D simulations that users enter, and communicate to the architect what should be changed in the design to fit the way they imagine it. They can discuss whether or not the windows should be bigger, or if the doors should be wider. In buildings such as museums or shopping malls, the way space behaves if only one person is present, or if instead a group of people are in it, could be simulated. After that, conclusions could be drawn about the room's, or even the whole building's, structure—without even being built. Of course, there are norms and conditions that need to be observed in this, but all participants could exchange about them and the actual user (at least in housing) could be a decision-maker.

Another aspect of game development that could be (re)transferred to designing real spaces is the examination of storytelling and "pathfinding." Francine Rotzetter, a former student of the Zurich University of the Arts (ZHdK), points out that guidance systems, or pathfinding systems, in games originate from real-life architecture, which is why they can also be transferred back into reality. Both the architect and the game designer are

6 | Mzo Tarr Architects, "About the studio," https://www.mzotarr.com/about/ (accessed June 17, 2019).

mindful of the user's guidance, and as such, strategically plan the user's or inhabitant's perception from their arrival to their departure. Moreover, in public places, guidance systems must quickly lead many people to a lot of destinations. If a system of guidance is ambiguous or misleading, the system's effectivity suffers.[7] This is the reason why reaching or creating intuitive guidance in architecture, rather than using signs, is worth striving for. Le Corbusier's (1887-1965) concept of the *promenade architecturale* deals with a viewer-oriented path through built space, and is a central element of his architectural and urban planning designs. He realized that linear guidance systems trigger the strongest architectural experience. Using "tree" structures or "foldback" structures, which are used in a lot of games as storytelling techniques, could, for example, impact a promenade, as well as what happens to it and the buildings around it, if a visitor suddenly has more paths to walk along. Thus, the visitor's experience and memory concerning the architecture could be reinforced. Maybe including rewards and achievements could be something to consider, too. A visitor to a museum could receive a reward, such as an impressive view, discover a special shortcut, or earn a souvenir for choosing a path that is not clearly obvious. The visit becomes more and more interesting, and remains present in their mind, because the visitor experienced something unexpected. Not everyone will find that inconspicuous pathway—but may come back later and begin to search for the path that brings a reward. With the help of augmented reality, a visitor could even collect points or see exhibits through a smartphone, experiencing some form of virtual museum.

Architecture in games is very focused on an event and is structured accordingly. As such, virtual designers concentrate on interactivity and the actual use of space and elements. The design of virtual worlds and its elements are deduced from their function or purpose. Although this principle may remind one of the "form follows function" maxim touted by Louis Henry Sullivan (1856-1924)—perhaps the most famous sentence a former student of architecture like me can recall—the aspect of interaction is often inadequately addressed in architecture. Because game spaces need to steadily mesmerize or captivate the player and always be interest-

---

7 | Francine B. R. Rotzetter, *Game Guidance—Nonverbale Leitsysteme in Open-World-Games*, unpublished Ph.D. dissertation (Zurich: Zurich University of the Arts (ZhdK), 2017), p. 83.

ing, the placement of elements as well as the entire architectural structure is linked to activity. The spaces we come across in games are dynamic: we interact and engage with elements, we can change and reposition things. If architects keep this in mind, we would, for example, have more urban spaces that enable activity, or in which events can take place. In reality, architects may need to create more architecture with which users can interact and change their world. These aspects are not new to architecture, but still they are not considered and implemented in every case.

WHY ARCHITECTS AND GAME DESIGNERS MAKE FOR GREAT SYMBIOSIS

In game spaces, architecture takes an important role; it is often decisive for the atmosphere and gameplay, which is why it needs to be developed and designed in consultation and with regard to its function within the game. Games can be made so realistically that players are able to immerse themselves in the virtual world. When games are designed to refer to real life, our real architecture provides great potential for inspiration. Game designers already consider typologies and psychologies of spaces, as well as building history and culture, and use them as reference material. Games like *Assassin's Creed II* (2009) or *The Witness* (2016) show how great a collaboration between game designers and architects can be.

In *Assassin's Creed II*, Maria Elísa Novarro, who teaches the history and theory of architecture, worked with the company *Ubisoft's* game designer team in Montreal. Her assignment was to verify contemporary clothing and the character's weapons, to correct architectonic mistakes that were possibly made while translating real-life architecture into virtual space, and to elaborate the details of the buildings.[8] The game takes place between 1476 and 1504, and contains elements of the Italian Renaissance. A player meets Niccolò Machiavelli (1469-1527) and Leonardo Da Vinci (1452-1519) while walking through Florence, Venice, and San Gimignano. For the gameplay design—which primarily consists of architecture in

---

8 | Maria Elísa Novaro, "What It's Like to Be an Architectural Consultant for Assassin's Creed II," interview by Manuel Saga, translated by Matthew Valata (October 7, 2015), https://www.archdaily.com/774210/maria-elisa-navarro-the-architectural-consultant-for-assassins-creed-ii (accessed June 17, 2019).

Assassin's Creed—as well as for character design, the team had to become acquainted with the Italian Renaissance. A player's path not only leads through streets and alleys, but the player also interacts with the environment and climbs up the buildings. Because being very close to the architecture as a player is so important, and because *Ubisoft* emphasizes authenticity in general, the architecture must be executed in accordance with the era.

Fig. 95: The detailed architecture in the concept art from Assassin's Creed II, 2009

The Witness, for which the game developer Jonathan Blow sought advice from architects, is another great example of a successful collaboration: "[Jonathan] wanted an architect who was a praciticing architect, not a video game artist or someone who was in that industry. I think he feels that that is how you actually start to elevate games to a higher level, an art form, by breaking out of certain ways of thinking".[9] This architect, Deanna van Burren, convinced Blow that no building can or could be designed without including the landscape, especially because the game's plot and environment is a desert island, which comprises more landscape than buildings. Eventually, architects, landscape architects, and virtual artists from *Fletcher Studio* and *FOURM* design studio worked together to perfect the game.

9 | Deanna Van Buren, "Behind the scenes of 'The Witness', a video game designed by architects," interview by Nicholas Korody, *Archinect* (August 23, 2016), https://archinect.com/features/article/149964654/behind-the-scenes-of-the-witness-a-video-game-designed-by-architects (accessed June 17, 2019).

At the time the architect joined the game's team, the game was already playable—but only assembled with buildings that fulfilled their purpose, and didn't really look realistic. With the help of the architects, the buildings were integrated to the landscape: textures, details, and the scale of the objects were fixed and placeholders such as buildings, which were only cubic volumes, were finely rendered with regard to their function and structure within the game.

Fig. 96: *Placeholders for buildings in a quarry in The Witness, 2016*

Fig. 97: *The buildings and quarry after involving architects in the design process, 2016*

In return, architects also need to see and use the creative potential that games provide. They need to experiment with space, form, and dimension within the virtual worlds that offer seemingly unlimited possibilities. With the help of games, architects can even approach and involve broader civil societies in their design process.

ENGAGING CIVIL SOCIETY TO CREATE AND UNDERSTAND THE COMPLEXITY OF THEIR SURROUNDINGS

Block'hood (2017) is a strategic city-building and management-simulator video game by architect, programmer, and game designer Jose Sanchez. The game conveys its players the essentials of architecture, economy, and ecology, focusing on ideas of interdependence and decay. Players can choose from around two hundred modules to build their own compact city; they must be able to place the bricks side by side, or one below another. They must arrange the modules such that the bricks work together as an ecological system and none of them decays. *Block'hood* is based on the real concepts of ecology and entropy, which is why the modules require both "input" and "output" to survive.

Trees need water, an apartment needs electricity and water, and so on. Just like in reality, these elements have specific requirements to survive; in return, they produce an output. The player has to keep the input and output in balance, and is thus able to understand complex dependencies of elements in a city. Sanchez believes that games like *Block'hood* can serve as new tools to solve the global challenges facing architecture. He sees the potential of games as tools to get experts and society to call attention to complex issues in urban design and architecture, in order to solve them together: "Games are great for understanding systems because they simulate interactions. [...] Being able to see how interactions play out is achieved through simulation".[10]

---

10 | Jose Sanchez, "Designing the Metaverse: The Role of Architecture in Virtual Environments," interview by Susan S. Szenasy, *Metropolis Magazine* (July 19, 2017), https://www.dezeen.com/2016/03/07/jose-sanchez-block-hood-video-game-tools-solve-global-challenges-architecture/ (accessed June 17, 2019).

Fig. 98: Jose Sanchez, Ecological dependence of elements in Block'hood, 2017

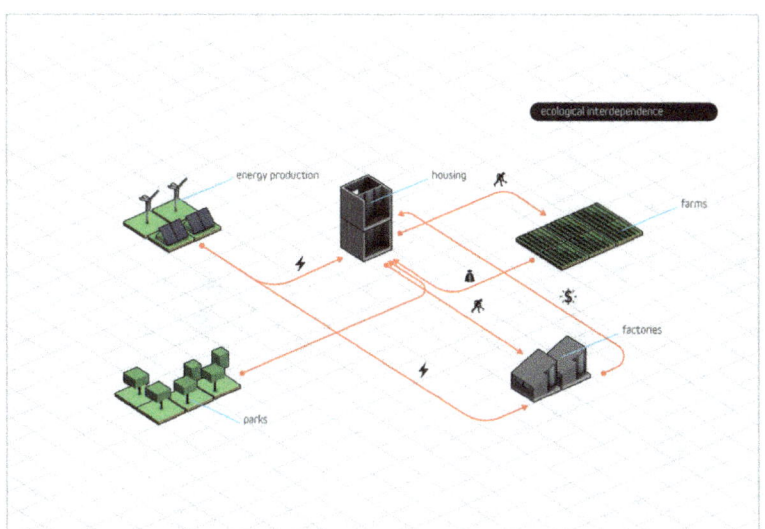

*BlockWork*s is doing exactly that. For *The Guardian*, a British daily newspaper, they created the "Climate Hope City" in *Minecraft* based on real and sustainable green technologies and prototypes, to show how a city can and should operate. They used vertical farms, kinetic pavements, and green roofs. Players interact with elements, turning them on and off to see their impact on the city. The goal was to visualize the challenges of climate change in an easy and understandable form, and to illustrate that, with technologies that already exist, it is possible to combat climate change and create a real word that can be almost emission-free. Another project by *BlockWork*s is the charity called *Block by Block*. *Minecraft* (2009) is used in workshops to get members of civil society to work on their own environment and city.

The advantage of *Minecraft* is not only that it is played online, but that it contains the potential to exchange and work in real-time. Architect Bjarke Ingels (*1974) says, in a movie filmed for the *Future of Storytelling* summit in 2014, that *Minecraft* brings a more democratic and populistic approach to architecture—and that nowadays, more than one hundred million people populate *Minecraft*, where they can build their own worlds and inhabit them through play. He emphasizes that architecture needs to do more to allow the public to change and interact, to truly transform their own environments.

Fig. 99: A "Place for Play" in East Jerusalem by 50 resident youth engaged by Block By Block, 2016

UNDERSTANDING GAME SPACES AND GAMES AS TOOLS FOR BETTER ARCHITECTS

Today, games are part of society's everyday life, and they have developed into a cultural artifact independent of age and gender. Virtual spaces as well as real spaces have their specific functions and claims on aesthetics. Game designers already draw on known styles of real architecture; they craft structures based on reality, and they have realized that architectural skills are valuable to their industry. Architects and city planners are taking more and more notice of games as a medium with which to communicate. Of course, games are not a replacement for the architect's CAD tools—but these tools are not made for their clients. Games can allow the architect to approach more people, because games are quite easy to understand and even entertain people. Beyond this, games can be used as more than a tool to involve society or all participants in planning. Structures and storytelling techniques in games are strong qualities that architects also need to take note of. Through digital games, we can expose people to challenges of architecture while improving the visual literacy of the population. Presently, many members of our global society are spending time in well-designed digital environments. If we harness the power of games, we can reverse-engineer the effect of starting to expect more from our real environments.

Augmented Play, Art, and Space

The Cognitive Coupling of Avant-Garde Games with Unexpected Mental Spaces

Margarete Jahrmann

Based on experiences in pervasive play[1] in media arts, this chapter questions the relationship between spatial perception and computer games from the perspective of playful, cognitive, and activist interventions. Today, in creating the artistic aspects of video games—what is known as "game art"—space is thematized as an almost meditative experience. In a series of artistic games, the concept of "flow" is induced by what are known as "walking simulators" in the architecture of games. Currently, the genre of game art is resurging in specific relation to the flow experience of virtual space, entangled with the physically experiential real space. This provides an opportunity to learn from the fields of performance art, staging, and motivational design. This is demonstrated by the art avant-garde gaming scene.

In the design and connection of digital and real space—known as "hybrid reality games"—the themes of corporeality, cognition, and superimposed spatial perception become virulent. As such, a new urban game activism can be identified: one focused on bodily experience, cognition, and spatial experience. The phenomenon is slightly shifted through augmented reality, which has become standard on contemporary mobile phone devices. The political dimension of playing as a form of resistance poses a model for the future and stands for hope at the forefront of a new, meaningful play movement—which, last but not least, would also beget new fields of artistic research.

---

1 | The term "pervasive play" refers to playful experiences of everyday life, which take place in both physical and virtual spaces and are mediated by technology.

CTRL-SPACE: GAMES AS SIMULATION OF SPATIAL ORIENTATION IN INTERACTION SITUATIONS

The curator and game art researcher Stephan Schwingeler[2] points out that flow—the complete immersion in a game—only occurs in a longer, more emotionally-influenced perception of game content. Such touching subject matters are spatially located. In sum, the simulation of spatial orientation in situations of interaction is a special feature of computer games, as artistic artefacts in a "space machine":

This aspect of space is central to understanding computer games as a medium. Historically, since the game *Tennis for Two* in 1958, the computer game image has moved ever further into space—from simple, two-dimensional representations to highly complex, three-dimensional environments. [...] The subjective view of the user into the space of the computer game is called the arbitrary perspective. This new kind of gaze concludes the exploration of the computer game as a space machine.[3]

Schwingeler has also researched spatial perception in games.[4] From this point of view, spatial perception appears as equally interesting in games and art perception. As part of the groundbreaking game art exhibition he curated at the Karlsruher Zentrum für Medienkunst (ZKM) in 2014, Schwingeler shows a game by the artist group Jodi, *CTRL-Space* (2001) as a flat projection on a screen.[5] Tucked between two pillars of the high halls of this former industrial building, which now serves as an exhibition space, abstract lines become visible. They cut the game into its essential components. White lines and surfaces can be rotated and turned by the

---

2 | This section was originally published in my article "Kriegsspiele und kognitives Mapping. Sensomotorische Erfahrung und ihre spielerische Schärfung," in *Medien – Krieg – Raum*, ed. Lars Nowak (Paderborn: Fink Verlag, 2018), pp. 451–470.

3 | Stephan Schwingeler, *Die Raummaschine. Raum und Perspektive im Computerspiel* (Boizenburg: Werner Hülsbusch, 2008) p. 3.

4 | Stephan Schwingeler, *Kunstwerk Computerspiel – digitale Spiele als künstlerisches Material, Eine bildwissenschaftliche und medientheoretische Analyse* (Bielefeld: transcript, 2014), p. 53.

5 | New reference required and are now part of ZKMs permanent collection.

player, but do not permit perspective view or spatial experience. 3D becomes a surface. *LinX3D*, by Max Moswitzer and Margarete Jahrmann—in the original version of the same exhibition (Netcondition 2000)—uses a replica game console in the exhibition space to show similar surfaces that had been altered and cleared of space by circular feedback.[65] In this work, the artists transformed "unreal" shooter space into an aestheticized flat world, more reminiscent of constructivist and deconstructed pictorial worlds of abstract painting. Nevertheless, it was exhibited as a real arcade-style game console, in which visitors to the exhibition could become players between real and virtual spaces—which was then digitized in front of the console through a hidden camera.

As an experiential space, it was flat—but it could be experienced as a three-dimensional movement in space by means of the cursor joystick or the mouse, freely rotated in real space. 2D and 3D were thus linked in an endless feedback loop.

Fig. 100: Margarete Jahrmann and Max Moswitzer, LinX3D, Netcondition Raum, 2000

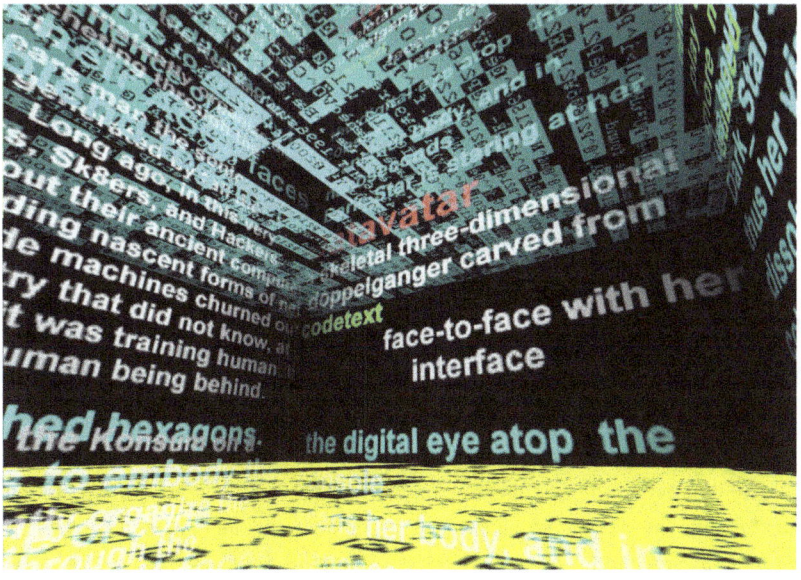

---

6 | The game console and flat-space screenshot for the *LinX3D* project can be accessed here: https://zkm.de/en/artwork/linx3d (accessed July 16, 2019).

Projected on a screen—no longer playable, and instead running in a loop, the game becomes reminiscent of a panel painting. In its reduced form, however, it is a cut that become visible—matching a cut into the surface of the canvas, like a protest against the art establishment. These cuts, entitled *Cuttings*, were spread in art history as an avant-garde technique, and also taken up in fashion, including the costumes of Ellio Petri's feature film *La Decima vittima* (1965)—in English, meaning "the tenth victim".[76] The plot of the movie is a game that society organizes. In a fictionalized future live TV game, the architecture of Rome is played to life and death. The climax of the film takes place in the ancient arena of the gladiators in Rome: the Colosseum. Interestingly, the game mechanics shown in the film are an anticipation of reality games as we know them from the productions of experimental theater groups, such as Sigma or Machina Ex. These occurred in the presence of real games and escape rooms, informed by game cultures. In *Decima vittima*, however, private spaces are connected with public architecture. In a shooter scene, the protagonist—the huntress, played by the Swiss actress Ursula Andress—shoots targets that resemble picture frames. She appears as a model in game clothing, with slits and cutouts in the scenography of a designer living room. Then, the wall of the room moves, and the old-fashioned living room of the parents of her opponent, played by Marcello Mastroiani, appears behind it. Spaces and times frame each other in this game film, staged as a game show. Erving Goffman's (1974) theory of framing becomes visible here directly in the image motif of a real-spatial game.[8] It refers to various cultural spaces of social play that spatialize themselves as systems of reference.

---

7 | In order to control human aggression and exploit it economically, governments and companies have developed a worldwide game show in the twenty-first century. "The Big Hunt" promises wealth and honor to the winner. A computer randomly selects players and turns them into hunters and victims. The hunters follow their victims around the world to kill them and move on to the next round. The victims are allowed to kill the hunters. The goal is to survive ten rounds: five as hunters, five as victims. See Robert Sheckley, *Das zehnte Opfer* (Bergish-Gladbach: Bastei Lübbe, 1985).

8 | Erving Goffman, *Frame Analysis: An Essay on the Organization of Experience* (New York NY: Harper & Row, 1974).

Fig. 101: Ellio Petri, La Decima Vittima, Photograph of Game Scenography Set Design, 1965

Artist Paolo Pedericini[97] compares works of game art with the works of American artist Gordon Matta-Clark (1943-1978), in which the artist creates large holes and cuts through existing architecture. At the edges of these interventions, the building's materials used become visible. The structure of this architecture thus becomes visible. In this sense, both game art works and Matta-Clark's *Cuttings* (1970s) reveal the underbelly of their respective systems.

---

9 | See the statement by artist Paolo Pedercini in: Schwingeler, 2014, p. 297.

Computer Game Space: Surface and Subsurface

In the Ph.D. thesis entitled *MODDING Künstlerische Forschung in Computerspielen*[10], which I supervised and which was defended in 2018, German game artist and theorist Thomas Hawranke argues how the architecture of "modding," or the creative change of computer games by players themselves, can be explained as a spatial structure. Referencing the early computer artist Frieder Nake, he describes the space of the computer game between surface and subsurface as two places in which the computer image is interpreted.[11] The algorithmic signal is processed on the subsurface—by the hardware—and the character is generated on the surface— on the visible interface. He chooses examples from the pioneering period of game art, which was characterized, above all, by the deconstruction of games and the experience of space. The aforementioned work *SOD*, by Jodi (1999), can also be interpreted according to these parameters. It shows the "inside" of a computer game; its invisible collision detectors and graphically-represented variables.[12] As Hawranke describes:

Figurative appearance and narration disappear and abstraction reveals how computer games actually work. Deprived of its stagings and atmospheres, SOD allows the viewer to perceive the underlying code that emerges through the simple geometric forms and visualizes the interplay of surface and subsurface.[13]

---

10 | Thomas Hawranke, "MODDING. Künstlerische Forschung in Computerspielen" (Ph.D. diss., Bauhaus-Universität Weimar, 2018), https://e-pub.uni-weimar.de/opus4/frontdoor/deliver/index/docId/3788/file/Hawranke_Thomas_Modding.pdf

11 | Frieder Nake, "Surface, Interface, Subface. Three cases of interaction and one concept," in *Paradoxes of Interactivity. Perspectives for Media Theory, Human-Computer Interaction, and Artistic Investigations*, eds. Uwe Seifert, Jin Hyun Kim, and Anthony Moore (Bielefeld: transcript, 2008), pp. 92–109, here p. 105.

12 | Pit Schultz, "Jodi als Software-Kultur," *Install.Exe – Jodi, [Plug In] Kunst und Neue Medien*, ed. Tilman Baumgärtel (Basel: Christoph Merian Verlag, 2002) pp. 31–39.

13 | Hawranke, 2018, p. 140.

This exciting approach of understanding space as the surface and subsurface of a technological object—a program that coincides with an artefact, simultaneously becoming the simulated and the simulacrum—will now be explained using examples from the artistic implementation of computer games as works of art in space. I will apply this approach to current hybrid games in the field of augmentation, be they in the city, part of a topographical experience, or in an exhibition space as a means of receiving art.

Fig. 102: David O'Reilly, Everything, Screenshot, 2017

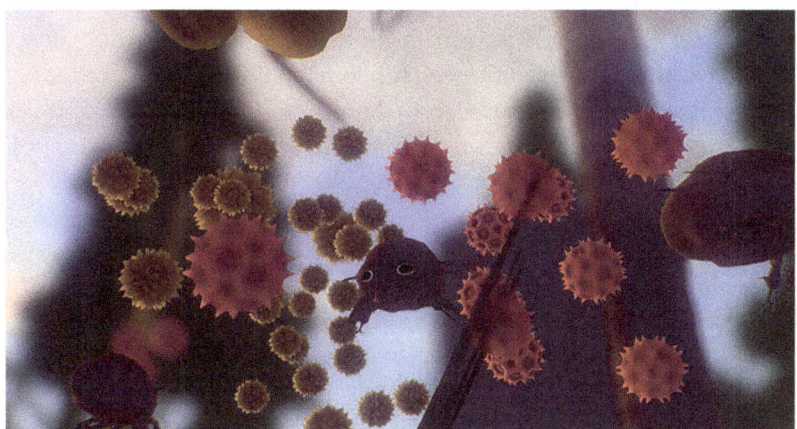

Starting Point: Walking Simulator

In games described as walking simulators, the perception of space remains fragmentary; the environment is explored, and possible courses of action are examined.[14] New concepts for navigation through three-dimensionally defined space are formulated in the critical practice of artistic modification of games—as cultural resistance to the established aesthetics of the game space as a space for action. Newly discovered interest in walking simulators within the independent game scene, as well as in the award-winning art world, can be discussed using the example of a multiple award-winning game: *Everything*, by the well-known 3D-animator David O'Reilly, was presented at the 2017 Berlin Film Festival and was

---

14 | Katie Salen Tekinbas and Eric Zimmerman, *Rules of Play. Game Design and Fundamentals* (Cambridge MA: MIT Press, 2003), p. 559.

awarded a prize at Ars Electronica.[15] It is a good example of a new artistic game that succeeds by allowing minimal action through pure spatial perception. In a flowing space, one constantly changes one's own form of identification and representation. Shifting scenarios and iridescent spaces, as well as a constantly-changing representation of one's own physicality, permit unorthodox interpretations of the fundamental conditions of being. Holistic philosophical content is conveyed through quotations by the philosopher Allan Watts, using his original voice. All of this results in a new sense of space in the game, defined by the form of artistic expression that refers to the realities of daily life, and the tropes and aesthetics of computer games. Thought patterns are tested in game flow and "creative flow," interpreted through current research into happiness and understanding contexts.[16] Meaning is processed from the absurd. The aim of the game is a walk toward insight and into fundamental questions of human existence, which extend from a micro-level of inner being into the macro-universe of perception.

REAL WALKING FLOW: AR GAMES IN ART SPACE

"Play, radically broken from a confined ludic time and space, must invade the whole of life. [...] play: the common creation of selected ludic ambiances. The central distinction that must be transcended is that established between play and ordinary life; play kept as an isolated and provisory exception."
Guy Debord, 1958[17]

---

15 | Everything is a beautiful interactive experience created by David O'Reilly, and narrated by the late, great philosopher Alan Watts. This PlayStation 4 and PC game lets you transform yourself into a thousand different things. Access more online: http://www.everything-game.com (accessed July 16, 2019).

16 | Mihaly Csikszentmihalyi, *Flow: The Psychology of Optimal Experience* (New York/London: Harper Perennial, 2008).

17 | Guy Debord, "Contribution to a Situationist Definition of Play," *Internationale Situationniste* No 1 (June 1958), trans. Reuben Keehan (Situationist International Online), http://www.cddc.vt.edu/sionline/si/play.html (accessed July 16, 2019).

Games, as a twentieth-century art form, are comparable to the political spatial games of Situationism. These performative games of twentieth-century century art were based on movements in real space, and defined public space as play space.[18] City maps acted as game-rule carriers, but did not correspond to the real topographies n which play was conducted. For example, a city map of London was used to stroll through Paris. It was a matter of connecting the maps with one's own psychological constitution. This is why the term "psychography" was introduced for these performance games in public space. These Situationist performances correspond to today's games in the form of "virtual cards"; these combine a fictitious reality with real topographies, by pretending to move through a narrative game space.

Augmented reality gaming in art can illuminate the relationship between spatial perception and computer games on different levels. Henry Jenkins, American cultural theorist and long-time director of the Comparative Media Studies Gamelab at the Massachusetts Institute of Technology (MIT), describes "game design as narrative architecture".[19] In the three-year international research project *Play and Prosume* (2013), we were able to investigate these interrelationships with an international team. The result was an augmented reality game exhibition installed in the Vienna Kunsthalle, in the form of a spatialized computer game.[20] The interplay of real space, walking, and research was specifically staged as a game plan for this exhibition. Researched content for individual monitoring and influencing was not only presented, but the exhibition itself was a tool for the research team. It was a test facility, aiming to obtain data on visitors touring the space. The game was played with mobile trays and an alternate reality application. Specially-developed textile patterns were transposed

---

18 | In the field of Situationist art from the twentieth century, such "inner maps" were created as automatic recordings of perceived movements. The founder of Situationist International, Guy Debord, advocated an activist definition of the game in his 1958 essay "A Situationist Definition of Play." See Debord, 1958.

19 | Electronic Book Review, review of Game Design as Narrative Architecture, by Henry Jenkins (October 7, 2004), http://electronicbookreview.com/essay/game-design-as-narrative-architecture/ (accessed July 16, 2019).

20 | See my personal website for further details: http://www.margaretejahrmann.net (accessed July 16, 2019).

into software codes. The aim of the game was to explore physical experience and knowledge generation.

Fig. 103: Play & Prosume, Augmented Reality Game, Kunsthalle Wien,
Photograph of Exhibition, 2013

The physical experience of space through the exploration of topographies in motion was also introduced into the experimental urban gaming scene by Katie Salen (2003), with her project *Big Urban Games.*[21] As a reference of my own—which I allow myself as a practical theorist who is herself active in artistic game design—I would like to cite a series of urban games

---

21 | The *Big Urban Game* was commissioned by the Design Institute of the University of Minnesota as a part of its Twin Cities Design Celebration, with the goal of encouraging the residents of Minneapolis and St. Paul to see their surroundings in a new way, and to think about the design of urban space. See Margarete Jahrmann "The Big Urban Game, Re-Play and Full city tags: Art game conceptions in activism and performance," in *Performing the Digital. Performativity and Performance Studies in Digital Cultures*, eds. Martina Leeker, Immanuel Shipper and Timon Beyes (Bielefeld: transcript, 2016), pp. 171–188. https://www.transcript-verlag.de/978-3-8376-3355-9/performing-the-digital/ (accessed July 16, 2019).

by the Ludic Society Collective.[22] The project served to promote hybrid and artistic urban games, which were performed at international media art festivals. The game performances were documented in a series of magazines, the *Ludic Society Magazines*, which can be downloaded online. This game, which combined technology and real spatial experience into a form of pervasive game, was based on the concept of situated play.[23] Hybrids of virtual technologies and physical realities allowed the testing of real experiential game architecture. As precursors to the commercialized application of hybrid augmented reality games in urban space, such as *Pokémon Go*, they can be found in among society in contemporary works of game art. Examples include the group Blast Theory, with groundbreaking works like *Can You See Me Now* or *Uncle Roy Is All Around You*. An excellent example of this is the current urban game by Blast Theory, entitled *A Cluster of 17 Cases* (2019).[24]

In contemporary games by groups oriented more toward theater, such as *machina eX* or *Invisible Playground*, fictional computer games are retold as real-spatial experiences, in order to explore a gray area between game design and participatory art. Such modulations of cause and effect, in technologically expanded environments where simulation and reality overlap, and where real space and play space become one, can be discovered more and more frequently in such theatrically staged games today. The purpose of *Invisible Playground* is described as follows:

By referencing playful traditions like video games and sports, we connect to something known and remix it to something new and one-of-a-kind. Our games are post-digital. They use technology, but know of the power of bodies in shared spaces and at a specific site. By creating games that make stories and histories of places and very different people playable,

22 | See this link to the Ludic Society for further information: http://ludic-society.net (accessed July 16, 2019).

23 | See Akira Baba, "Situated Play" *Conference of DiGRA*, the Digital Games Research Association (September 24-28, 2007, Tokyo, Japan).

24 | Blast Theory, "A Cluster of 17 Cases" (New York NY/Hong Kong: Museum of the City of New York, September, 2018-January 2019), https://www.blasttheory.co.uk/projects/a-cluster-of-17-cases/ (accessed July 16, 2019).

we aspire to contribute to the development of play as a cultural technique and an art.[25]

Prior to these productions, however, there were games that directly connected theater and urban space. These included the game *Evening of the Ludic Society* (2007) by Max Moswitzer, René Bauer, Olli Leino, Doris C. Rusch, and F.E. Rakuschan, among others, which was presented as *Import Export Game* at the Dutch Electronic Arts Festival in Rotterdam.[26] Evenings at the renowned Rotheater Rotterdam, a play was performed that refined a new way of experiencing urban space. Staged as a psycho-therapy-oriented setting—with a carpet over a couch borrowed from Sigmund Freud's original practice—a renowned game theoretician from MIT Gamelab, Dr. Carmen Rusch, led a conversation with her game-addicted friend whom she had learned to love in Ultima Online.

Fig. 104: Evening of the Ludic Society, RFID Tagging Game, Rotheater Rotterdam, 2007

25 | See Invisible Playground, "Games," http://www.invisibleplayground.com/en/category/games (accessed July 16, 2019).

26 | See "The Evening of the Ludic Society," DEAF07 (Rotterdam: Ro heater, April 12, 2007) https://v2.nl/events/the-evening-of-the-ludic-society (accessed July 16, 2019).

For about half of the season, after an introduction and lectures, half of the audience was invited outside into the surrounding urban space. In front of a half-empty theater hall, the performance continued in parallel on stage. The players in the city were equipped with mobile phones and had to carry out orders in small groups, which did allowed the individual players to remain in this immersive social experience. However, the urban space was perceived differently: as play space. On the stage, with an old Bakelite telephone, calls from the players were answered. Accompanied by an operator, they placed objects in the real space of the next street and found them again on a predefined area near the theater. Using radio frequency technology (RFID)—which at the time had become as omnipresent as the Internet of Things—everyday objects such as cups and glasses in pubs were marked. These everyday objects thus became objects of knowledge in the game, artefacts. They could be read as "objects of desire," like in the Import/Export game for game-capable phones—specifically, Nokias, which were already equipped with near-frequency readers (NFC) by 2007. This resulted in a form of technological augmentation with the help of RFID technology, which, of course, was not intended to be used this way by those who initiated the technologies. However, it led to the introduction of the spatial perception of the city as game architecture. But what role does the human condition—the physical and mental constitution of the players—play?

BODILY ARCHITECTURE AND SPATIAL EXPERIENCE: COGNITIVE MAPPING THROUGH VIRTUAL GAME SPACES

Recently, a new "cut" has been made into the architecture of the body. Biofeedback games and self-optimization applications collect data and generate a fictitious form of bodily architecture. The mapping of movement patterns creates a psychogeographic representation of individual movements in space, which then generates a sort of "data body," which must constantly be optimized. Features of mobile interfaces, such as gyro sensors and geographic mapping, are used to collect data about an individual—and then to generate an "architecture of the self" within the context of the game. Coupled with direct bodily interfaces, such as the Apple Watch and mobile biofeedback sensors, the innermost self and its data become part of new urban spaces.

Games provide the advantage of what is known as "motivational design," meaning the active consent of a person to have their data collected in order to allegedly improve one's physical well-being. As with all health-related positive aspects of self-measurement, there are also justified criticisms of the quantified self, and of the obvious topic how personal data is financialized.[27] In contrast, the potential of art as activism is represented by many works of game art.[28] Elements of the virtual game can be used as experimental stimuli in real space-time experiments. An example of this is the installation *I Want to See Monkeys*, shown at the 2017 Ars Electronica exhibition entitled *AI*. In a performative setting, this work combines elements of artificial intelligence, artificial neural networks, and the dramaturgical *mis en scène* of a neuroscience laboratory. The structural coupling of methods and disciplines offers a new form of discourse in the public sphere of art on the stage of game art exhibitions.

The cognitive mapping of spatial realities associated with a spatial experience must be considered separately in hybrid games of the augmented reality genre. At the 2016 Berlin Bernstein Conference, neuroscientist Daphne Bavelier presented a study that demonstrates the importance of computer games for spatial perception, as well as the corresponding potential to train cognitive abilities in stressful situations.[29] Software testing the detection of three-dimensional objects in moving environments, by utilizing a computer model, was completed by participants who had previously achieved the highest scores playing the computer game *Call of Fortress* ten hours a week. Bavelier calls increasing these skills through three-dimensional action games "brain-boosting." The neurophysiological formulation of internal representations of space, based on the recording of spatial information through multiple sensory impressions, is a promising future field of investigation—especially in regard to the connection between real spatial and virtual game worlds. Experiences of movement in virtual space, however, can only be interpreted as perceptions of move-

27 | Simon   Schaupp,   *Digitale   Selbstüberwachung.   Self-Tracking   im kybernetischen Kapitalismus* (Heidelberg: Verlag Graswurzelrevolution, 2016).

28 | Molleindustria and Blast Theory are examples of this. See their websites: http://www.molleindustria.org and https://www.blasttheory.co.uk (accessed July 16, 2019).

29 | Daphne Bavelier and C. Shawn Green, "The Brain-Boosting Power of Videogames," *Scientific American* 315, no. 1 (July 2016), pp. 26–31, here p. 26.

ment to a limited extent, since some forms of sensory input are missing in comparison to physical movement, which contains all sensory feedback mechanisms.[30]

Fig. 105: Margarete Jahrmann and Stefan Glasauer, I Want to See Monkeys, Area7lab, installation, Ars Electronica, 2017

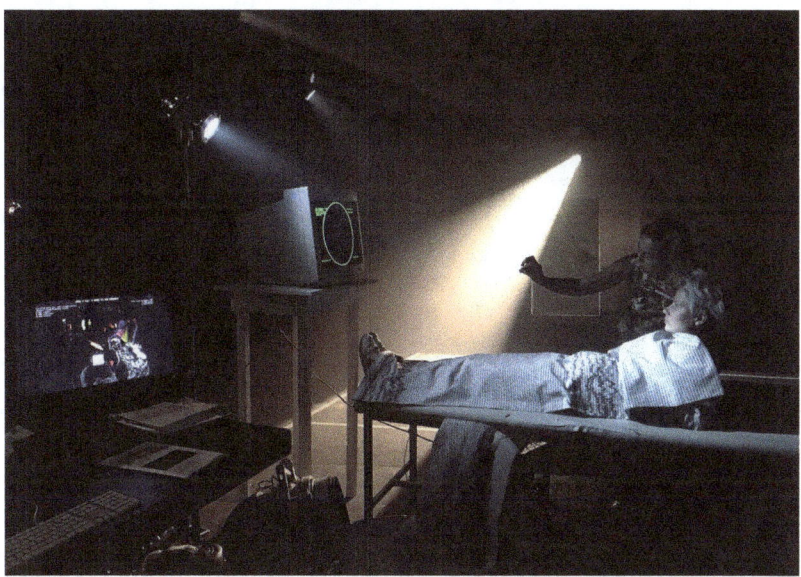

Thus, cognitive representations and abilities derived thereof are only obtained by a movement reduced into one or more components. The strategies conveyed in hybrid games demonstrate, however, how an individual not only performs representative actions in the game, but even becomes capable of action in concrete geographical reality. This connection should

30 | As described by Jeffrey Taube, Stephane Valerio, and Ryan Yoder: "[...] when participants perform a virtual navigation task in a scanner, they are lying motionless in a supine position while viewing a video monitor. Here, we provide evidence that spatial orientation and navigation rely to a large extent on locomotion and its accompanying activation of motor, vestibular, and proprioceptive systems." See Jeffrey Taube, Stephane Valerio, and Ryan Yoder, "Is Navigation in Virtual Reality with fMRI Really Navigation?" *Journal of Cognitive Neuroscience* XXV/7 (July 2013), pp. 1008–1019, here p. 1018.

be investigated further—in games, using extended body interfaces as an artistic research practice.

Play the City

Dungeons and Dragons for Cities

Ekim Tan

Games are as old as society, yet when a spatial designer enters the world of games, a new world opens—bright with novelty and possibility, a relatively unexplored instrument for shaping spaces that are more meaningful to humans. How much can an architect or an urbanist learn from games? Can games teach them about trust and ownership, as platforms with transparent rules valid for everyone, and with common goals? Can games teach them about learning and engagement, having fun with strangers while constantly being challenged individually and collectively? Can games teach them about training and strategizing for the real world, as they fail but are allowed the chance to restart? Can games teach them about communication and avoiding jargon, with their effective visual environment and simple language?

From IBM's *CityOne* (2010) to Will Wright's *SimCity* (1989), and from Richard Duke's *Metropolis* (1969) to Buckminster Fuller's *World Game* (1961), a long list of games are predicated on cities in their staging, or these games take place directly in real urban areas. Some, as single-player games, run on predefined algorithms and quantitative feedback loops; others provide a multiplayer environment. Rules for the organization and composition of cities emerge from negotiations among multiple actors; an open system where new rules can be invented or unused rules abandoned, rather than a closed game with a predefined algorithm, are particularly promising for spatial designers.

Perhaps better than a city-themed game, an environment that can be modified by the players could be useful in the pursuit of spatial designers learning from video games—environments that can host a wide range of players and do not focus on winning or losing, but rather, on building experience and partnerships as their rewards. At first glance, *Dungeons and Dragons* (1974), a role-playing and story-building adventure game, seems to have little to do with urban development, yet it could serve as a game system for trying to understand and develop cities. This was the case for the game-evaluation method which was invented for the 2009 Play the City project, implemented by a serious gaming company focusing on the research and development of urban spaces.

Fig. 106: Play the City, Circular Amsterdam Game, 2016

Not one person controls urban development processes, but many "players" influence them. In *Dungeons and Dragons* (D&D), there are many characters, each with unique properties. They come together to build a collective adventure and carry out careful research before they meet to play; for instance, they determine the era and location of the adventure, their character's powers, and who they need to supplement to reach their goals.

The ability to build several unique, personal stories, which can be based on data and players' knowledge, is the most striking property of *Play the City's* games. Similar to the setup of D&D, we introduced a wide range of city-maker roles and specific influences on our city game. Both the usual and unusual suspects of urban development were included, with powers ranging from unlocking legal rules or finding investments, to mobilizing crowds, shaping streets and squares, vetoing speculations, calculating carbon dioxide reductions, and so forth. As the game system matures, we have observed that more realistic and applicable outcomes are achieved when players act out their everyday, real-life roles in the game. As in D&D, play becomes much more advanced when players already know about their mission and conditions, yet are given the chance to develop, expand, and apply an evolving understanding of their roles in an interactive, creative setting with other players.

After achieving a meta-game structure, the *Play the City* method has been adapted for dozens of city challenges. This includes topics and locations such as urban renewal in Rotterdam, circulation in Amsterdam, township development in Cape Town, urban transformation in Istanbul, economic transition in Shenzhen, affordable housing in Dublin, urban safety in The Hague, mass-migration in Europe, mobility in Marmara Region. The list continues to grow.

Fig. 107: Play the City, Affordable Housing Game, 2018

JUST A GAME, IS IT?

Our *Play the City* team, comprising many architects experimenting with gaming as a design method, is thrilled to have discovered a world with many new avenues to explore. However, we are aware that we have entered risky territory. Conservative decision-makers preoccupied with securing predictable results in the field of urban planning are particularly threatened. The first meeting we managed to schedule—a meeting with the alderman of Amsterdam's Noord borough—was particularly memorable. Looking back, I realize that he was doing his best by spending time with young urbanists, who argued that they could help him reactivate a stalled master plan by playing a city game. Listening to our city-gaming pitch left him quite puzzled, but still he decided to finance and join the game.

However, convincing his project office of the process, or our colleagues who designed the master plan, was even more difficult. The office's technical advisors responsible for the project refused to join the game or to discuss alternatives outside the walls of their office. At the time, it was not uncommon for planners to think: "It is just a game, and we do not comprehend the real purpose of a game in such serious matters." Was it correct to spend their time on a game, when no one knew what the outcome would be? Confrontations with our colleagues at city halls proved to be a real challenge over the years. While delving into the world of games had been enriching and eye-opening, we faced an image problem. Was it really a good idea to call our method a game? "Playing games with someone" is considered manipulative, and "playing the game" refers to someone who acts a part. Not only in English, but most languages, have similar, suspicious phrasing regarding games. As we have introduced our method to cities around the world, we remain surprised to see how comparable the jokes cracked about gaming are, each and every time.

GAMES IN REALITY, REALITY IN GAMES

At the heart of the matter lies a tension between reality and gaming. How close and how distant are the "game world" and the "real world" from one another? Can they influence each other's progress? I believe the key to explaining how games can perform as real-world problem solvers lies in the particular ways that games and reality connect. There are several ways the two relate:

The most common relation is when games conduct their fictional narrative in an environment the player recognizes from real life; for example, when the popular video games *Grand Theft Auto III* and *IV* (200/2008) depict New York City. Thanks to its realistic rendering, a New Yorker notices particular details about their city, while a teenager from Amsterdam would be able orient himself upon first arrival in New York. Today, gaining familiarity with complex subjects without even being conscious of them is effectively used as an entertaining learning mechanism.

A more direct link to reality is using gaming to fix a real problem, while simultaneously exploiting its escapism. Games can remain fictional, but the very act of playing the game will alter aspects of reality. A telling example of this relationship comes from the ancient Greek era, when, in order to survive a severe famine that lasted eighteen years, King Croesus of Lydia ordered everyone to indulge in games on one day and eat or work on the next.

Game dynamics can be introduced into real life, as with Nike's running application: a digital interface encourages users to exercise regularly to improve their health, and then congratulates them for it. Thus, the game is introduced through feedback loops into an individual's life. It can also connect these players with each other, to make the daily workout more fun and engaging, and less tiring and boring.

Games can be constructed in alternate realities to help initiate real life challenges. This can be done by taking real-life quests, such as global warming, migration, or inequality, and changing some of their conditions to generate what-if scenarios. Reminiscent of Buckminster Fuller's *World Peace Game*, in which all nation-state borders disappear, players can trade world resources and move freely. By altering the condition of country borders, the game is able to show that the deadlock is not scarcity, but rather, an unfair distribution of resources. Hence, a more equitable and peaceful world becomes not only visible, but also possible, by testing out alternatives.

Last but not least, a real-life challenge can be introduced into a game (i.e. the reverse of the third kind of relation). Thus, in safe gaming environments, testing and mastering collaborative solutions becomes possible. Real actors can play through out-of-the-box solutions, while mistakes can be made and learned from, in order to potentially reduce risks.

As such, games can be inserted into reality and reality into games. Whether games are constructed as an aspiration resembling the real world, or built to escape from it or fix it, they are a reality for those who play them, and games can influence their lives in the ways elaborated above. New theories of play, such as those from the literature on pervasive and ambient gaming, bring games right into the heart of the real world, blurring the boundaries of Johan Huizinga's (1872-1945) "magic circle." In her groundbreaking book *Reality is Broken*, Jane McGonigal invited everyone to design games to repair reality.[1] Almost every day, a new game emerges for education, in the health sector, the defense industry, entertainment business, personal development, and for making more open, collaborative cities.

Among the five mechanisms relating games to reality, *Play the City's* gaming method is most closely aligned with the final category. All city games are modeled on real urban challenges and are played by their actual stakeholders. In this model, by playing, responsible actors train for reality by considering and testing various options, or by making mistakes in the game environment. This allows them to avoid them, and articulate wiser decisions for widely negotiated urban processes, in the real world. The game helps generate collaborative solutions to collectively defined questions. During this process, the understanding of games as escapism is slowly shifting towards a playful confrontation with reality.

Fig. 108: Play the City Gaming Method

1 | Jane McGonigal, *Reality is Broken: Why Games Makes us Better and How They Can Change the World* (New York, NY: The Penguin Press, 2011).

NEW HORIZONS FOR CITY GAMING

What began as a simple design experiment with students slowly evolved into a mature and authentic city-making methodology, practiced daily at the *Play the City* office. Today, city games are becoming more and more prevalent in the everyday work of policy-makers, regulators, urban designers, smart-city experts, and architects. A decade ago, many local government agencies in the Netherlands would have been puzzled if they were advised to work with games. Using applied city games as a tool to resolve complex urban development processes was simply too unfamiliar.

Although it is not yet a mainstream practice, cities are now inviting game designers to come up with their own urban challenges to tackle with city gaming. Since 2010, several cities in the Netherlands—Amsterdam, Utrecht, The Hague, Almere, Eindhoven, among others—have increasingly been applying the city-gaming method to their own contextual challenges. Apart from *Play the City's* work, talented young designers are working on developing new city-gaming techniques and championing the method with clients unfamiliar to gaming, such as encouraging large, conservative construction companies to guide early design processes with city games. Another striking example of this is that city-game designers now occupy full-time positions in strategic planning departments at the local, provincial, and national levels. Besides progress with the Dutch government, well-respected academic institutions in the Netherlands have also been integrating gaming into their curricula and their architectural design methods, such the *Why Factory* at the Technical University of Delft.

Academic institutions worldwide have also been exploring the potential of game-based research and design in their educational curricula, including the ETH Zurich and MIT Media Lab, developing their own city-game methods and interfaces. Beyond the more well-known objectives of learning and education, cities are also beginning to play games to address complex and pressing urban challenges, channeling innovative solutions. In November 2016, the Mayor of Hamburg hired a game called *Finding-Places* to respond to a large and rapid influx of refugees in the city, engaging residents to co-develop a strategic settlement plan proposal through a hybrid game interface, which was then put to the City's planning department for approval. City-gaming methods are emerging and evolving with increasing frequency, often alongside technological advances, employing the collective intelligence of experts and non-experts toward more informed and sustainable city-making solutions. A comprehensive, world-wide overview of city-games is mapped on the *Games for Cities* platform. From Boston to Bangalore, Moscow to Istanbul, Shenzhen to Sydney, and Cape Town to Nairobi, city games are tackling complex urban issues through the active engagement of their people.

Fig. 109: A Collection of Worldwide City-Games

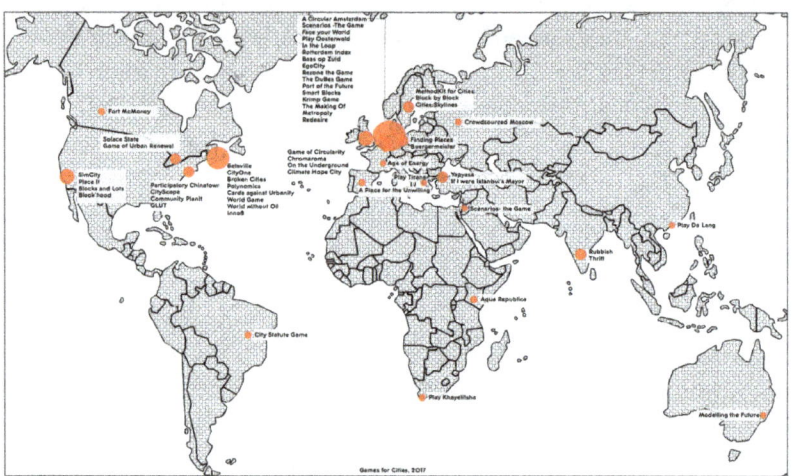

These games address common challenges of urban planning departments, such as delivering affordable housing, providing quality public spaces, preventing water scarcities and floods, developing ports sustainably, maintaining urban safeties, adapting to a circular economy, mitigating climate change, and accommodating increased migration flows. Across the spectrum of city-game topics, games and urban planning share two common properties: they require a combination of multiple experts and kinds of tacit knowledge, and are concerned with a highly diverse set of stakeholders, who require effective communication and cooperation in order for successful outcomes to emerge. While capable of distilling and interpreting knowledge from all players, the expertise involved is necessary to carry proposals forward, transforming collective ideas into uniquely tailored solutions.

An interesting future step would be linking games with distinct topics to one another, as an inter-operable platform of games, each tackling their own city-making elements in a system and plugging into one another. Imagine if a game about the circular economy could feed back into the affordable housing game, and could receive input from the urban transformation game, and so on. A number of players active in the flood game are relevant to the circular economy game, and stakeholders that focus on urban development in the circular economy game could provide input to corresponding game sessions in the affordable housing arena. A connected and layered set of city games could thus facilitate exponential increases to creativity and collective solution-making. I believe there is significant untapped potential in future attempts that would try build a circular system of games, in which the players and their decisions in one game can act as input to another game, increasing the complexity of each individual game (and its topic of inquiry) as the input is enriched and become more nuanced.

Just as the challenges that can be addressed by city-gaming diversify, the technologies that support gaming interfaces also vary greatly and evolve rapidly. City games running on digital game engines provide 2D and 3D geographic visualizations, and produce real-time, data-driven software simulations. This property is superior to conventional analog games, in terms of the quantity of data that can be processed before and during game sessions. However, fully digital game environments have come under scrutiny for the individualist nature of play, as well as their limited capacity for building trust, due to a lack of interaction between players and the emergent qualities of such interactions. Individual players are isolated in analyzing and interpreting the large sum of data with which they are interacting, unable to remold their own perspectives based on others, or to contribute towards shared narratives. This divide need not be so black and white. Hybrid games can employ both analog and digital components, formulating an optimal mix of their respective attributes, as appropriate for each specific challenge and context. While analog 3D-environments, which are modeled with game blocks based on real urban geographies, help players interact face-to-face and negotiate on solutions, 3D scanners and software tailored to urban simulations read the color and height information from physical model, depicting land use, square-meter price, density, parking, and so forth. This technology fosters increased and accelerated opportunities for making sense of complex datasets, and generating responsive, real-time feedback on player moves.

Technology is also transforming the pervasiveness of city games, accessing players in public spaces, or even in their own homes. For example, in a playful public space experiment in Istanbul, RFID scanners transformed local public transport cards into digital voting devices for a public poll. When used correctly, in this sort of way, technology can increase the social, economic, and political inclusivity of active engagement strategies. On top of this, digitally integrated gameplay decisions can be embedded within social media platforms to engage a wider community, as well as to support the systematic recording of game outcomes. Engaging online communities not physically present during the "game" can generate valuable external commentary and discussion regarding a game's outcomes, and potentially even trigger face-to-face meetings between interested parties. Hybrid systems that link digital and analog game elements have the potential to achieve a better integration between game interfaces and real-world planning and city-making.

Fig. 110: If I were the Mayor of Istanbul

The *Games for Cities* database provides the necessary evidence that city games are considered an effective method of engagement for collaborative city-making. As it continues to become more widely accepted, we expect its instruments to spread, variegate, and mature. While it would not be wise to claim that it can guarantee solutions, city-gaming has the potential to go beyond traditional planning methods when intense and effective communication is called for, when complexity is high due to the involved parties, or when a conflict needs to be taken into account in planning and designing. For technically complicated cases—such as urban development according to circular economy logic—or for integrating different disciplines, games prove to be effective as a common language that all disciplines can relate to, and appropriate to serve their own means. Inaccessible, "expert" jargon is removed from the debate, and relayed to players as a form of tangible and tractable logic to be played with. Knowing the strengths of games, as well as appropriate combinations of digital and analog components, and using them accordingly, is key to successfully applying the method. Empirical research on implementing games as tools for addressing city-making challenges is rather sparse, as it is a relatively new field of inquiry. Simply put, more research is required, entailing the careful and continuous observation of games and analyses of their outcomes. This will allow the method to become more accurate and assertive, in regard to the benefits that games possess for urban development processes.

The horizons for city-gaming as a method will continue to expand, as long as there remains a need to involving people in conversations about their city. However, the evolution of this approach is also dependent on more young and innovative designers joining this movement; they must convince open-minded cities to implement this method for urban challenges globally, and apply the right combination of analog and digital elements for their individual contexts and objectives. This is also an imperative step in contesting preconceived notions of gaming as "not serious enough" a method for serious urban issues. There is some progress in this regard, with city officials becoming increasingly likely to embrace gaming as a relevant, interactive, fun-but-serious, and effective planning tool. While it may be too early to declare city-gaming as an established method for engaging with urban development, there is no doubt that the method is gaining ground. We need to adapt our methods of inquiry to suit a new generation of regulators and policymakers—ones born into a world that not only contains, but is reshaped by, the likes of *Minecraft* (2009), *Pokemon Go* (2016) and *Foursquare* (2009) on a daily basis. Interactive digital maps, 3D-virtual environments, and multiplayer settings are simply the new media and technologies through which an entire generation perceives the urban world. Imagine a future where cities are modeled, tested, designed, and reshaped through interactive, collaborative games. At *Play the City*, we are working towards creating this future. This generation's city officials will not need convincing: they will speak the language of games and they will play to plan their cities.

Democracy, Video Games, and Urban Design

Minecraft as a Public Participation Tool

James Delaney

Participation in urban design is essential to creating inclusive, sustainable and democratic cities. The creation of public space, in particular, should involve those whom that space will serve at some point, or else it is unlikely to meet their needs and interests. Young people, as a demographic group, face an additional challenge in this area. They are often under-represented in the planning process, resulting in political alienation as well as the creation of city spaces that do not sufficiently address their needs.

Our cities are growing at an unprecedented rate, as is the proportion of young people within those cities. By 2030, it is estimated that sixty percent of the world's population will be living in cities—and by the same year, sixty percent of urban dwellers will be under the age of eighteen due to rapid population growth, especially in Africa, despite ageing trends in high-income and medium-income countries.[1] Additionally, there has been a dramatic increase in access to the internet. Worldwide, fifty percent of the population was online as of 2017.[2] In this context, the importance of participation in urban design and governance—and youth participation,

---

1 | United Nations Department of Economic and Social Affairs, Population Division, *World Population Prospects: The 2015 Revision* (July 2015), https://www.un.org/en/development/desa/publications/world-population-prospects-2015-revision.html (accessed May 28, 2018), p. 7.

2 | International Telecommunications Union, *ICT Facts and Figures* (2017). https://www.itu.int/en/ITU-D/Statistics/Documents/factsICTFactsFigures2017.pdf (accessed May 28, 2018), p. 2.

in particular—cannot be overstated. In this chapter, I propose that information and communication technology (ICT), and more specifically the computer game *Minecraft* (2009), can both improve and facilitate public engagement in the planning process, unlike traditional consultation processes.

DIGITAL ENGAGEMENT

The ICT revolution has transformed the way in which both individuals and communities communicate, interact, and engage. Youth are at the center of this technological revolution and are twice as likely to be online than the global population. This gap is even more pronounced in developing countries, where youths are three times more likely to be online than the general population.[3]

This shift in methods of communication has generated both a need and an opportunity to change the way in which we engage, and how we invite the people that the built environment serves to participate.[4] According to Michael Kohn, CEO of the online participation platform *Stickyworld*, this opportunity comes at a time when three trajectories align. Firstly, the "user experience" has become mainstream—meaning the success and viability of all products, services, and processes are now underpinned by good design and ease-of-use, without which people quickly disengage. Secondly, the internet and open data have transformed information access, allowing users to be informed about and engaged with any topic relevant to them, wherever they go. Thirdly, the resurgence of localized legislation and devolved decision-making power (particularly regarding the built environment) has helped authorities to understand and engage

---

3 | Daniella Ben-Attar and Tim Campbell, *Urban Governance and Youth, Report 4: Global Youth-Led Development Report Series* (Nairobi: UN-Habitat, 2015), http://www.youthpolicy.org/wp-content/uploads/library/2012_ICT_Urban_ Governance_Youth_Eng1.pdf (accessed May 28, 2018) p. 5.
4 | Michael Kohn, *Designing Democracy and Democratising Design* (London: The Design Commission, 2015) https://s3-eu-west-1.amazonaws.com/dcfw-cdn/Designing_Democracy_Inquiry-March-20151.pdf (accessed May 28, 2018), p. 77-78.

with citizens on a granular level.[5] As a result, the need and potential to use digital solutions for public consultation is greater than ever. The most commonly used and most thoroughly studied digital solutions come in two forms: the use of online platforms or virtual discussion forums, and the use of virtual reality and visualization technology.

Virtual reality (VR) technology has generated the widest range of possibilities for visualization within the decision-making process. Given its use in many different contexts, it is tricky to provide a precise definition of this technology. Aukstakalnis and Blatner determined a general definition of VR in 1992: "Virtual Reality is a way for humans to visualise, manipulate and interact with computers and extremely complex data".[6] Since then, the field of VR has experienced massive growth with the development of computer and graphics technology, in particular, the graphics cards of personal computers. Thanks to this technology, VR devices can now simulate a fully immersive and interactive environment—and more importantly, provide the capacity to explore this environment as a user would in real life. There are two benefits of VR for public consultation: firstly, creating a more realistic (and neutral) presentation for members of the public to experience the existing and proposed situation; secondly, on a higher level, it offers enhanced interaction, such as the ability for citizens to offer comments on a virtual model—a kind of "digital graffiti" inscribed into the existing and proposed environments.[7]

While mature VR-software has been specifically developed for 3D city-model representations and for urban planning, most software is reserved for professionals, and lacks even the most basic public consultation features. The most accessible and easy-to-use VR technology has, instead, been developed by the computer game industry, which now leads the market in the development and production of VR technology. Currently, at least ninety percent of all content built for VR is created with the video

---

5 | Ibid., p. 78.

6 | Steve Aukstakalnis and David Blatner, *Silicon Mirage: The Art & Science of Virtual Reality* (Berkeley CA: Peachpit Press Inc., 1992).

7 | T.L.J. Howard and Nicolas Gaborit, "Using Virtual Environment Technology to Improve Public Participation in Urban Planning Process," *Journal of Urban Planning and Development*, Vol. 133, Nr. 4 (2007), pp. 1–28.

game engine *Unity*.[8] In 2016, Microsoft released a new version of *Minecraft* specifically tailored for VR, such that users could experience existing *Minecraft* environments as VR environments, as well as design new ones using the software. Although this was an expected and seemingly obvious development for Microsoft, the consequence of this version was, arguably, to make *Minecraft* the most effective and easily available participatory design tool on the market—one that combines the social networking and communication aspects of online discussion forums with the immersion and interactivity of virtual environments used in VR technology.

DESIGN AND PLAY

> "For, to mince matters no longer, man only plays when he is in the fullest sense of the word a human being, and he is only fully a human being when he plays."
> Friedrich Schiller, 1794[9]

There is a rich history of using games and play for serious tasks, and significant literature upon which this idea is founded. Our philosophical understanding of games and play has been elaborated upon by many thinkers—Schiller's sentiment is echoed by Johan Huizinga's (1872-1945) *Homo Ludens* (1938) in which he presents play not as an aspect of culture, but culture itself as a manifestation of play.[10] Roger Caillois' (1913-1978) *Man, Play and Games* (1958)[11], and Jean Piaget's (1986-1980) *Play, Dreams and Imitation in Childhood* (1945) also provide insight into games and play

---

8 | John Gaudiosi, "This company dominates the VR business, and it's not named Oculus," *Fortune online* (March 19, 2015), http://fortune.com/2015/03/19/unity-virtual-reality/ (accessed March 19, 2018).

9 | Friedrich Schiller, *On the aesthetic education of a man in a series of letters* [1794], fifteenth letter, ed. and transl. by Elizabeth M. Wilkison and L.A. Willoughby (Oxford: Clarendon Press, 1967), p. 107.

10 | Johan Huizinga, *Homo Ludens: A Study of Play-Element in Culture* [1938] (Abingdon: Routledge & Kegan Paul, 1949).

11 | Roger Caillois, *Man, Play and Games* [1958] (New York: Free Press of Glencoe, 1961).

from the perspectives of philosophy, sociology, and psychology, revealing a wide range of possible uses for games in real-life tasks.[12]

The importance of play in creative processes was truly appreciated by the founders of the Bauhaus: Weimar, Germany's iconic, modernist school. One of the school's professors, László Moholy-Nagy (1895-1946) played a crucial role in understanding the relationship between play and creativity—and the importance of maintaining the spirit of play that is lost in adulthood. As he describes: "The method is to keep in the work of the grown-up the sincerity of emotion, the truth of observation, the fantasy and creativeness of the child".[13] The work of Moholy-Nagy, among others, identifies play as one of the most important companions of creativity, and an essential element of the creative problem-solving process.

Among the many reasons for play's value in creativity is its self-rewarding nature. Playing games is an autotelic experience, engendering positive emotions that provide the motivation to solve creative problems. Psychologist Mihály Csikszentmihályi (*1934) describes this as "the optimal experience of flow"—the enjoyable experience of creative activity that induces "an almost automatic, effortless, yet highly focused state of consciousness".[14]

Another benefit of play as a creative process is that the cost of failure in games is typically low. In the context of design, the "safe space" created by games provides an opportunity to experiment and test design ideas without fear of criticism of failure. Ambiguity is also an important aspect of play. By its very nature, play involves uncertainty—the play theorist Brian Sutton-Smith (1924-2015) explains how the ambiguous nature of play removes the constraints of what we know to be possible, allowing us to explore creative possibilities that would otherwise be suppressed by the limits of reality.[15] In the design process, play stimulates associations between elements, which are usually disparate. In other words, play results

---

12 | Jean Piaget, Play, *Dreams, and Imitation in Childhood* [1945] (New York NY: W.W. Norton & Co., Inc., 1962).

13 | László Moholy-Nagy, *The New Vision* (New York: W.W. Norton & Co., Inc., 1938), pp. 20–21.

14 | Mihály Csikszentmihályi, *Creativity: Flow and the Psychology of Discovery and Invention* (New York NY: Harper Collins Publishers, 1996), p. 110.

15 | Brian Sutton Smith, *The Ambiguity of Play* (Cambridge MA: Harvard University Press, 1997).

in things being put together in new ways—thus making the designer aware of new ideas and creative solutions.

The links between design and play are well established. However, the question that remains is which methods and types of play are most beneficial to the design process. I believe that the computer game *Minecraft* best suits this task; specifically, it contains intrinsic features that render it useful for the design process in the context of public consultations.

MINECRAFT AND PUBLIC PARTICIPATION

The easiest way to describe *Minecraft* is as a form of "digital Lego." It is a "sandbox game," an open world without a pre-determined course for players to follow. The player makes up their own rules and can play the game in any way they wish. It is also a "voxel world." Voxels are 3D pixels—the entire *Minecraft* universe is generated upon a 3D grid and made up of blocks, which can be placed or destroyed by the player. Crucially, players can animate these blocks, or add characters and objects—all of which the player can interact with. The versatility of *Minecraft* allows new games and fully interactive experiences to be created within the game, which challenges us to consider *Minecraft* as a game design tool rather than a game itself.

Fig. 111: Mojang AB/Microsoft, A "vanilla" Minecraft world, 2018

Minecraft is the most successful video game in history, with over 250 million users worldwide—and counting. If all the *Minecraft* players in the world were to form a country, it would be the world's fifth most populous. Minecraft is almost gender equal in its userbase (45% female, 55% male)—unusually balanced for a video game. The game's audience also has an enormous age range, from children as young as five to adults of fifty or older. *Minecraft's* consistent growth since its release in 2009 demonstrates its long-lasting appeal; it retains the game's loyal fan base, while continually attracting a growing younger audience. In all senses of the word, *Minecraft* is a phenomenon. It has defied all expectations of the video game industry, and clearly resonates much more with its players than many of its competitors.

Minecraft has also caused a sensation on social media and other digital communication platforms. Curiously, more people watch videos of other people playing *Minecraft* than play the game themselves. In 2014, the most searched-for term on YouTube was "music." The second was *Minecraft*.[16] This game has a highly developed online community that frequently shares, adapts, and collaborates on digital environments created within in the game itself. On one popular *Minecraft* community website, over 440,000 digital environments have been uploaded and shared amongst the game's users from around the world.[17]

"Notch [the creator of the game] hasn't just built a game, he's tricked 40 million people into learning to use a CAD program." This quote from MIT Media Lab's Cody Sumter, only one year after the game's release, suggests looking at *Minecraft* from another perspective. In the right hands, *Minecraft* transforms from a computer game into a computer-aided design tool, and moreover, it acts as an entire language of digital design, with the potential to overcome the barriers of communication between professionals and laypeople.

If we consider *Minecraft* a CAD program, an interesting comparison can be made with other available CAD software, putting the scale of *Minecraft* into perspective. John Bacus, Product Management Director of

---

16 | Google Trends: YouTube Search, 2014. https://trends.google.com/trends/explore?date=2014-01-01%202014-12-31&gprop=youtube&q=music,minecraft (accessed March 28, 2018).

17 | Planet Minecraft. https://www.planetminecraft.com/ (accessed March 28, 2018).

SketchUp, claims *SketchUp* is the most widely used 3D modeling software product in the world, with 35 million unique users as of 2016.[18] *AutoDesk* software (including the programs *Revit* and *AutoCAD*) claims subscriptions of 3.11 million users for its products, as of 2017.[19] If *Sketchup's* claim to be the world's most-used 3D design software is true, then with over twice as many users, deeming *Minecraft* a CAD program would, in fact, make it world's most popular—and by a significant margin. It is therefore also true that more digital environments have been created through *Minecraft* than any other tool or software program. Despite this, research into the nature of the environments being created in *Minecraft*, and the game's potential use for real-world architectural and urban applications, remains woefully thin.

BlockWorks, a company I established in 2012, uses *Minecraft* to educate, facilitate engagement, and enable participation in arts projects, local planning, and architecture-related processes. The first step towards this unusual use of a computer game came about through the exploration of the game's potential as a tool for sculpting, architectural design, and landscape design.

Fig. 112: BlockWorks, Hedgeland Exeter Model, Royal Albert Memorial Museum, June 5, 2017

18 | John Bachus, Sketchup/Trimble User Presentation (3D Basecamp Steamboat Springs, 2016). https://youtu.be/N5PojLA71KM?t=5907 (accessed March 28, 2018).

19 | Autodesk, Corporate Info. https://www.autodesk.com/company/newsroom/corporate-info (accessed March 19, 2018).

In recent years, the role of architecture and architects in the design of video games has been given much attention; game developers have sought the advice and assistance of trained architects, in order to create increasingly more convincing and engaging virtual environments. On the other hand, little attention has been paid to how video games and game developers might benefit the field of architecture. *Minecraft* stands as a paradigmatic example of this potential, and is, in my opinion, the most convincing argument for why the collaboration between the fields of architecture and video games should become a reciprocal and mutually beneficial cooperation.

Fig. 113: UNHabitat Block by Block workshop, Surabaya, Indonesia, July 2016

As such, what could *Minecraft's* role be in citizen participation and urban design? There are several characteristics of the game that make it a valid and potentially successful tool for architectural design, not only for use in citizen participation but also by architects themselves. Firstly, *Minecraft* is an adept, accessible, and effective tool for visual communication. It is quick to learn, easy to use, and—most importantly—can be used both by professionals and non-professionals. Unlike many existing design and visualization tools, *Minecraft* does not discriminate between those with architectural training and those without it—an essential factor in any open, democratic design consultation. Not only does *Minecraft* allow participants to easily see and engage with the content created by professionals, but it provides them with the agency to adapt that content and submit their own ideas and proposals in a 3D form. The flexible and adaptive nature of the game makes it easy to test and change proposals; nothing is permanent in *Minecraft*, and the speed with which such changes can be made contributes to its strength as a visualization and design tool.

Even those who are entirely unfamiliar with the game can easily be taught during a short teaching session, as I discovered during my facilitation of a UN-Habitat *Minecraft* workshop in Surabaya, Indonesia. At this workshop, I was tasked with teaching a community group how to use *Minecraft*. Despite difficulties in translation and technology (many of the workshop participants were entirely unfamiliar with the use of computers in any form), almost all of the participants were fluent in *Minecraft* within two to three hours. As expected, teaching younger participants in this workshop was considerably faster.

Another benefit to using *Minecraft* in architectural design is that it provides a new way of designing and constructing within a digital workspace. When you build in Minecraft, you do so from the perspective of your avatar, a virtual character that represents you inside of the game. All interactions within a *Minecraft* world must be conducted through this avatar: for example, to build a wall, you must walk to where you want the wall and place blocks in front of you. Although this is a common interface for players to use in video games, it is never used in design software and digital tools. On the other hand, architects using CAD have a "birds-eye" view. It look down on the design from above, and the architect has no agency or avatar within the program to represents a human presence. As a result, it is very easy to lose a sense of scale or human perspective with traditional design software, whereas *Minecraft* users are entirely immersed in the environment they are designing, moving through their designs as they create them.

The multiplayer feature of the game allows users to access the same virtual environment remotely, from anywhere in the world, and interact with the environment in real-time. For instance, a change made by one user will be seen by all other users in the same environment without delay. This kind of responsive technology does exist in the professional design field, with software such as Building Information Modeling (BIM). However, Minecraft also allows users to view the avatars of other users as they adapt the environment. This makes collaborative design in Minecraft far more fluid and natural, resulting in 3D models that are more coherent in their final design.

Fig. 114: BlockWorks, Atropos—The Walking City, 2014

Minecraft is also unique in its playful approach to design. Existing CAD software has been designed specifically to create technical drawings. However, they provide no consideration for conceptualization or experimentation of design ideas in a playful manner. As previously mentioned, the links between design and play are well documented; play is a natural mechanism for humans to solve problems—albeit while enjoying the activity at the same time. The similarity of the nature of play with real-life situations has generated a whole field of study, led by thinkers such as Johan Huizinga and Jean Piaget, examining how game and play can complement our real-life tasks. The concept of "playful design" is something with which all *Minecraft* users are familiar; *Minecraft* is a game without instructions, and when left without instructions, a player is forced to come up with creative solutions to the design problems they face in their world. Finally, *Minecraft* allows users to create a narrative in and around the environments they build. Traditional CAD software requires users to create their designs on a blank digital canvas; prior to the user's interaction with the program, there is no existing context or environment. Conversely, *Minecraft* users design and build within a universe, which has existing environmental features and assets. This includes, for instance, a day and night cycle allowing players to experience their designs in changing lighting; weather conditions roughly match real-life environments. Players can also add characters, animals, written books, and other content into their environments, with which they can adapt and interact. When used in this way, *Minecraft* becomes a narrative-based design tool, which facilitates the creation of inhabited, living digital spaces rather than the inoperative and unresponsive 3D models—which are the product of traditional design software.

It is also worth considering the limitations to using *Minecraft* in the consultation process. *Minecraft* was never intended to be used in this way, and the game's low resolution makes it ineffective for producing technical models or detailed proposals. While there are creative benefits to using a game for design, there is also a potential for distraction: young children may struggle to focus on a set task inside a gameplay environment. The use of *Minecraft* also risks the potential alientation of different age groups. Rather than mediating between older and younger participants, older participants may be limited by their technical competence, while younger participants, who are more familiar with *Minecraft* or game environments in general, could dominate the process.

CASE STUDY: VICTORIA & ALBERT MUSEUM MINECRAFT WORKSHOP

To celebrate the opening of the Victoria & Albert Museum's (V&A) *Exhibition Road Entrance* in June 2017, *BlockWorks* was asked to develop and run a *Minecraft* workshop at the V&A Museums's new learning center.[20] The workshop was hosted on the same weekend that the Exhibition Road Entrance was first opened. Thus, the workshop presented an opportunity to help children engage with the architecture of this new space and develop their own response to it.

First, we recreated architect Amanda Levete's (*1955) new design in *Minecraft*. For the workshop, we had fifteen available laptops with *Minecraft* installed. Attendee sessions were limited to thirty minutes each, allowing

20 | Olivia Rickman, V&A gets set to open new Exhibition Road Quarter by Amanda Levente. June 15, 2015, http://www.vam.ac.uk/blog/network/hello-exhibition-road (accessed 28/03/18).

us to reach a total of 200 attendees over the course of the weekend. The vast majority of attendees were children between ages seven and eleven. Each laptop station also had printed instructions on how to use *Minecraft*, so attendees with little or no experience could also participate. Each laptop contained our pre-built *Minecraft* version of the Exhibition Road Entrance and, upon arrival, attendees were encouraged to look around this model and then to adapt it based on their ideal version of a museum entrance. No further creative instruction was given, and there were no limits or guidelines on what attendees could create.

Fig. 115: Minecraft/BlockWorks, V&A Exhibition Road Entrance Minecraft Model, 2017

This workshop provided a unique opportunity to judge young people's reactions to a newly designed space; the entrance had only opened that same weekend; as such, the proposals created in *Minecraft* were a "gut reaction" to this new place. Out of a huge variety of creative, fantastical and controversial proposals, there was a noticeable trend toward additional green space. Over seventy-five percent of the attendees placed trees, water, or plants in the courtyard entrance—and in some cases, they forested the entire area. This is an understandable response, considering that the actual design of the entrance is a dazzling, tiled, white surface made from concrete and polished ceramic tiles—yet suggests an instinctive reaction among children that a softer, greener design may prove a more inviting environment.

Despite this passive criticism of the courtyard design from the majority of children who attended the workshop, architect Amanda Levete's design was described by critics as "a triumph" and received widespread critical acclaim.[21] For an internationally renowned museum with the stated aim of "inspiring the next generation",[22] it would seem that youth consultation for the design of the new museum entrance may have facilitated the development of a more child-oriented space, welcoming to youths as well as adults.

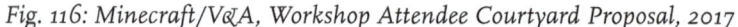

Fig. 116: Minecraft/V&A, Workshop Attendee Courtyard Proposal, 2017

The design of a fifty million pound public space and museum entrance is an enormously complex task, necessitating the use of a myriad of specialist design tools and kind of software. *Minecraft* is by no means a full replacement for such tools. However, as we learned with the V&A project, the use of the game in the early planning stages would at least have given the youth some agency and voice in the design process.

This workshop showed that children were highly engaged—requiring them to leave at the end of each thirty-minute session was a most difficult

21 | Ellis Woodman, "The V&A's new £48m Exhibition Road Quarter is a triumph," *The Telegraph*, June 28, 2017.

22 | *V&A Museum. Annual Review 2016-2017*. September 6, 2017, https://www.vam.ac.uk/info/reports-strategic-plans-and-policies#strategic-plans (accessed March 28, 2018), p.21.

process, with almost all of the children indicating that they would have preferred to stay longer. The workshop was also successful in demonstrating *Minecraft's* potential as a communication platform. Although none of the children verbally expressed dislike of the new entrance space, their intuitive response of adding trees and greenery described an opinion which only came to be through use of the program. This case study is one example of many from companies such as *BlockWorks* and other institutions that have used *Minecraft* to great effect. Also of note is the *Block by Block Foundation*, a UN-Habitat, Microsoft and Mojang collaboration, which uses *Minecraft* as a community participation tool in urban design, focusing on poor communities in developing countries.

Conclusion

Observations from case studies such as the one outlined in this chapter indicate that *Minecraft* can be a powerful tool in the design consultation process. It is particularly effective in engaging youth, improving visual communication during consultations, and giving people the ability and platform to contribute their own ideas in three dimensions. This ability is usually only available to specialists and professionals. Although designed as a computer game, and never intended for use in public consultation, the features of *Minecraft* make it an effective tool that can improve the consultation process. While *Minecraft* is not an appropriate program to use throughout the urban design process, I would argue that future design software intended for use in consultation should look to *Minecraft* as an example which, though unorthodox, has produced useful results in a variety of design consultation processes. Based on my own experiences, I have found that the structure and format of consultation workshops is essential to maximizing the potential benefits of *Minecraft*. Firstly, a sufficient provision of laptops and access to *Minecraft* must be made. When possible, all attendees should have access to the game to enable equal opportunities. Secondly, consultations should make use of the collaborative aspect of the game. Attendees should use the multiplayer feature to design and build in the same digital space at the same time, thus promoting negotiation, mediation, and interaction between participants. Thirdly, attendees should not be limited by rules or practical considerations. The most creative proposals often emerge from states of play, and participants should be allowed to explore design proposals in the playful manner that *Minecraft* so brilliantly provides. Finally, it is also evident that the greatest opportunity *Minecraft* presents is in regard to youth engagement. Nowhere is this more important than in developing countries, where a growing young population is being increasingly marginalized due to their lack of involvement in decision-making processes. When used in the correct manner, *Minecraft* provides a platform for all stakeholders to present their views equally—it is a tool for a more democratic approach to urban design that would greatly enrich public participation processes.

Video Game Urbanism

How we Design Virtual Game Spaces to Engage new
Audiences with the Architecture of Tomorrow

Luke Caspar Pearson

We do not have to look far to see that most contemporary videogames are highly spatial, both thematically and in their mechanisms of play. *Mine-craft* (2009) is the most notable example, producing numerous collab-orative building practices straddling the virtual and physical. But even the phenomenon *Fortnite* (2017), which is ostensibly just a "battle-royale," last-person-standing shooter game, lets players recycle materials to build structures within the game world. The most talented players are equally adept in shooting and construction, in order to shield themselves or access better vantage points. Other games challenge architecture in different ways, such as presenting caricatures of urban planning systems—*Cities: Skylines* (2015)—integrating scanned real-world geometry into virtual en-vironments—*The Vanishing of Ethan Carter* (2014)—creating spaces that defy logic—*Manifold Garden* (2019)—or even new forms of spatial practice through generative world-building—including games by indie developer *Strangethink* since 2011. As games are a meeting of computational and vi-sual arts cultures, and their tools, both the world and the rules that struc-ture it are designed together. In this sense, game spaces become architec-tural representations that are highly programmatic and specific.

It is in this context that I will discuss my work with Sandra Youkha-na, as leaders of the Videogame Urbanism studio at the Bartlett School of Architecture, University College London. Over the last three years we have established a research studio that uses game engine technologies to conceptualize and realize urbanism projects. This has produced over forty games (and counting!) of various complexities and scopes. Students arrive in our studio with backgrounds ranging from architecture to urban and landscape design, but have no prior knowledge of game software. Our research together examines how the future of cities—and how they are regulated—can be communicated to new audiences and challenged through game technologies. We use speculative game scenarios, drawn from real-world research, that incorporate narrative as well as architectural theory into their structure. Using games as pedagogical tools allows our students to understand the forces and systems that shape contemporary urbanism, manipulating them to explore how the educational and immersive qualities of game environments can be used to challenge those existing power structures.

We see game spaces as reminiscent of Bernard Tschumi's (*1944) notion of *event architecture*, in which "actions qualify spaces as much as spaces qualify actions".[1] These actions place architecture into a productive contingency, where the spaces of games support *failure* as well as success against the game's rules. This might present itself as a gap to jump in *Fez* (2012), environmental puzzles in *The Witness* (2016), or the more complex architectural ecologies of a game such as *Frozen Synapse 2* (2018), which uses procedurally generated building floor plans. This architectural context exists because, as game theorist Jesper Juul (*1970) has argued: "Video games are the art of failure, the singular art form that sets us up for failure and allows us to experience and experiment with failure".[2] Game systems and the architecture contained therein are therefore generally not tools for problem-solving in the conventional sense, but can also be problem-*producing*. However, their responsive systems can also be highly reflective. As Greg Costikyan (*1959) argues, "in designing games, a degree of uncertainty is essential",[3] and this uncertainty allows us to echo the complexities of urban environments and their future in new and innovative ways. Much of our research involves exposing urban systems to scrutiny, allowing for a deeper critique of how cities are shaped, rather than simply proposing another modernist reinvention of the city.

---

1 | Bernard Tschumi, *Architecture and Disjunction* (Cambridge MA/London: MIT Press, 1996), p. 123.

2 | Jesper Juul, *The Art of Failure: An Essay on the Pain of Playing Video Games* (Cambridge MA/London: MIT Press, 2013), p. 30.

3 | Greg Costikyan, *Uncertainty in Games* (Cambridge MA/London: MIT Press, 2015), p. 16.

The intellectual basis of our research reflects upon the properties of video games as a medium and places them within the wider architectural discourse. In our studio, we discuss game structures as tools for learning and engagement, but also how game environments resonate with experimental approaches and architectural projects from the past. We also examine games as cultural objects, drawing from the work of other architects who quantified the effects of pop-cultural technology upon the discipline. In the 1950s, Alison Smithson (1928-1993) and Peter Smithson (1923-2003) remarked "but today we collect ads",[4] arguing that the "pace-setting" of the advertisement industry's creation of public desire through "impulses" challenged architectural design. Likewise, Denise Scott Brown (*1931) and Robert Venturi's (1925-2018) *Learning from Las Vegas* fieldwork was predicated upon "form analysis as design research"[5] of the city, in order to understand how it worked through attraction and iconography. Half a century later, escapist equivalents to the Las Vegas strip can be found in the innumerable virtual worlds we can inhabit, widely and rapidly communicated through *YouTube* and *Switch*. The pace-setting and iconography of game spaces challenges architecture in new ways, which we examine and then apply to our own design research.

PLAYFUL PRECEDENTS

We position our work within the wider field of historical, conceptual architectural design. While the ability to synthesize worlds using free game engine technology is relatively new, the "virtual" environment—or unrealized architectural project—is not. In 2017, our studio ran a brief called *Playing the Metropolis of Tomorrow*, a direct reference to the 1929 book by Hugh Ferriss (1889-1962), which contained his famous zoning diagram drawings from 1922.[6] These drawings show the architectural form of real legal rules, published alongside imaginary city designs. Such a relationship between rules, representation, and narrative is key to the construc-

---

4 | Alison Smithson and Peter Smithson, "But Today We Collect Ads," in *Ark Magazine* Nr.18 (November 1956), pp. 49–50.

5 | Stephen Izenour, Denise Scott Brown and Robert Venturi, *Learning From Las Vegas* (Cambridge MA: MIT Press, 1977), p. xi.

6 | Hugh Ferriss, *The Metropolis of Tomorrow* (New York: Washburn, 1929).

tion of virtual game spaces; moreover, Ferriss shows that such relationships have existed for a long time.

Fig. 117: Yingying Zhu, Beyond "The Bubble," 2017, Digital Screenshot Drawing from Game, Bartlett School of Architecture, UCL

The task outlined in this brief asked students to recreate seminal, unrealized urban projects from the past as game spaces. These ranged from superstructures such as Constant's (1920-2005) *New Babylon* or Arata Isozaki's (*1931) *Clusters in the Air* (1960-62) to the polemics of Superstudio's *Continuous Monument* (1969), the spatial compositions of Kazimir Malevich's (1879-1935) *Architectons* (1923), and Iakov Chernikov's (1889-1951) *Architectural Fantasies* (1925-33)—alongside the social visions of Frank Lloyd Wright's (1867-1959) *Broadacre City* (1932) and even Walt Disney's (1901-1966) *EPCOT* (1966). Using these projects as precedents not only quickly introduces students to experimental and conceptual urbanism, but also demonstrates the ways in which a game space can be used to establish a critique that goes beyond the formal, interrogating the ways of *being* proposed in these historical projects.

The games produced in this eight-week study moved far away from simple virtual reproductions. *Living with the Continuous Monument* (2017) extrapolated individual Superstudio collages to investigate how different cultures would react to the monument, by providing a series of scenarios and tools with which to engage the blank grid. And *Beyond 'The Bubble'* (2017) took Disney's idea for a city encapsulated under a dome, turning it into a spherical urbanism using miniature planetary gravity.

Precedents can also be textual and theoretical. A prior project entitled *Back Up Culture* asked students to make games exploring the urban morphology of Los Angeles through key writings on the city. Renyer Banham's (1922-1988) conception of "autopia"[7] structured a car-based urbanism where pedestrianism had been eliminated at every scale. Michael Hardt (*1960) and Antonio Negri's (*1933) definition of "ether," the controlling influence of cultural production, underpinned a game that collapsed various movie spaces into their real-life locations. *Homestead* (2017) explored Banham's notion of housing in L.A. through a series of "case-study" homes in a suburban sprawl that responded to the user's interactions; *Temples of Consumption* (2017) created a *walking simulator* of an alternative L.A. with an urban design structured around consuming iconography and advertising.

Another game, *AirSpace* (2017), took writings on the internationalized aesthetics of *Airbnb* listings and coffee shops[8], creating a game in which the player entered and exited a generic café interior, while the city outside shifted from London or Tokyo to Tel Aviv or Taipei. And precedents can also be morphological, such as two games exploring Manhattan's urban configuration: *Greatest Grids* (2018), a "reverse city-builder," where players terraform Manhattan's island into a grid system allowing buildings to

---

7 | Reyner Banham, *Los Angeles: The Architecture of Four Ecologies* (Berkeley/ Los Angeles: University of California Press, 2009).

8 | Kyle Chayka, "Welcome to Airspace: How Silicon Valley helps spread the same sterile aesthetic across the world," *The Verge* (August 3, 2016), https:// www.theverge.com/2016/8/3/12325104/airbnb-aesthetic-global-minimalism-startup-gentrification (accessed June 22, 2019).

grow; and *Automonument* (2018) was a rhythm game where players would build ever-taller skyscrapers, inspired by Rem Koolhaas's (*1944) definition of Manhattan's monumentality.[9]

Fig. 118: Mingpei Liu, Yingying Zhu, Yu Zhu, Greatest Grids, 2018, Digital Screenshot Drawing from Game, Bartlett School of Architecture, UCL

The effect of such projects is twofold. Firstly, they give students a clear entry point into the use of game technologies, allowing them to focus on acquiring skills and expertise in the software, with precedents providing a basis for making design decisions. Secondly, and more importantly for their research, they establish platforms for understanding how the structure of game spaces can be applied as speculative and critical architec-

9 | Rem Koolhaas, *Delirious New York* (New York: The Monacelli Press, 1994).

tural practice. They also reinforce the validity and importance of design methods that use fictional worlds and narratives to make critical arguments about reality. This also allows us to establish a research agenda that reflects the structural capacity of game engines—which, as Ian Bogost (*1976) argues, move "far beyond literary devices and genres." For Bogost, "unlike cultural categories like the modern novel or film noir, game engines regulate individual videogame's artistic, cultural, and narrative expression".[10] Our use of *Unity* as a specific platform allows us to develop structures that can work across different types of game and research agendas, integrating real-world data into projects that reinvigorate the utopic as a vehicle for architectural experimentation.

Utopics vs. Engagement

The historical projects we reference often tackled issues of society's relationship to technology, labor, and play, which persist today despite technological shifts. In fact, they may have predicted an interchange between playful, engaged citizens and the modern smart city. For instance, Marie-Ange Brayer (*1964) argues that Constant's *New Babylon* is "a 'dynamic labyrinth' ... the forerunner of our globalized and dematerialized society, a purely informational system".[11] Of course, the inhabitants of Constant's structure were called *homo ludens* (people at play), not coincidentally after the title of Johan Huizinga's (1872-1945) seminal text on games and game playing.[12] The playful interaction with informational systems was a tacit structure of other experimental projects of the era, such as the work of Cedric Price (1934-2003), and most notably the Italian group Archizoom's *No-Stop City* (1969-1971). By creating a conditioned, isotropic grid that allowed citizens to assemble flexible elements in a free space, Francesca Balena Arista argues: "for Archizoom, the height of their

---

10 | Ian Bogost, *Unit Operations: An Approach to Videogames Criticism* (Cambridge MA/London: MIT Press, 2006), Kindle edition for iPad, Loc 784.

11 | Marie-Ange Brayer, "Work and Play in Experimental Architecture, 1960-70," *PCA-Stream*, https://www.pca-stream.com/en/articles/work-and-play-in-experimental-architecture-1960-1970-57, (accessed February 22, 2019).

12 | Johan Huizinga, *Homo Ludens: A Study of the Play-Element in Culture* (London: Routledge, 2003).

technology would instead be invisible technology, that is, electronics".[13] *No-Stop City* was utopian, but under a strict structure. Andrea Branzi (*1938) argued "nowadays the only possible utopia is quantitative",[14] which reinforces Arista's point that their imaginary, conceptual city closely resembles the logic of electronic systems.

Games, built on information and code, are almost entirely quantitative—underneath the surface, at least. McKenzie Wark (*1961) takes this further, claiming that game spaces should not be considered utopian but *atopian*. Wark argues that "if utopia thrives as an architecture of qualitative description, and brackets off quantitative relation, atopia renders all descriptions arbitrary. All that matters is the quantitative relations".[15] While I would argue that games do still retain qualitative descriptions, this emphasis on quantitative structure allows us to unpack urbanism in new ways. Our studio developed the game *Carbon Neutral Living* (2018) with a typical roleplaying game structure; however, the data profile of the player was built not on their mastery in swords or spells, but around their real-world carbon footprint (using World Wildlife Fund indicators).

As a player makes decisions in the game, it responds by calculating changes to their footprint, opening or foreclosing parts of the city in response. Another game, *The Ludic Sanitorium* (2018) suggested that a post-work society would be structured through play, replacing the individual meaning of labor. As the player undertakes different forms of "play-work," from logistics to proof-reading (by typing directly into the game), the qualities of work become encased in a quantitative world performed by rote.

While framing game spaces as utopian (even quantitative ones) could be seen as a retreat from the pressing issues of the real world, this offers the potential to conceptualize new architectural conditions that can challenge normative readings of the city. Graeme Kirkpatrick (*1963) argues that "all video games are a kind of opening up of the machine and begin the process of prising it away from the dominant historical narrative of

---

13 | Francesca Balena Arista, "Archizoom Associati," *Radical Utopias*, ed. Brugellis, Pettena and Salvadori (Rome: Quodlibet Habitat, 2017), p. 102.

14 | Andrea Branzi, *No-Stop City Archizoom Associati* (Orleans: HYX, 2006), pp. 176–179.

15 | McKenzie Wark, *Gamer Theory* (Cambridge MA/London: Harvard University Press, 2007), Note [119].

'technological progress'"[16]; similarly, when Ian Bogost calls algorithms "caricatures" of systems, he argues games are the only form that admits this truth.[17] -

Fig. 119: Zhibei Li, Shenghan Wu, Meiwen Zhang, The Playable Planning Notice, 2017, Digital Screenshot Drawing from Game, Bartlett School of Architecture, UCL

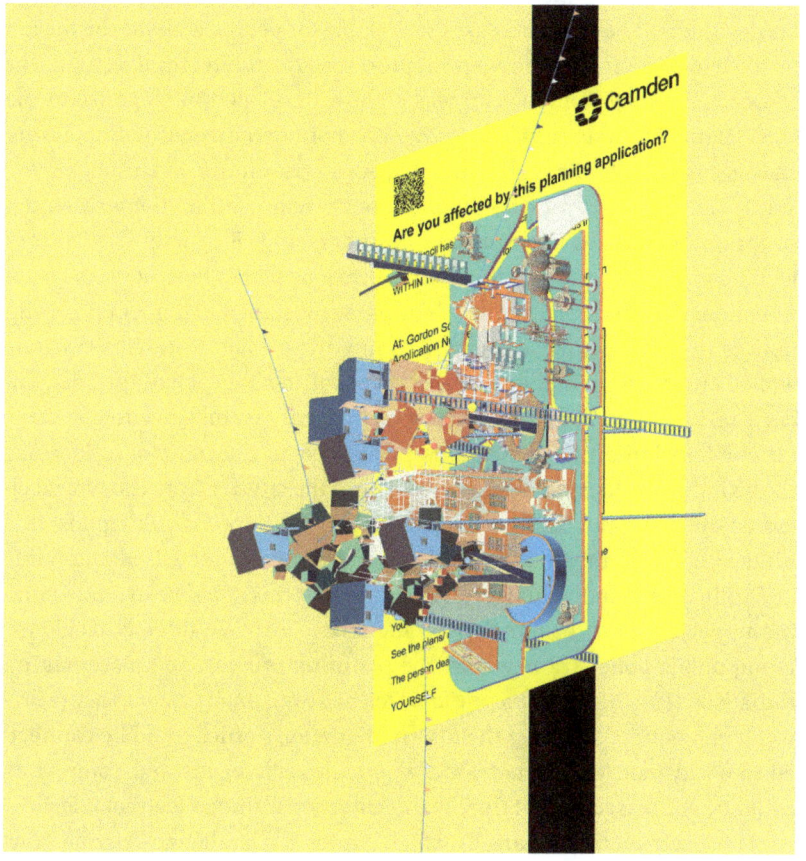

16 | Graeme Kirkpatrick, *Aesthetic Theory and the Videogame* (Manchester: Manchester University Press, 2011), p. 115.

17 | Ian Bogost, "The Cathedral of Computation," *The Atlantic* (Jnauary 15, 2015), https://www.theatlantic.com/technology/archive/2015/01/the-cathedral-of-computation/384300/ (accessed February 22, 2019).

Rather than seeing this playful and ironic use of computation as a deficit, our studio offers it as a counterpoint to trends in architectural discourse towards the pure modernist efficiency of smart city technologies, parametric simulation, or robotic fabrication. We see the potential of game spaces for architects to rethink the ambitions and ideas of architecture.

A part of these ambitions also resides in establishing new ways of engaging people with architecture and urbanism. Games offer us the opportunity to make tools that people can use, and that provide direct feedback for designers. They are also easily accessible for people without the means or voice to participate in the typical processes of architectural design. *The Playable Planning Notice* (2017) was a game developed in response to the U.K. planning system, which generally notifies citizens of impending changes to the city through laminated A4-notices hung on lampposts. While these notices provide links to applications online, the written description of changes is often hard to understand. Examples can be very technical, but also include things like "various works to various trees" or "erection of a plinth and statue." The game, designed using real planning notices in London, allowed players to prototype what terms like "various works" might mean and design divergent futures for each of the sites under consideration. While the game has a visual resemblance to construction or "city-building" games, it is positioned as a social tool to increase the visibility of changes taking place within the city, far from the typical elevated overview and control of "God games." As Kars Alfrink argues, this hints at a future in which "a gameful city promises increased autonomy and influence to individuals".[18] We believe that this could be extended into the upper echelons of our democratic structures. We directly tackle existing public policy frameworks, the planning process, and placemaking initiatives (*Play Making*, 2017; *Clone Town*, 2017). *Smart Democracy* (2017) was a game proposing that the Mayor of London's office could be connected to a citywide virtual network, where citizen's needs and complaints could be addressed in real time using Internet of things technologies.

However, another means by which games can challenge existing power structures is in how their worlds and systems are presented to players. *SimCity* (1989) or *Cities: Skylines* (2015) both frame urbanism from above,

---

18 | Kars Alfrink, "The Gameful City," *The Gameful World*, ed. Walz and Detarding (Cambridge MA/London: MIT Press, 2015), p. 556.

as a top-down construction. This is equally true of more socially engaged urban games such as *Block'Hood* (2016) or *Nova Alea* (2017), which use isometric cameras.

Fig. 120: Mingpei Liu, Yingying Zhu, Yu Zhu, Sub-Urban, 2018, Digital Screenshot Drawing from Game, Bartlett School of Architecture, UCL

Minecraft, in contrast, uses a first-person perspective, which is more reminiscent of pre-Renaissance architectural practices, in which the designer would directly participate by guiding building work on site. Perhaps this direct relationship to construction is why it has blossomed into such an effective tool of spatial design. While aerial viewpoints are appropriate for understanding the systems behind urbanism, our studio also explores divergent ways of seeing and experiencing the city. *E-London* (2017), for instance, uses a first-person perspective and multiple different cameras (rendering different layers of the game space) to explore life in a post-Brexit United Kingdom, where citizens can opt back in through augmented reality technologies. Inspired by Estonia's E-Citizenship system, the game explores the impact of Brexit on London's urban realm through its effect on people within the city rather than on larger organizational scales. Another game, *Sub-Urban* (2018), uses a spinning camera as the player builds underground infrastructure beneath London, producing a block of pure subterranean urbanism. This is not, of course, realistic, but instead represents a distillation of complex urban issues (such as "iceberg" houses excavated far beneath the city by the super-wealthy[19]) into a clear and accessible game space.

Non-Material Materials

Of course, the resolution and appearance of game worlds is inextricably linked to how they are seen by a virtual camera. Within the studio, we do not place an emphasis on "photorealistic" depictions of space, despite the architectural visualization industry increasingly using VR-game technologies to make realistic portrayals of urbanism for clients and stakeholders. In contrast, we disrupt the idea that such depictions will be the only future for game technologies in architecture, and instead explore new forms of materiality that are only possible in the virtual world.

Virtual materials in a game engine are entirely different to real-world materials, despite heavy investment in technology to simulate reality as convincingly as possible. Even the most realistic looking concrete or brick, upon which light falls believably in-game, will be constructed from multiple flat image files that contain information about color, reflectivity, shadows, and so on. This is still the case, even when the construction of game

---

19 | Oliver Wainwright, "Billionaires' basements: the luxury bunkers making holes in London streets," *The Guardian* (November 9, 2012), https://www.theguardian.com/artanddesign/2012/nov/09/billionaires-basements-london-houses-architecture (accessed June 22, 2019).

Fig. 121: Daniel Avilan, Aradhana Kapoor, Sanjana Samant, Snooper's Charter, 2017, Digital Screenshot Drawing from Game, Bartlett School of Architecture, UCL

worlds draws directly from the real, as in *The Vanishing of Ethan Carter*, which used photogrammetry techniques to scan real locations for the game.[20] As these raw models are much too detailed for use in a real-time game, the models were used to "bake" sets of shadow and texture information that would then be applied to more simple geometries.

As such, in game worlds, it is impossible to divorce architectural materiality from the regime of the image. With that in mind, we regularly employ materials and techniques that emphasize the unreal qualities of game spaces to explore the potential gap between representations and buildings, but also to suggest that there are now challenges to our normative conception of how materials and environments should behave. Because most of these material qualities are attached to values, they can be manipulated within the game. They can become roughly hewn or smooth; reflective, stretched or grossly distorted depending on the interactions of the player. Further techniques such as level of detail (LOD) allow us to nest multiple versions of a virtual building within the same space. This is typically used to replace complex models with simpler versions as the player moves further away, but we have often reversed this process, calling the resolution of visualization tools into question.

Many of our studio projects, such as the surveillance-based game *Snooper's Charter* (2017), use what are called "unlit" or "triplanar" shaders—materials that do not respond to virtual lights, and thus do not receive or cast shadows. This can subvert perspective and depth: when two objects with the same material coincide, they will be indistinguishable. This effect has been used in the game *Vignettes* (2017), where unlit materials allow objects rotated by the player to morph into different shapes at points where their silhouettes combine. It has also been used in the work of developers such as indie collective *Sokpop*. In our game *Projectives* (2018), for the Royal Institute of British Architects, we used four shifting "split-screen" panels with different camera angles that were combined by players into one perspective view.

Using these shaders produces an aesthetic that operates between the flat and the volumetric; this challenges the relationship between the two-dimensional matrix of the screen and the 3D model by removing its relationship to light and shadow. The effect of this is to emphasize the game-like qualities of these worlds, and to draw them away from "real-

---

20 | Andrzej Poznanski, Visual Revolution of The Vanishing of Ethan Carter, *The Astronauts* (March 25, 2014), http://www.theastronauts.com/2014/03/visual-revolution-vanishing-ethan-carter/ (accessed June 22, 2019).

istic" depictions of urbanism. However, if we recall Peter Eisenman's (*1932) contention that "real architecture" only exists in drawings",[21] then underlining the fact that these spaces are not buildings—nor are they designed to be—can be considered a technique of productive separation. Embracing the synthetic allows us to more clearly articulate messages about reality.

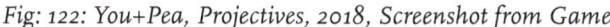

Fig: 122: You+Pea, Projectives, 2018, Screenshot from Game

In turn, many of our games might be considered to look "cute," which places them in stark contrast to both realistic depictions of architecture (which are rarely ever truly that) and the increasing ubiquity of "datascapes" and other means of spatializing computational information. Such cuteness is drawn from the technology of the game engine and the lineage of game aesthetics, but also allows us to develop a nuanced and layered relationship to the observer. As Simon May has argued: "Cute unsettles the habitual by toying with it from a position of playful vulnerability. It lightheartedly probes the established ways in which we invoke power to order our priorities and to understand who we are".[22] The "teasing indeter-

21 | Iman Ansari, Peter Eisenman, Architectural Review (April 20, 2013), https://www.architectural-review.com/essays/interview-peter-eisenman/8646893.article (accessed June 22, 2019).

22 | Simon May, *The Power of Cute* (Princeton/Oxford: The Princeton Press, 2019), p. 47.

minacy"[23] of many of our games is a conscious effort to explore these power structures. In another example, *Peep-Pop City* (2018)—a physical city-building game developed by Sandra and myself for *Now Play This 2018*, used five hundred candy-colored, 3D-printed pieces derived from London along with cue-cards for players to enact events in the city's urban morphology.

Through its cuteness, it was especially popular with children who visited the event allowing them to engage with urban power structures, even if unwittingly.

Fig. 123: You+Pea, Peep-Pop City, 2018, Photograph of Game

Despite the game industry's drive towards realism, many games now consciously reemphasize video game aesthetics in and of themselves. This is true in the new wave of game remasters, in which older worlds are updated with new textures and graphics in a similar way to buildings that are recreated with new technologies, such as Antoni Gaudí's (1852-1926) *Sagrada Familia*. Nightdive Studios work almost exclusively on updating game worlds from seminal titles such as *System Shock* (1994) using contemporary game engines. But, more realistic depictions can still be unpacked, such as in my research project *Noclip World*, in which I use architectural drawing and cheat codes to interrogate the construction of realistic-looking game worlds.

---

23 | Ibid., p. 27.

Fig. 124: Luke Caspar Pearson, NoClip World, 2015, Pen and Ink Drawing on Paper

This relates to John Sharp's readings of similar art practices as "a space for exposing the questioning the peculiar trajectory of 3D videogames toward even greater verisimilitude".[24] Such work can also be compared to that of artists such as Harun Farocki's (1944-2014) *Parallel I–IV* (2012–2014), and JODI's *Max Payne Cheats Only* (2006). They have also questioned the role of realism in games and how it can be subverted. What this suggests, and our studio promotes, is a new form of architectural practice that operates between the virtual and real, both in its tools and its aesthetic approach.

We also subvert traditional forms of architectural drawing by asking students to follow our own methods of screenshot-based collage. Screenshots are typically used by game designers to promote their games, capturing certain key moments and enticing the consumer towards a purchase. Certain figures such as Duncan Harris of *Dead End Thrills* have elevated screenshot-making into a form of photography, using various tools to push the fidelity of game worlds to their limit. Rather than taking inspiration from photography, we instead explore how multiple screenshots from our games can be composed into new forms of temporal architectural drawing that reflect the dynamic nature of the world. This allows us to establish a direct connection to the history of architectural representation and image-making, while also accounting for the aesthetic particularities of our game worlds. In our *Tokyo Backup City* (2016-) project we used screenshot drawings to explore the "afterglow" of a neon-lit city, suggesting an imprint on the retina, not unlike the moment a game world breaks down when we transgress its borders.

THE FUTURE OF VIDEO GAME URBANISM

Our research with the Videogame Urbanism studio has formed the basis for new ways of practicing spatial design, framing the video game as an alternative way of addressing computation in architecture. There are many technological developments that are and will reshape the urban, from machine learning and A.I. to the internet of things and big data. As designers, we can operate as mediators between all of the new information cities give us and the citizens who live within them. Games allow us

---

24 | John Sharp, *Works of Game* (Cambridge MA/London: MIT Press, 2015), p. 47.

to make complex and temporal systems visible, and create environments in which players and observers can interact with these to prototype new futures.

Fig. 125: You+Pea, Tokyo Backup City, 2016, Digital Screenshot Drawing from Game

Video game urbanism leverages games as a familiar medium, which allows for an increased level of engagement between designers and the public. But we also emphasize the importance of using games to dream and experiment with what cities can be. Game worlds are places where the improbable can become normal; environments where space can twist and gravity can flip; where entire actions and ways of being can be opened or closed to us. As we continue to move forward, we believe that games will change what it means to represent architecture, to inhabit architecture—and indeed, what it means to *realize* architecture. There is a whole cabinet of tools and a whole universe of worlds to come.

Bibliography/Ludography

Bibliography

Aarseth, Espen J., "I fought the Law: Transgressive Play and the implied Player" *Proceedings of the 2007 DiGRA International Conference: Situated Play*, 2007

Aarseth, Espen J., *Cybertext: Perspectives on Egodic Literature* (Baltimore MA: Johns Kopkins University Press, 2007)

Aarseth, Espen J., "Allegories of Space. The Question of Spatiality in Computer Games," in *Cybertext Yearbook 2000*, eds. Raine Koskimaa and Markku Eskelinen (Jyväskylä: University of Jyväskylä, 2001), pp. 44–47

Aarseth Espen J., "Virtual Worlds, Real Knowledge: Towards a Herme-neutics of Virtuality," *European Review* 9, no. 02 (2001), pp. 227–232

Abbott, Edwin Abbott, *Flatland: A Romance of many Dimensions* (London: Seeley & Co., 1884)

Adams, Ernest W., "Designer's Notebook: The Role of Architecture in Videogames" *Gamasutra*, October 9, 2002, https://www.gamasutra.com/view/feature/131352/designers_notebook_the_role_of_.php

Agotai, Doris, *Architekturen in Zelluloid, der filmische Blick auf den Raum* (Bielefeld: transcript, 2007)

Alexander, Leigh and Laura Hudson, eds., *Offworld* (19 Castles LLC, 2016)

Alfrink, Kars, "The Gameful City", in *The Gameful World*, eds. Walz and Detarding (Cambridge, MA and London: MIT Press, 2015), pp. 527-560

Anders, Peter, *Envisioning Cyberspace: Designing 3D Electronic Spaces*, (New York: McGraw-Hill Professional, 1998)

Ansari, Iman, *Interview: Peter Eisenman, Architectural Review*, 20. April 2013, https://www.architectural-review.com/essays/interview-peter-eisenman/8646893.article

Anthropy, Anna and Naomi Clark, *A Game Design Vocabulary. Exploring the foundational Principles behind good Game Design* (Upper Saddle River, NJ: Addison-Wesley, 2014)

Artaud, Antonin, *The Theater and Its Double*, trans. Mary C. Richard (New York: Grove Press, 1994)

Arista, Francesca Balena, "Archizoom Associati," *Radical Utopias*, ed. Brugellis, Pettena and Salvadori (Rome: Quodlibet Habitat, 2017), pp. 100-129

Augé, Marc, *Non-lieux: introduction à une anthropologie de la surmodernité* (Paris: Éditions du Seuil, 1992)

Aukstakalnis, Steve and David Blatner, *Silicon Mirage: The Art & Science of Virtual Reality* (Berkeley, CA: Peachpit Press Inc, 1992)

Austin, John L., *How to Do Things with Words* [1962] (Cambridge, MA: Harvard UP, 1975)

Babic, Edvin, "On the Liberation of Space in Computer Games," *Eludamos. Journal for Computer Game Culture* 1, no. 1 (2007)

Backe, Hans-Joachim, "Metareferentiality through in-game images in immersive simulation games," *Proceedings of Foundations of Digital Games (FDG 2018). 07.-10. August 2018, Malmö, Sweden* (2018), pp. 1–10

Banham, Reyner, *Los Angeles. The Architecture of Four Ecologies* (London: Allen Lane The Penguin Press, 1971)

Barthes, Roland, *Le plaisir du texte* (Paris: Éditions du Seuil, 1973)

Baudrillard, Jean, *Les stratégies fatales* (Paris: Éditions Grasset & Fasquelle, 1983)

Baudrillard, Jean, *Simulacres et simulation* (Paris: Galilée, 1981)

Bavelier, David, and C. Shawn Green, "The Brain-Boosting Power of Video games," in *Scientific American*, Juli, CCCXV/1 (2016), pp. 26-31

Bazin, André, "The Myth of Total Cinema," *What Is Cinema* 1 (1967), pp. 17–22

Benjamin, Walter, "Theses on the Philosophy of History," in *Illuminations*, trans. Harry Zohn (New York: Schocken Books, 1969), pp. 253-264

Benjamin, Walter, "L'œuvre d'art à l'époque de sa reproduction mécanisée," *Zeitschrift für Sozialforschung* 5, (1936), pp. 40-66

Bertol, Daniela, *Designing Digital Space: An Architect's Guide to Virtual Reality*, (New York: Wiley, 1996)

Bhabha, Homi, "The Third Space: Interview" in *Identity: Community, Culture, Difference*, ed. Jonathan Rutherford (London: Lawrence&Wishart, 1990), pp. 207-221

Binotto, Johannes, "Closed Circuits. Immanence as Disturbance in High Definition Cinema," in *Disruption in the Arts*, ed. Lars Koch (Berlin, Boston: De Gruyter, 2018), pp. 171-185

Bogost, Ian, "The Cathedral of Computation," *The Atlantic*, 15. Jan, 2015 https://www.theatlantic.com/technology/archive/2015/01/the-cathedral-of-computation/384300/

Bogost, Ian, *Persuasive Games. The Expressive Power of Videogames* (Cambridge: The MIT Press, 2007)

Bogost, Ian, *Unit Operations: An Approach to Videogame Criticism* (Cambridge, MA: The MIT press, 2006)

Bonner, Marc, "On Striated Wilderness and Prospect Pacing: Rural Open World Games as Liminal Spaces of the Man-Nature Dichotomy," *DiGRA 2018. The Game is the Message, University of Turin July 25-28 2018, Conference Proceedings* (2018), pp. 1–18

Bonner, Marc, "Erkundung als virtuell-fiktionale Immersionsstrategie – Das prospect pacing der Open-World-Computerspiele als Spiegel nicht linearer Spieler-Einbindung," in *Jahrbuch Immersiver Medien 2016. Interfaces – Netze – Virtuelle Welten*, ed. Institut für Immersive Medien Kiel (Marburg: Schüren, 2017), pp. 38–57

Bonner, Marc, "Architektur als mediales Scharnier – Medialität und Bildlichkeit der raumzeitlichen Erfahrungswelten Architektur, Film und Computerspiel," *Image. Zeitschrift für interdisziplinäre Bildwissenschaft* 21, no. 1, (January 2015), pp. 5–22

Bonner, Marc, "Analyzing the Correlation of Game Worlds and Built Reality: Depiction, Function and Mediality of Architecture and Urban Landscapes," *DiGRA Conference 2014, University of Utah*, August 03-06. 2014, Conference Proceedings (2014), pp. 1–14

Borden, Iain, *Skateboarding and the city: architecture and the body* (Oxford: Berg 2001)

Boullée, Etienne Louis, *Architecture, Essay on Art*, ed. Helen Rosenau, trans. Sheila de Vallée (Academy Editions, 1976)

Boulton, Eli and Colin Cremin, "The sociology of videogames," in *Being Cultural*, ed. B. Cohen (Auckland: Pearson 2011), pp. 341-355

Brandes, Jennifer Hepler, ed., *Women in Game Development. Breaking the Glass* (Boca Raton: CRC Press, 2017)

Branzi, Andrea, *No-Stop City Archizoom Associati* (Orleans: HYX, 2006)

Braun, Wilhelm Alfred, *Types of Weltschmerz in German Poetry* (New York, NY: Columbia University Press, 1905)

Brosterman, Norman, *Inventing Kindergarten* (New York: Harry N. Abrams, 1997)

Burton, Robert, *Anatomy of Melancholy* [1621] (Amsterdam: Theatrum Orbis Terrarum, 1971)

Caillois, Roger, *Man, Play and Games* [1958] ([New York]: Free Press of Glencoe, 1961)

Calleja, Gordon, *In-Game, From Immersion to Incorporation* (Cambridge/London: MIT Press, 2011)

Calvino, Italo, *Lezioni americane. Sei proposte per il prossimo millennio* [1988] (Milano: Arnoldo Mondadori Editore, 1993)

Canadian Centre for Architecture, *Toys and the Modernist Tradition* (Montréal: CCA, 1993)

Card, Orson Scott, *Ender's Game* (New York: Tor Books, 1985)

Carpo, Mario, "Building with Geometry, Drawing with Numbers," in When Is the Digital in *Architecture?*, ed. Andrew Goodhouse (Montréal: Sternberg Press, 2017), pp. 33–44

Carpo, Mario, "The Art of Drawing," *Architectural Design* 83, no. 5 (September 1, 2013)

Carpo, Mario, *The Alphabet and the Algorithm* (Cambridge, Mass: The MIT Press, 2011)

Clegg, Brian, *A Brief History of Infinity: The Quest to Think the Unthinkable*, UK ed. edition (London: Robinson Publishing, 2003)

Cogburn, Jon and Mark Silcox, *Philosophy through Video Games* (New York, NY/London: Routledge, 2009)

Costikyan, Greg, *Uncertainty in Games* (Cambridge MA & London: MIT Press, 2015)

Coyne, Richard, "Mindless repetition: Learning from computer games," *Design Studies*, vol. 24, no. 3 (May 2003): pp. 199-212

Csikszentmihályi, Mihály, *Creativity: Flow and the Psychology of Discovery and Invention* (New York: Harper Collins Publishers, 1996)

Davis, Erik, "Acoustic Cyberspace," *Xchange On-Air Session*, November 11, 1997, https://techgnosis.com/acoustic-cyberspace/

Debord, Guy, *La société du spectacle* (Paris: Buchel/Chastel, 1967)

Debord, Guy, "Contribution to a Situationist Definition of Play", in: *Internationale Situationniste* 1 (Juni 1958), http://www.cddc.vt.edu/sionline/si/play.html (accessed 26.01.2017)

Deleuze, Gilles, *Difference and Repetition* [1968], (Bloomsbury Academic, 2014)

Deleuze, Gilles, Félix Guattardi, *L'Anti-Oedipe. Capitalisme et schizophrénie* (Paris: Minuit, 1972)

Derrida, Jacques, "Chora," in *Chora L Works. Jacques Derrida and Peter Eisenman* [1987], eds. Jeffrey Kipnis and Thomas Leeser (New York, NY: Monacelli Press, 1997), pp. 15-32

Dimopoulos, Konstantinos and Maria Kallikaki, *Virtual Cities* (London: Unbound, 2019)

Duke, Richard D., *Gaming: The Future's Language* [1974] (Bielefeld: W. Bertelsmann Verlag, 2014)

Duke, Richard D., *Gaming-simulation Studies in Urban Land Use Allocation*, Ph.D. (The University of Michigan, 1964)

Dünne, Jörg and Stephan Günzel, *Raumtheorie: Grundlagentexte aus Philosophie und Kulturwissenschaften* (Frankfurt am Main: Suhrkamp 2015)

Dyer-Whiteford, Nick and Greig de Peuter, *Games of Empire. Global Capitalism and Video Games* (Minneapolis: University of Minnesota Press, 2009)

Edgerton, Samuel Y., "Brunelleschi's Mirror, Alberti's Window, and Galileo's' Perspective Tube'," *História, Ciências, Saúde-Manguinhos* 13 (2006): pp. 151–179

Edgerton, Samuel, "The Renaissance Development of the Scientific Illustration," in *Science and the Arts in the Renaissance*, eds. John William Shirley and F. David Hoeniger (Plainsboro, NJ: Associated University Presses, 1985), pp. 168–197

Eichenbaum Adam, Daphné Bavelier and C. Shawn Green, "Video games: play that can do serious good," *American Journal of Play*, vol. 7, no. 1, (2014), pp. 50-72

Einstein, Albert, *Geometrie und Erfahrung* (Berlin: Verlag von Julius Springer, 1921)

Erickson, Thomas, "From Interface to Interplace: the Spatial Environment as a Medium for Interaction," in *Spatial Information Theory A Theoretical Basis for GIS. COSIT 1993. Lecture Notes in Computer Science*, eds. Andrew U. Frank and Irene Campari (Berlin, Heidelberg: Springer), pp. 391-405

Euler, Leonhard, "From the Problem of the Seven Bridges of Königsberg," in *Classics of Mathematics* [1736], ed. Ronald Calinger (Englewood Cliffs, NJ: Prentice Hall, 1995), pp. 503-506

Fassone, Riccardo, *Every Game is an Island: Endings and Extremities in Video Games*. (Bloomsbury Publishing, USA, 2017)

Fassone, Riccardo, *Every Game Is an Island: Borders, Endings, Extremities in Video Games* (Doctoral thesis discussed at the department of humanistic studies of the University of Turin, Turin, Italy, 2013)

Ferreira, M. Jamie: „Faith and the Kierkegaardien leap," in *The Cambridge Companion to Kierkegaard*, ed. Alastair Hannay, Daniel Marino Gordon (Cambridge: Cambridge University Press, 1998), pp. 207-235

Ferriss, Hugh, *The Metropolis of tomorrow* (New York: Washburn, 1929)

Feyerabend, Paul, "Brunelleschi and the Invention of Perspective," in Conquest of *Abundance: A Tale of Abstraction Versus the Richness of Being*, ed. Bert Terpstra, New (Chicago: University of Chicago Press, 1999), pp. 89–128

Flanagan, Mary, *Critical Games: Radical Game Design* (Cambridge, MA: The MIT Press 2009)

Fleischmann, Monika and Wolfgang Strauss, "The House of Illusion: Extending the Boundaries of Space," in *1st International Conference Proceedings*, ed. K. Nys et al.(AVOCAAD, Brussels, : Hogeschool voor Wetenschap en Kunst, 1997)

Fleischmann, Monika and Wolfgang Strauss, "Implosion of Numbers_ Performative Mixed Reality," in *Disappearing Architecture: From Real to Virtual to Quantum*, ed. Georg Flachbart and Peter Weibel (Basel: Birkhäuser Architecture, 2005), pp. 119–31

Flusser, Vilém, *Dinge und Undinge, Phänomenologische Skizzen* (München: Carl Hanser Verlag 1993)

Fraser, Benjamin, "Why the Spatial Epistemology of the Video Game Matters: Metis, Video Game Space and Interdisciplinary Theory," *Journal of Gaming & Virtual Worlds* 3, no. 2 (2011): pp. 93–106

Frederick, Matthew, *101 Things I Learned In Architecture School* (Cambridge MA: MIT Press, 2007)

Gagnon, Diana, "Videogames and Spatial Skills: An Exploratory Study," in *ECTJ*, Vol 33, No. 4 (1985), pp. 263-275

Gauss, Karl Friedrich: *General Investigations of Curved Surfaces* [1827] (Mineola, NY: Dover Publications, 2005)

Gerber, Andri, Michal Berkowitz, Beatrix Emo, Stefan Kurath, Christoph Hölscher and Elsbeth Stern, "Does Space Matter? A Cross-Disciplinary Investigation upon Spatial Abilities of Architects," in *Research Culture in Architecture. Cross-Disciplinary Collaboration*, eds. Cornelie

Leopold, Christopher Robeller, Ulrike Weber (Basel: Birkhäuser Verlag, forthcoming)

Gerber, Andri, Tibor Joanelly and Oya Atalay Franck, eds., *Proportions and Cognition in Architecture and Urban Design* (Berlin: Reimer Verlag, 2019)

Gerber, Andri and Philippe Koch, "Architektur muss als Ruine gedacht werden (um politisch zu sein)," *Archithese* no. 4, (2017), pp. 8-16

Gerber, Andri, *Metageschichte der Architektur. Ein Lehrbuch für angehende Architekten und Architekturhistoriker* (Bielefeld: transcript, 2014)

Gerber, Andri and Brent Patterson eds., *Metaphors in Architecture and Urbanism. An Introduction* (Bielefeld: transcript, 2013)

Gilpin, William, *Three essays on the Picturesque* [1792] (London: R. Blamire,1792)

Gleiter, Jörg H., Norbert Korrek, Gerd Zimmermann, eds., *Die Realität des Imaginären. Archhitektur und das digitale Bild*, 10. Internationales Bauhaus-Kolloquium Weimar (Weimar: Verlag der Bauhaus-Univer-sität, 2008)

Goffman, Erving, *Frame Analysis: An Essay on the Organization of Experience* (Harper & Row, New York, 1974)

Goodman, Nelson, *Languages of Art: An Approach to a Theory of Symbols* [1968] (Indianapolis, IN: Hackett 1976)

Goffman, Erving, *Encounters. Two Studies in the Sociology of Interaction* [1961] (Middlesex, England: Penguin University Books, 1972)

Götz, Ulrich, "Rules Shape Spaces – Spaces Shape Rules," in *Games and Rules. Game Mechanics for the "Magic Circle,"* eds. Beat Suter, Mela Kocher, and René Bauer (Bielefeld: transcript, 2018), pp. 259–65

Götz, Ulrich, "Load and Support. Architectural Realism in Video Games," in *Space Time Play. Computer Games, Architecture and Urbanism: the Next Level*, eds. Friedrich von Borries, Steffen P. Walz and Matthias Böttger (Basel: Birkhäuser, 2007), pp. 134–37

Granic, Isabela, Adam Lobel and Rutger C. M. E Engels, "The Benefits of Playing Video Games," *American Psychologist* (January 2014), pp. 66-78

Grusin, Richard, "Radical mediation", *Critical Inquiry*, vol. 42, No. 1 (Autumn 2015): pp. 124-148

Gualeni, Stefano, *Virtual Worlds as Philosophical Tools: How to Philosophize with a Digital Hammer* (Basingstoke, UK: Palgrave Macmillan, 2015)

Günzel, Stephan, *Egoshooter: das Raumbild des Computerspiels* (Frankfurt am Main: Campus, 2012)

Günzel, Stephan, "The Spatial Turn in Computer Game Studies," in *Exploring the Edges of Gaming* (Vienna games Conference 2008-2009, Vienna: Braumüller, 2010), pp. 147–56

Harvey, David, "Space as a Keyword," in *Inaugural Conference* (Marx and Philosophy Conference, Institute of Education, University of London: University of London, 2004)

Hawranke, Thomas, *MODDING. Künstlerische Forschung in Computerspielen* (Bauhaus-Universität Weimar, Fakultät Kunst und Gestaltung, Promotionsstudiengang Medienkunst, 2018)

Henderson, Linda Dalrymple, "Einstein and 20th-Century Art: A Romance of Many Dimensions," in *Einstein for the 21st Century: His Legacy in Science, Art, and Modern Culture*, eds. Peter Galison, Gerald Holton, and Silvan Schweber, Reprint edition (Princeton University Press, 2018), pp. 101–29

Henderson, Linda Dalrymple, *The Fourth Dimension and Non-Euclidian Geometry in Modern Art* [1983] (Cambridge, MA/London: MIT Press, 2013)

Herder, Johann Gottfried, *Auch eine Philosophie der Geschichte zur Bildung der Menschheit* (Riga: Hartknoch, 1774)

Hoffmann, Heinrich, *König Nussknacker und der arme Reinhold* (Frankfurt am Main: Literarischen Anstalt Rütten & Löning, 1851)

Hollein, Hans, "Alles ist Architektur," in *Bau. Schrift für Architektur und Städtebau*, Nr. 1/2 1, (1968), pp. 1-28

Horatius Flaccus, Quintus, *His Art of Poetry*, trad. Ben Johnson (Amsterdam: Theatrum Orbis Terrarum, 1974).

Howard, T.L.J. and N. Gaborit, "Using Virtual Environment Technology to Improve Public Participation in Urban Planning Process," *Journal of Urban Planning and Development* (2007), pp. 1-28

Huizinga, Johan, *Homo Ludens: A Study of Play-Element in Culture* [1938] (Routledge & Kegan Paul, 1949)

Huizinga, Johan, *The Waning of the Middle Ages. A Study of the Form of Life, Thought and Art in France and the Netherlands in the XIVth and XVth centuries* [1919] (New York: Doubleday Anchor Books, 1954)

Husserl, Edmund, „Philosophy as Rigorous Science" [1910], in: *Phenomenology and the Crisis of Philosophy*, ed. Quentin Lauer (New York: Harper & Row, 1965)

Ihde, Don, *Technology and the Lifeworld: from Garden to Earth* (Bloomington: Indiana University Press, 1990)

Izenour, Stephen, Denise Scott Brown and Robert Venturi, *Learning From Las Vegas* (Cambridge MA: The MIT Press, 1977)

Jackendorff, Ray, *The Architecture of the Language Faculty* (Cambridge: MIT Press, 1997)

Jahrmann, Margarete, "Kriegsspiele und kognitives Mapping. Sensomotorische Erfahrung und ihre spielerische Schärfung" in *Medien-Krieg-Raum*, ed. Lars Novak (Paderborn: Fink Verlag), pp. 451-470

Jaspers, Kristine, "Alice im Wunderland, Die Gestaltungskunst des Szenenbildners Uli Hanisch," *film-dienst* 14, 2009, pp. 6–10

Jay, Martin, "Scopic Regimes of Modernity," in *Vision and Visuality*, ed. Hal Foster (Seattle: The New Press, 1999), pp. 3–28

Jenkins, Henry, "Game Design as Narrative Architecture," *Computer* 44 (2004)

Johnston, David, "The making of Dust: Architecture and the Art of Level Design", in *The State of Play. Creators and Critics on Video Game Culture*, eds. Goldberg, Daniel, Larsson, Linus (New York: Seven Stories Press, 2015), pp. 169-182

Juul, Jesper, *The Art of Failure: An Essay on the Pain of Playing Video Games* (Cambridge MA, London: MIT Press, 2013)

Juul, Jesper, "The Open and the Closed: Games of Emergence and Games of Progression," in *Computer Games and Digital Cultures Conference Proceedings*, ed. F. Mäyrä (Tampere, Finland: Tampere University Press, 2002), pp. 323–29

Kahn, Louis, "Space and the inspirations," [1967] in: *Louis Kahn, Essential Texts*, ed. Robert Twombly (New York: W.W. Norton, & Company Inc., 2003), pp. 220-227

Kant, Immanuel, *The Critique of judgment* [1790] translated with Analytical Indexes by James Creed Meredith (Oxford: Clarendon Press, 1989)

Kant, Immanuel, *Critique of pure reason* [1781], translated and edited by Paul Guyer and Allen W. Wood (Cambridge: Cambridge University Press, 1998)

Kelly, Kevin, "Virtual Reality: An interview with Jaron Lanier," *Whole Earth Review*, 1989, pp. 108-119

Kirkpatrick, Graeme, *Aesthetic Theory and the Videogame* (Manchester: Manchester University Press, 2011)

Kleist, Heinrich von, *Sämtliche Werke und Briefe*, zweiter Band (München: Carl Hanser Verlag, 1993)

Kline, Morris, *Mathematics in Western Culture* (London: Oxford University Press, 2008)

Koolhaas, Rem and Bruce Mau, *Small, Medium, Large, Extra-large. Office for Metropolitain Architecture* (Rotterdam: 010 Publisers, 1995)

Koolhaas, Rem, *Delirious New York* (New York: The Monacelli Press, 1978)

Krauss, Rosalind, "Sculpture in the Expanded Field," *October* no. 8 (1979), pp. 31–44

Latour, Bruno and Albena Yaneva, „Give me a gun and I will make all buildings move: an ANT's view of architecture," *Explorations in architecture: Teaching, Design and Research*, ed. Reto Geiser (Basel: Birkhäuser, 2008), pp. 80-8

Le Corbusier, *Le Modulor [I], Essai sur une mesure harmonique à l'échelle humaine applicable universellement à l'architecture et à la mécanique* (Boulogne: Edition de l'Architecture d'aujourd'hui, 1950)

Le Corbusier, *Une Maison – Un Palais* (Paris: G. Crès, [1928])

Lefebvre, Henri, *The Production of Space* [1974]) (Oxford/Cambridge, MA: Blackwell, 1991)

Lemerle, Frédérique, "L'émergence de l'hôtel particulier à Paris," in *Marquer la ville, Signes, traces, empreintes du pouvoir (xiiie-xvie siècle)*, ed. Patrick Boucheron and Jean-Philippe Genet (Paris/Rome: Publications de la Sorbonne, 2013), pp. 109-123

Leuenberger, Theresia, *Architektur als Akteur? Zur Soziologie der Architekturerfahrung* (Bielefeld: transcript, 2018)

Licht, Michael Stuart, "An Architect's Perspective On Level Design Pre-Production," *Gamasutra*, June 3 (2003), https://www.gamasutra.com/view/feature/131257/an_architects_perspective_on_.php.

Longo, Giuseppe, "Mathematical Infinity 'in Prospettiva' and the Spaces of Possibilities," *Visible, a Semiotics Journal* no. 9 (2011): pp. 1-10

Lynch, Kevin, *The Image of the City* (Cambridge: Technology Press, 1960)

Macklin, Colleen and John Sharp, *Game, design and play: A detailed Approach to iterative Game Design* (Upper Saddle River, NJ: Addison-Wesley, 2016)

Majsova. Natalija, "Outer Space and Cyberspace: An Outline of Where and How to Think of Outer Space in Video Games," *Teorija in Praksa* 51, no. 1 (2014), pp. 106-122

May, Simon, *The Power of Cute* (Princeton and Oxford: The Princeton Press, 2019)

McArthur, John A., *Digital Proxemics, How Technology Shapes the Ways We Move* (New York: Peter Lang Publishing, 2016)

McGonigal, Jane, *Reality is Broken: why Games Makes us Better and how they can Change the World* (New York: Penguin, 2011)

McGregor, Georgia Leigh, "Situations of Play: Patterns of Spatial Use in Videogames," *Situated Play, Proceedings of Digra 2007 Conference,* 539

Miklaucic, Shawn, "Virtual Real(i)ty: SimCity and the Production of Urban Cyberspace (2001)" in *Game Research: The Art, Business and Science of Computer Games,* 2006, game-research.com/index.php/articles/virtual-reality-simcity-and-the-production-of-urban-cyberspace

Moholy-Nagy, László, *The New Vision* (New York: W.W. Norton & Co., 1938)

Morgan, Diane, *Kant Trouble. The Obscurities of the Enlightened* (London and New York: Routledge, 2000)

Muriel, Daniel and Garry Crawford, *Video Games as Culture. Considering the Role and Importance of Video Games in Contemporary Society* (London: Routledge, 2018)

Murray Janet H., *Hamlet on the Holodeck: The Future of Narrative in Cyberspace* (New York, NY et al.: Free Press, 1997)

Nake, Frieder, "Surface, Interface, Subface. Three Cases of Interaction and one Concept", in *Paradoxes of Interactivity. Perspectives for Media Theory Human-Computer Interaction, and Artistic Investigations,* eds. Anthony Moore, Jin Hyun Kim et. al. (Bielefeld: transcript, 2008), pp. 92–109

Newcombe, Nora S., "Picture this. Increasing Math and Science Learning by Improving Spatial Thinking," *American Educator,* vol. 34, no. 2, (2010), pp. 29-35

Nitsche, Michael, *Video Game Spaces. Image, Play, and Structure in 3D Worlds* (Cambridge/London: MIT Press 2008)

Novak, Marcos, "Liquid Architectures in Cyberspace," in *Cyberspace: First Steps,* ed. Michael Benedikt (Cambridge, Mass.: MIT Press, 1992), pp. 225–54

Novaro, Maria Elísa, "What It's Like to Be an Architectural Consultant for Assassin's Creed II," interview by Manuel Saga, translated by Matthew Valata, October 7, 2015, https://www.archdaily.com/774210/maria-elisa-navarro-the-architectural-consultant-for-assassins-creed-ii

Oechslin, Werner, "'A parte per parte – a membro per membro'. Die Konkretisierung der architektonischen Form", *Archithese* no. 26, March/April (1996), pp. 15-18

Oechslin, Werner, „'Poetando'; ‚nous poétisons'. TEXTE - wissenschaftliche und andere: TEXTE!" *SCHOLION* 9 (2012), pp. 5-23

Pallasmaa, Juhani, *The Embodied Image. Imagination and Imagery in Architecture* (Chichester: John Wiley & Sons Ltd., 2011)

Panofsky, Erwin, "Iconography and Iconology: An Introduction to the Study of Renaissance Art," in *Meaning in the Visual Arts: Papers in and on Art History* [1939] (Garden City, NY: Doubleday 1955)

Pasqualini, Isabella, „The Architectonic Avatar – Multisensory Aspects of Architecture," in *Proportions and Cognition in Architecture and Urban Design*, eds. Andri Gerber, Tibor Joanelly and Oya Atalay Franck (Berlin: Reimer Verlag, 2019), pp. 95-108

Pedercini, Paolo, "Invisible Walls, puffy Clouds, and the unheavenly World behind them," *Blog post*, April 1 (2014), http://www.molleindustria.org/blog/invisible-walls-puffy-clouds/

Penny, Simon, "Virtual Reality as the Completion of the Enlightenment Project," in *Culture on the Brink: Ideologies of Technology*, ed. Gretchen Bender and Timothy Druckrey, Discussions in Contemporary Culture 9 (Seattle: BayPress, 1994), pp. 231–48

Piaget, Jean, *Play, Dreams and Imitation in Childhood* [1945] (W,W, Norton & Co., 1962)

Poznanski, Andrzej, *Visual Revolution of The Vanishing of Ethan Carter, The Astronauts*, March 25 (2014), http://www.theastronauts.com/2014/03/visual-revolution-vanishing-ethan-carter/

Repton, Humphrey, *The Art of Landscape Gardening. Including his Sketches and Hints on Landscape Gardening and Theory and Practice of Landscape Gardening* [1794], ed. John Nolen (Boston and New York: Houghton Mifflin Company, 1907)

Riemann, Bernhard, *On the Hypotheses Which Lie at the Bases of Geometry* (University of Göttingen, 1854)

Rotzetter, Francine B. R., *Game Guidance - Nonverbale Leitsysteme in open-World-Games*, Unpublished MA thesis (Zurich University of the Arts (ZhdK), 2017)

Roussel, Raymond, *Comment j'ai écrit certains de mes livres* (Paris: Alphonse Lemerre, 1935)

Russell, Bertrand, *An Essay on the Foundations of Geometry* (CreateSpace Independent Publishing Platform, 2018)

Sale, James, "From dark souls to manifold garden: how games tell stories through architecture," interview by Thomas McMullen, *Alphyr*, https://www.alphr.com/games/1002937/from-dark-souls-to-manifold-garden-how-games-tell-stories-through-architecture

Salen, Katie and Eric Zimmermann, *Rules of play: game design fundamentals* (Cambridge, Mass.: The MIT Press, 2004)

Sanchez, Jose, "Designing the Metaverse: the Role of Architecture in Virtual Environments," interview by Susan S. Szenasy, *Metropolis Magazine*, July 19, 2017, https://www.dezeen.com/2016/03/07/jose-sanchez-block-hood-video-game-tools-solve-global-challenges-architecture/

Schiller, Friedrich, *On the aesthetic education of a man in a series of letters* [1794], ed. and transl. by Elizabeth M. Wilkison and L. A. Willoughby (Oxford: Clarendon Press, 1967)

Schmitt, Gerhard et al., "Toward Virtual Reality in Architecture: Concepts and Scenarios from the Architectural Space Laboratory," *Presence: Teleoper. Virtual Environ.* 4, no. 3 (January 1995), pp. 267–285

Schmitt, Gerhard, *Information Architecture: Basics of CAAD and Its Future* (Basel ; Boston: Birkhauser, 1999)

Schultz, Pit, "Jodi als Software-Kultur", in *Install.Exe – Jodi, [Plug In]*, ed. Tilman Baumgärtel (Basel: Kunst und Neue Medien, 2002), pp. 31–39

Schützeichel, Rainer, *Die „Theorie der Baukunst" von Herman Sörgel: Entwürfe einer Architekturwissenschaft* (Berlin: Reimer, 2019)

Schwingeler, Stephan, *Kunstwerk Computerspiel – digitale Spiele als künstlerisches Material, Eine bildwissenschaftliche und medientheoretische Analyse* (Bielefeld: transcript, 2014)

Serres, Michel, "The Origin of Geometry," in *Hermes: Literature, Science, Philosophy* (Baltimore: The Johns Hopkins University Press, 1983), pp. 125–33

Sharp, John, *Works of Game* (Cambridge MA, London: MIT Press, 2015)

Shaw, Philip, *The sublime* (Abingdon: Routledge, 2006)

Schnell, Jesse, *The Art of Game Design. A Book of Lenses* (Boca Raton: CRC Press, 2008)

Smithson, Alison and Peter Smithson, "But Today We Collect Ads," in *Ark Magazine* no.18 (November 1956), pp. 49-50

Soja, Edward W., *Thirdspace: Journeys to Los Angeles and Other Real-and-Imagined Places* (Cambridge, MA/Oxford: Blackwell, 1996)

Soja, Edward W., *Postmodern Geographies: The Reassertion of Space in Critical Social Theory* (London/New York, NY: Verso, 1989)

Solitaire, Marc, *Au retour de la Chaux-de-Fonds: Le Corbusier-Froebel* (Martigues: Éditions Wiking, 2016)

Spielmann, Yvonne, *Video: The Reflexive Medium* (Cambridge, MA, MIT Press, 2010)

Steets, Silke, *Der sinnhafte Aufbau der gebauten Welt: eine Architektursoziologie* (Berlin: Suhrkamo, 2015)

Stockburger, Axel, *The Rendered Arena: Modalities of Space in Video and Computer Games*, Dissertation (London: University of the Arts 2006)

Strange, C. Carney and James H. Banning, *Educating by Design, Creating Campus Learning, Environments That Work* (San Francisco: Jossey-Bass/Wiley & Sons, 2001)

Subrahmanyam, Kaveri and Patricia M. Greenfield, "Effect of Video Game Practice on Spatial Skills in Girls and Boys," *Journal of Applied Developmental Psychology* 15, no. 1 (1994), pp. 13–32

Sutherland, Ivan E., "A Head-Mounted Three Dimensional Display," in *Proceedings of the December 9-11, 1968, Fall Joint Computer Conference, Part I* (ACM, 1968), pp. 757–764

Sutherland, Ivan E., "The Ultimate Display," in *Proceedings of the IFIP Congress* (New York, 1965), pp. 506–508

Sutherland, Ivan E., "Sketch Pad a Man-Machine Graphical Communication System," in *Proceedings of the SHARE Design Automation Workshop* (ACM, 1964), pp. 6–329

Sutton Smith, Brian, *The Ambiguity of Play* (Cambridge, Massacgusetts: Harvard University Press, 1997)

Tafuri, Manfredo, *Teorie e storia dell'architettura* (Bari: Laterza, 1968)

Tan, Ekim, *Play the city: games informing the urban development* (Heijjningen: Jap Sam Books, 2017)

Tan, Ekim, *Negotiation and design for the self-organizing city: gaming as a method for Urban Design* (Delft: Delft University of Technology, 2014)

Taube, Jeffrey S., Stephane Valerio and Ryan M. Yoder, "Is Navigation in Virtual Reality with fMRI Really Navigation?" *Journal of Cognitive Neuroscience* XXV, July 7 (2013), pp. 1008-1019

Terlecki, Melissa and Nora S. Newcombe, "How Important Is the Digital Divide? The Relation of Computer and Videogame Usage to Gender Differences in Mental Rotation Ability," *Sex Roles*, Vol. 53, No. 5/6, (September 2005), pp. 433-44

Tönnesmann, Andreas, *Monopoly: das Spiel, die Stadt und das Glück* (Berlin: Wagenbach, 2011)

Tschumi, Bernard, *Architecture and Disjunction* (Cambridge MA & London: MIT Press, 1996)

Van Buren, Deanna, "Behind the scenes of 'The Witness', a Video Game designed by Architects," *Archinect*, interview by Nicholas Korody, August 23, 2016, https://archinect.com/features/article/149964654/behind-the-scenes-of-the-witness-a-video-game-designed-by-architects

Vasylevska, Khrystyna, Iana Podkosova, and Hannes Kaufmann, "Walking in Virtual Reality: Flexible Spaces and Other Techniques," in *The Visual Language of Technique* (Springer, 2015), pp. 81-97

Vella, Daniel, "No Mastery Without Mystery: Dark Souls and the Ludic Sublime," *Game Studies*, Vol. 15 issue 1, July (2015)

Vico, Giambattista, *Cinque Libri de'Principj d'Una Scienza Nuova* (Napoli: Felice Mosca, 1730)

Vico, Giambattista, *De Antiquissima Italorum Sapientia, Ex Linguae Latinae Originibus eruenda Libri Tres* (Napoli; Felice Mosca, 1705)

Giacomo Barozzi da Vignola, *I cinque ordini d'architettura* [1562] (Firenze: Giuseppe Molini, 1834)

Wagner, Mark, *The Geometries of Visual Space* (Mahwah, N.J: Routledge, 2006)

Wainwright, Oliver, "Billionaires' Basements: the luxury Bunkers making Holes in London Streets," *The Guardian*, 9 November, (2012), https://www.theguardian.com/artanddesign/2012/nov/09/billionaires-basements-london-houses-architecture

Walz, Steffen P., *Towards A Ludic Architecture* (Carnegie Mellon University/Pittsburgh: ETC Press, 2010)

Wark, McKenzie, *Gamer Theory* (Cambridge MA, London: Harvard University Press, 2007)

Warren, William H., "Non-Euclidean Navigation," *Journal of Experimental Biology* 222 (2019), https://doi.org/10.1242/jeb.187971.

Warren, William H. et al., "Wormholes in Virtual Space: From Cognitive Maps to Cognitive Graphs," *Cognition* 166 , September 1, (2017), pp. 152–63,

Wertheim, Margaret, "Lost in Space: The Spiritual Crisis of Newtonian Cosmology," in *Seeing Further: 350 Years of the Royal Society and Scientific Endeavour* (Harper Collins Publ. UK, 2010), pp. 42–59

Wertheim, Margaret, "The Illusionistic Magic of Geometric Figuring," *Cabinet Magazine*, Summer 2007

Wycoff, Mick, "Margaret Wertheim: Complexity, Evolution and Hyperbolic Space," *Evolution: Education and Outreach* 1, no. 4 (2008), pp. 531–535

Yagou, Artemis, *Modernist Complexity on a small Scale: The Dandanah glass building Blocks of 1920 from an object-based research perspective* (München: Deutsches Museum, 2013)

Zimmerman, Eric, "Gaming Literacy: Game Design as a Model for Literacy in the Twenty-First Century," in *The Video Game Theory Reader 2*, eds. Bernard Perron and Mark J. P. Wolf (New York: Routledge, 2008), pp. 253–71

Ludography (chronological order)

Buckminster Fuller, *World Game*, 1961

Allan G. Feldt, *CLUG – Community Land Use Game*, 1966

Richard D. Duke, *Metropolis,*1969

Cedric Green, *INHABS (Instructional Housing and Building Simulation)*, 1970

Atari, *Pong*, 1972

Gary Gygax and Dave Arneson, *Dungeons and Dragons*, 1974

William Crowther and Don Woods, *Adventure*, 1976

Steve Perrin and Greg Stafford, *RuneQuest*, 1978

Atari, *Asteroids* 1979

Infocom, *Zork*, 1980

Sandy Petersen, *Call of Cthulhu*, 1981

ZX Spectrum, *The Hobbit*, 1982

Cinematronics, *Dragon's Lair*, 1983

Nintendo, *Mario Bros.*, 1983

Sandy White, *Ant Attack*, 1983

Matthew Smith, *Manic Miner*, 1983

Epyx, *Summer Games*, 1984

Epyx, *Winter Games*, 1985

Steve E. Meretzky, *A Mind Forever Voyaging*, 1985

Nintendo, *Legend of Zelda*, 1986

Technos, *Double Dragon*, 1987

Capcom, *Street fighter*, 1987

Will Wright/Maxis Software, *SimCity*, 1989

Dynamix, *Rise of the Dragon*, 1990
LucasArts, *Monkey Island 2: LeChuck's Revenge*, 1991
Sierra On-Line, *Space Quest IV*, 1991
Sensible Software, *Sensible Soccer*, 1992
Id Software, *Doom*, 1993
LucasArts, *Star Wars: TIE Fighter*, 1994
Looking Glass Technologies/Origin Systems, *System Shock*, 1994
id Software/GT Interactive, *Quake*, 1996
Blizzard Entertainment, *Diablo*, 1996
Stainless Software, *Carmageddon*, 1997
Interplay, *Fallout*, 1997
Valve Corporation/Sierra Entertainment/Valve, *Half Life*, 1998
Konami/Kojima Productions, *Metal Gear Solid*, 1998-2015
Rockstar Games, *Grand Theft Auto III*, 2001
Ubisoft/Gameloft, *Tom Clancy's Splinter* Cell, 2002-2013
LucasArts, *Star Wars: Bounty Hunter*, 2002
Illusion Softworks, *Mafia*, 2002
Linden Lab, *Second Life*, 2003
CCP, *EVE Online*, 2003
Blizzard Entertainment, *World of Warcraft*, 2004
Valve Corporation, *Half-Life 2*, 2004
Tarr and Zach Adams, *Dwarf Fortress*, 2006
2K Games, *BioShock*, 2007
FogValve Corporation, *Portal*, 2007
Digital Illusions CE, *Mirror's Edge*, 2008
Rockstar Games, *Grand Theft Auto IV*, 2008
Ubisoft, *Assassin's Creed II*, 2009
Mojang/Microsoft, *Minecraft*, 2009
IBM, *CityOne*, 2010
Wargaming.net, *World of Tanks*, 2010
Stabyourself, *Not Tetris*, 2010
Rockstar San Diego, *Red Dead Redemption*, 2010
IQ Interactive, *Kane and Lynch 2 Dog Days*, 2010
From Software, *Dark Souls*, 2011
Eidos Montreal/Square Enix, *Deus Ex: Human Revolution*, 2011
Polytron Corporation, *Fez*, 2012
Johnson, M., *Ultima Ratio Regum*, 2012
Massive Entertainment/Ubisoft, *Far Cry 3*, 2012

IO Interactive/Square Enix, *Hitman: Absolution*, 2012

King Digital Entertainment, *Candy Crush*, 2012

Jonas & Verena Kyratzes, *The Sea Will Claim Everything*, 2012

Rockstar Games, *Grand Theft Auto V*, 2013

Mossmouth LLC., *Spelunky* (remake), 2013

Demruth, *Antichamber*. 2013

Droqen, *Starseed Pilgrim*, 2013

Santa Ragione, *Mirrormooon EP*, 2013

Santa Ragione, *Fotonica*, 2014

Ubisoft, *Assassin's Creed Unity*, 2014

Creative Assembly, *Alien: Isolation*, 2014

The Astronauts, The *Vanishing of Ethan Carter*, 2014

Colossal Order, *Cities: Skylines*, 2015

CD Project, *Witcher 3: Wild Hunt*, 2015

Zack Grossbart *The Seven Bridges of Königsberg*, 2015

Ubisoft, *Assassin's Creed Syndicate*, 2015

CD Projekt RED, *The Witcher 3: Wild Hunt*, 2016

Arkane Atudios/Bethesa, *Dishonored 2*, 2016

SIE Japan Studio, *The Last Guardian*, 2016

Thekla, *The Witness*, 2016

Hello Games, *No Man's Sky*, 2016

Niantic, *Pokemon GO*, 2016

IO Interactive/Square Enix/Warner Bros. Interactive, *Hitman*, 2016

Molleindustria, *Nova Alea*, 2016

Molleindustria, *A short history of the gaze*, 2016

Michael Brough, *Cinco Paus*, 2017

Outbounds, *Memory of a broken dimension*, 2017

PUBG Corporation, *PlayerUnknown's Battlegrounds*, 2017

Plethora Projects, *Block'hood*, 2017

People Can Fly/Epic Games, *Fortnite*, 2017

Mode 7 Games, *Frozen Synapse 2*, 2018

IO Interactive/Warner Bros. Interactive, *Hitman 2*, 2018

William Chyr, *Manifold Garden*, 2019

Frogwares, *The Sinking City*, 2019

Blast Theory, *A Cluster of 17 Cases*, 2019

Image Copyrights

Introduction
Fig. 1: Hoffmann, Heinrich, *König Nussknacker und der arme Reinhold*
(Frankfurt am Main: Literarischen Anstalt Rütten & Löning, 1851)
Fig. 2: © Aram Bartholl
Fig. 3: © Ulrich Götz
Fig. 4: © Ulrich Götz

Werner Oechslin
Fig. 5-10: © Bibliothek Werner Oechslin
Fig. 11: Johann Gottfried Grohmann/ Friedrich Gotthelf Baumgärtner
eds., *Ideenmagazin für Liebhaber von Gärten, Englischen Anlagen und
für Besitzer von Landgütern* (Leipzig) © Bibliothek Werner Oechslin

Paolo Pedercini
Fig. 12-16: © Paolo Pedercini/Molleindustria

Konstantinos Dimopoulos
Fig. 17: © Konstantinos Dimopoulos, Maria Kallikaki and Unbound
Fig. 18-20: © Konstantinos Dimopoulos, Maria Kallikaki
Fig. 21: © Konstantinos Dimopoulos

Johannes Binotto
Fig. 22: © Harun Farocki
Fig. 23: © Juan Campanella
Fig. 24: © Michael Mann
Fig. 25: © David Fincher,
Fig. 26: © Makropol, by courtesy of the artist

Fig. 79: God as Architect/Builder/Geometer/Craftsman, The Frontispiece of Bible Moralisee. circa 1220-1230, source: https://commons.wikimedia.org/wiki/File:God_the_Geometer.jpg

Fig. 80: Triumph of St. Ignatius of Loyola, ceiling fresco by Andrea Pozzo, church Sant'Ignazio, Rome, 1685, https://commons.wikimedia.org/wiki/File:Frescos_of_Ignatius_of_Loyola_HDR.jpg

Fig. 81: © Richard Leacock

Fig. 82: https://medium.com/@johnlakness/case-study-decentralizing-the-flat-earth-society-44cf45be850e

Ulrich Götz

Fig. 83: © Ulrich Götz

Fig. 84: © Rockstar Games

Fig. 85: © Outbounds

Fig. 86: © Bram Wisman/MAI.

Marc Bonner

Fig. 87: © Marc Bonner

Fig. 88: https://www.flickr.com/photos/9160678@N06/2650386807/, photo: Villa Savoye 19.JPG by Scarletgreen, CC BY 2.0.

Fig. 89: Jean Marot, *Recueil des plans, profils et élévations des [sic] plusieurs palais, chasteaux, églises, sépultures, grotes et hostels, bâtis dans Paris, et aux environs, avec beaucoup de magnificence, par les meilleurs architectes du Royaume* (Paris), p. 84

Fig. 90: Author's screenshots taken from http://hitmanmaps.com/paris, interactive map made by reddit user "u/Winterbirds", 2016

Fig. 91: Author's screenshots taken on PS4; IO Interactive, Square Enix 2016

Fig. 92: Author's screenshots taken from http://hitmanmaps.com/sapienza, interactive map made by reddit user "u/Winterbirds", 2016

Fig. 93: Author's screenshots taken on PS4; IO Interactive, Square Enix 2016

Sinem Cukurlu

Fig. 94: Michael Stuart Licht, "An Architect's Perspective On Level Design Pre-Production," Gamasutra (June 3, 2003), https://www.gamasutra.com/view/feature/131257/an_architects_perspective_on_.php

Fig. 95: © Ubisoft Montreal

Authors

Johannes Binotto is researcher in cultural and media studies. After studying literature and philosophy at the University of Zurich, he was visiting professor for media studies at the Universities of Basel and Lucerne and is now senior lecturer for film theory at the Lucernce School of Art and Design and for English and American literature at the University of Zurich and also works as film journalist and video essayist. His research focuses on the intersections between media theory, philosophy of technology, architecture and psychoanalysis. Among his numerous publications are the two books *TAT/ORT. Das Unheimliche und sein Raum in der Kultur* (Diaphanes 2013) and the edited volume *Film/Architektur. Perspektiven des Kinos auf den Raum* (Bauwelt Fundamente 2017). Personal Homepage: http://www.medienkulturtechnik.org

Marc Bonner is a media scholar and art historian with focus on game studies. He studied art history, history of the modern age and information science at Saarland University. In 2013, he received his doctorate on the topic of "Architecture of Distant Worlds – Santiago Calatrava's Sculptural Understanding of Architecture and the Graphic Quality of his Buildings and Interdependency with Advertising, Film, Music, Computer Games and Fashion". From 2009 to 2013 he was lecturer at Saarland University at the Institute for Art History and at a special BA division with the focus on European Studies. From 2013 to 2017 he was lecturer at the Department of Media Culture and Theatre at University of Cologne. Since 2017 he leads the research project *Open World Structures: Architecture, City- and Landscape in Computer Games* funded by the German Research Foundation (DFG). His research interests include history and theory of architecture of the 19th, 20th und 21st century as well as the spatiotemporal depiction and use of architecture, cityscapes and natural landscapes in computer games and films (especially science-fiction films). Thus, he broaches the issue of transdisciplinary correlations between architecture, film and computer games by including disciplines like urbanism, philosophy, landscape theory and anthropogeography, among others.

François Charbonnet is co-founder, along with Patrick Heiz, of the architecture studio Made in, based in Geneva and Zurich, Switzerland. After graduating from the ETH Zurich with a thesis supervised by Prof. Hans Kollhoff, he collaborated with Herzog & de Meuron and OMA, Rem Koolhaas before setting up their own office in 2003. François Charbonnet has been a visiting professor at the EPF Lausanne (2010-2011), at the ETH Zurich (2011-2013) and at the Accademia di Archittetura, Mendrisio (2014-2015). Since 2018 he is Professor for Architecture and Design at ETH Zurich. In addition to its academic activity, Made in works as an operative practice at redefining the outline of the architectural project through an extensive range of private commissions, as well as competition entries, challenging the common acceptation of elaborate design. As frequent lecturers in Switzerland and abroad, Made in is a prominent agent of the debate on contemporary architecture and advocates for a critical and transversal insight of present contingencies and demands.

Sinem Cukurlu studied architecture at the University of Applied Sciences in Bochum from 2012 on and and finished her master's degree in 2018. Being fascinated by video games, she decided to focus on the process of creating virtual spaces which resulted in the content of her master thesis. Cukurlu examined that the exchange of ideas between virtual and real designers offers mutual inspiration. She realized that both disciplines can learn from each other and profit from interdisciplinary collaboration.
After an employment in an office for architecture in Bochum she switched to working in an online marketing agency in Dortmund. In future, she aims to work in the marketing sector, more specifically in the gaming industry, to connect her passion with her professional life.

James Delaney is the founder and Managing Director of *BlockWorks* – a collective of over 60 designers, animators, artists and developers from around the world with a shared passion for Minecraft. BlockWorks has grown from an informal group of friends playing their favourite game, to a large design studio and consultancy working for some of the largest film studios, marketing firms and educational institutions from around the world. The team's use of *Minecraft* as a design tool rather than a game underlines their work, which is usually characterised by large scale immersive environments and unique gameplay which seems to stretch Minecraft to its limits. James also studied architecture at Cambridge University and now pursues a particular interest in the correlation between architecture and video games, Minecraft in particular, which is explored through educational projects inside the game as well as in theoretical discussions and proposals. In 2019, James joined the Board of Directors of the *Block by Block Foundation*, a partnership between UNHabitat, Mojang and Microsoft which uses Minecraft as a community participation tool in urban design, with a focus on poor communities in developing countries. Since 2012, the Foundation has funded and activated dozens of public space projects in more than 30 countries, with Minecraft at the core of these projects' designs.

Konstantinos Dimopoulos is an urban planner and geographer, engineer, and game urbanist. He studied at the National Technical University of Athens, Greece, where he also received his MSc in urban and regional planning. In 2010 he was awarded a doctorate in urban planning and city geography. In 2012 he published with Kyttaro Games his first commercial game Droidscape: BAsilica for iOS. Since 2014 he has started working to lay the foundations for the field of game urbanism. He has worked on several games either as a consultant on urban matters and as a level/city designer, and is talking about game cities in conferences around Europe, while also writing books and articles.

Andri Gerber is an architectural and planning historian and an urban metaphorologist. He studied architecture at the ETH Zurich and was a project architect and project manager for Peter Eisenman in New York. In 2008, he received his doctorate from the ETH Zurich, for which he was awarded the ETH Medal. From 2008 to 2011 he was an assistant professor at the Ecole spéciale d'architecture in Paris. Since 2011 he has been a lecturer and since 2017 professor in urban planning history at the Zurich University of Applied Sciences (ZHAW). He completed his habilitation in 2016 at the ETHZ's gta Institute, funded by an SNSF Ambizione Scholarship. Gerber has been a visiting professor and is private lecturer at the

ETHZ since August 2017. His research interest turns around space and metaphors, specifically from a cognitive perspective.

Ulrich Götz is professor at the Zurich University of the Arts (ZHdK), heading the ZHdK Subject Area in Game Design since 2004. He was trained as an architect at the Berlin University of the Arts and the Escola Técnica Superior D'Arquitectura in Barcelona. He discusses comparable strategies of spatial design in architecture and game spaces in publications, public and university lectures. He has built up extensive experience in research and development of serious & applied games over years of cooperation with numerous partners from medical, therapeutical, educational and economic contexts. His university teaching focuses on the analysis and design of game mechanics, game concepts, motivation design, and spatial design in virtual environments.

Stefano Gualeni is a philosopher who designs digital games and a game designer who is passionate about philosophy. Among his best-known playable works are the digital games *Tony Tough and the Night of Roasted Moths* (1997), *The Horrendous Parade* (2012), and *Something Something Soup Something* (2017). Stefano is currently an Associate Professor in Game Design at the Institute of Digital Games (University of Malta) where he works in the intersections between continental philosophy and the design of virtual worlds. In summer, he is a Visiting Professor at the Laguna College of Art and Design (LCAD) in Laguna Beach, California. Regardless of his location on the planet, he uses virtual interactions as tools to practically experience and manipulate ideas, world-views, and thought-experiments.

Stephan Günzel is a media scholar and game researcher. He studied philosophy at the Universities of Bamberg, Manchester and Magdeburg and received his docotrate in 2000 from the University of Jena with a thesis on Nietzsche's Geophilosophy. His habilitation was completed in 2011 with a thesis on the spaceimage of computer games in Cultural and Media Studies at the University of Potsdam. There, in 2008, he also co-founded the Digital Games Research Center. He was a visiting professor at the Humboldt-University Berlin and at the Universities of Basel, Göttingen, Kassel, Trier. Right now he is visiting professor and head of the Media Studies program at the Technical University of Berlin as well as permanent professor for Media Theory at the University of Applied Sciences Europe in

Berlin. Here he founded the BA-program on Game Design in 2014. His research interests are on theories of space, image, games and media.

Patrick Heiz is co-founder, along with François Charbonnet, of the architecture studio Made in, based in Geneva and Zurich, Switzerland. After graduating from the ETH Zurich with a thesis supervised by Prof. Hans Kollhoff, he collaborated with Herzog & de Meuron before setting up their own officce in 2003. Patrick Heiz has been a visiting professor at the ETH Zurich (2011-2013) and at the Accademia di Archittetura, Mendrisio (2014-2015). Since 2018 he is Professor for Architecture and Design at ETH Zurich. In addition to its academic activity, Made in works as an operative practice at redefining the outline of the architectural project through an extensive range of private commissions, as well as competition entries, challenging the common acceptation of elaborate design. As frequent lecturers in Switzerland and abroad, Made in is a prominent agent of the debate on contemporary architecture and advocates for a critical and transversal insight of present contigencies and demands.

Margarete Jahrmann Ph.D., artist and researcher. She is professor for game design at the Zurich University of the Arts and for artistic research at the PhD in Arts program of the University of Applied arts Vienna. In her research she developed a practical take on play as principal and designed numerous augmented reality games, game art installations and performances. Her works include deep dreaming algorithms, AI and neuro-epistemology experiments and a specific ludic method. In 2006 she founded pervasive and urban game design and research association ludic society, 2016 she and Max Moswitzer presented the ultimate VOID Book at Cabaret Voltaire Zurich. They edit a ludic arts research journal on playful methods in artistic research, the Ludic Society Magazine. In her collaborative projects she now works with neuroscientists, philosophers and early adopters of technologies, from augmented reality to artificial intelligence and science theory. She exhibits internationally and presents at artistic research and arts events. In 2019, she was invited as research fellow at the CAS Center of Advanced studies LMU Munich and Art|Sci Center Los Angeles.

Constantinos Miltiadis is an architect, programmer, researcher and media artist. He has studied architecture at NTU-Athens and philosophy and computation at the Chair for Computer Aided Architectural Design at ETH Zurich. Since 2015, he is assistant professor at the Institute of Architecture and Media of TU Graz. Constantinos' research is experimental and inter-disciplinary, aiming to expand the scope of architecture and its aesthetics. His work has been presented in exhibitions, seminars, published in aca-demic conferences as well as by international press, and received awards in international competitions. He has taught creative programming and experimental computational in undergraduate and post-graduate levels, as well as in conferences and festivals. At IAM he founded the Virtual Spaces Design Studio, to introduce experimental design in VR in architecture education. He is the founder and curator of the IAM Open Lecture Series since 2015. In his sabbatical in 2019, he studied Computer Music at the Institute of Electronic Music of the University of Music and Performing Arts of Graz. Constantinos' work can be found at studioany.com

Werner Oechslin was born on 3 October 1944 in Einsiedeln. He stud-ied art history, archaeology, philosophy, and mathematics in Zurich and Rome. From 1971 to 1974 he was a scientific assistant at the University of Zurich. He then taught at MIT in Cambridge, MA in 1975 and 1978, and at RISD in Providence in 1979. After a brief period teaching at the Freie Universität Berlin from 1979 to 1980, where he completed his habilitation in 1980, he was appointed to professor in Bonn (1980–1985). In 1985, he taught at the Ecole d'Architecture in Geneva. From 1985 to 2010, Werner Oechslin was Full Professor of Art and Architectural History at the ETH Zurich. In 1987, he was a visiting professor at Harvard University. From 1987 to 2006 he was head of the Institute for the History and Theory of Architecture (gta). From 1996 to 2002, he headed the selection committee of the CCA Montréal's Study Centre and was also a member of the Board of Trustees. He is a member of the consiglio scientifico of the Centro In-ternazionale di Studi di Architettura Andrea Palladio in Vicenza. During its founding, he was a member of the consiglio scientifico of the Scuola di Architettura in Mendrisio. Werner Oechslin is founder and patron of the Werner Oechslin Library in Einsiedeln (www.bibliothek-oechslin.ch).

Luke Caspar Pearson is a Lecturer at the Bartlett School of Architecture, University College London where he is the Director of the Architecture undergraduate programme. He is the founding partner of the design re-search practice You+Pea with Sandra Youkhana (www.youandpea.com), and together they run the Videogame Urbanism studio as part of the Bartlett's MArch Urban Design programme. He received his doctorate from the Bartlett with a thesis exploring the interrelation between virtual game spaces and architectural design practices. Luke is the editor of *AD: Re-Imagining the Avant-Garde* (Wiley, 2019) and *Drawing Futures* (UCL Press, 2016). His writings on games and architecture have been published in *e-flux Architecture, Thresholds, The Journal of Architectural Education,* and *Architectural Research Quarterly* alongside architecture and games industry publications such as *Frame, EDGE Magazine* and *Heterotopias.* Recent game-based architectural commissions include *Playing the Picturesque* (2019) at the Royal Institute of British Architects, *Church of Colocation* (2019), *Architecture (AFTER GAMES)* (2017) at the Victoria and Albert Museum and *Peep-Pop City* (2018) at Somerset House. He has lectured widely on his research including at Strelka Institute, Global Design Forum, Shibaura House Tokyo, New York University Games Lab and the Victoria and Albert Museum.

Paolo Pedercini teaches foundational media production courses and an experimental game design class. His artistic practice deals with the relationship between electronic entertainment and ideology. He often works under the project name "molleindustria" producing video games addressing various social issues such as environmentalism, food politics, labor and gender. His work is enjoyed by millions of non-art oriented people over the net and has been exhibited in art contexts from over seventeen countries around the world. He lectured in several universities in Europe and US and in venues ranging from the oldest squat in Italy to the Centre Pompidou in Paris. Paolo's work has been received wide international coverage by major media including The Guardian, El Pais, BBC, Liberation, Der Standard, New York Times, Washington Post, Business Week, Playboy Brazil, ARTE' TV, The Times among the others. Paolo is the director of LIKELIKE, a neo-arcade devoted to independent games and playful art in Pittsburgh, PA.

Francine Rotzetter is an architect, game designer and VR expert. She studied architecture at the ETH Zurich. In 2015 she received her MA in architecture. From 2016 to 2017 she studied game design at the Zurich University of the Arts, completing a further MA degree in game design in 2017. In her game design master's thesis, she dealt with "Non-verbal guidance systems in open-world games". Rotzetter has been VR project manager at Raumgleiter AG since January 2018.

Philipp Schaerer visual artist and architect, 1994 - 2000 study of architecture at the Swiss Federal Institute of Technology in Lausanne (EPFL). Architect and knowledge manager at Herzog & de Meuron (2000-06), taught the postgraduate course for CAAD headed by Prof. Ludger Hovestadt at the Swiss Federal Institute of Technology in Zürich (ETHZ). Since 2010, Philipp Schaerer has been teaching at various Swiss universities and, as of 2014, is visiting professor at the Faculty of Architecture of the EPFL in the discipline Art and Architecture. His work has been published and exhibited widely and is represented in several private and public collections – among others in The Museum of Modern Art MoMA in New York, The Centre Pompidou in Paris, The Museum of Contemporary Photography in Chicago (MoCP), The Center for Art and Media Technology in Karlsruhe (ZKM) and The Fotomuseum in Winterthur. Philipp Schaerer lives and works in Zurich and Steffisburg/CH. www.philippschaerer.ch; www.constructingtheview.org

Silke Steets is a sociologist and Heisenberg Fellow at the Institute for the Study of Culture at Leipzig University. Her current research project revolves around a cross-cultural comparison of religious cognitive minorities in Germany and Texas. In 2007, Silke earned a PhD from Technical University Darmstadt with an empirical study on the spatial effects of the evolving creative industries in Leipzig. In her habilitation thesis *Der sinnhafte Aufbau der gebauten Welt* (Suhrkamp, 2015) she developed a knowledge-sociological approach to architecture extending Peter L. Berger and Thomas Luckmann's *The Social Construction of Reality* to the built world. Her research interests include the relationship between space, popular culture, religion, contemporary art, materiality and the city.

Ekim Tan is an architect from Istanbul based in Amsterdam. Born in Istanbul, she relocated to the Netherlands after having worked and studied in the United States, Syria and Egypt. Being trained as an architect, her growing interest and passion in cities and games led to a doctoral degree at the Delft University of Technology, titled *Negotiation and Design for the Self-organizing City: Gaming as a Method for Urban Design*. In 2008, she founded Play the City, an Amsterdam and Istanbul based city consultancy firm that helps governments and market parties effectively collaborate with stakeholders. Since developing the City Gaming method during her doctoral research at the TU Delft, it has been applied in projects worldwide, among others, in Istanbul, Amsterdam, Dublin, Shenzhen, Tirana, Cape Town and Brussels. In my role at the Play the City, I stay well-informed about the latest developments in societies and technologies worldwide. This helps me give the right direction to a young and growing firm. Meanwhile, I regularly travel to lecture and give trainings about cities and games; amongst which are the Technical University of Delft, Aleppo University for Arts and Sciences, Rotterdam Architecture Academy, Amsterdam Architecture Academy, Copenhagen Business School, and Middle East Technical University. Following the book on her doctoral research [2014], I published 'Play the City: Games Informing Urban Development' (2017) sharing special knowledge and experiences developed through the Play the City practice.

Architektur und Design

Annette Geiger
Andersmöglichsein. Zur Ästhetik des Designs

2018, 314 S., kart., zahlr. Abb.
29,99 € (DE), 978-3-8376-4489-0
E-Book: 26,99 € (DE), ISBN 978-3-8394-4489-4

Andrea Rostásy, Tobias Sievers
Handbuch Mediatektur
Medien, Raum und Interaktion als Einheit gestalten.
Methoden und Instrumente

2018, 456 S., kart., zahlr. Abb.
39,99 € (DE), 978-3-8376-2517-2
E-Book: 39,99 € (DE), ISBN 978-3-8394-2517-6

Christoph Rodatz, Pierre Smolarski (Hg.)
Was ist Public Interest Design?
Beiträge zur Gestaltung öffentlicher Interessen

2018, 412 S., kart., z.T. farb. Abb.
34,99 € (DE), 978-3-8376-4576-7
E-Book: kostenlos erhältlich als Open-Access-Publikation, I
SBN 978-3-8394-4576-1

Architektur und Design

Gerrit Confurius
Architektur und Geistesgeschichte
Der intellektuelle Ort der europäischen Baukunst

2017, 420 S., kart.
34,99 € (DE), 978-3-8376-3849-3
E-Book: 34,99 € (DE), ISBN 978-3-8394-3849-7

Eduard Heinrich Führ
Identitätspolitik
»Architect Professor Cesar Pinnau«
als Entwurf und Entwerfer

2016, 212 S., kart.
24,99 € (DE), 978-3-8376-3696-3
E-Book: 21,99 € (DE), ISBN 978-3-8394-3696-7

Thomas Hecken, Moritz Baßler, Robin Curtis, Heinz Drügh,
Mascha Jacobs, Nicolas Pethes, Katja Sabisch (Hg.)
POP
Kultur & Kritik (Jg. 7, 2/2018)

2018, 176 S., kart., zahlr. z.T. farb. Abb.
16,80 € (DE), 978-3-8376-4455-5
E-Book: 16,80 € (DE), ISBN 978-3-8394-4455-9

GPSR Authorized Representative: Easy Access System Europe, Mustamäe tee 50, 10621 Tallinn, Estonia, gpsr.requests@easproject.com

www.ingramcontent.com/pod-product-compliance
Lightning Source LLC
Chambersburg PA
CBHW061554120626
46550CB00004B/1487